A Global Force

A Global Force
War, Identities and Scotland's Diaspora

Edited by David Forsyth and Wendy Ugolini

EDINBURGH
University Press

Edinburgh University Press is one of the leading university presses in the UK. We publish academic books and journals in our selected subject areas across the humanities and social sciences, combining cutting-edge scholarship with high editorial and production values to produce academic works of lasting importance. For more information visit our website: www.edinburghuniversitypress.com

© editorial matter David Forsyth and Wendy Ugolini, 2016, 2017
© the chapters their several authors, 2016, 2017

Edinburgh University Press Ltd
The Tun – Holyrood Road
12 (2f) Jackson's Entry
Edinburgh EH8 8PJ

First Published in hardback by Edinburgh University Press 2016

Typeset in 10/12 Goudy Old Style by
Servis Filmsetting Ltd, Stockport, Cheshire,
and printed and bound in Great Britain by
CPI Group UK (Ltd), Croydon CR0 4YY

A CIP record for this book is available from the British Library

ISBN 978 1 4744 0273 6 (hardback)
ISBN 978 1 4744 2930 6 (paperback)
ISBN 978 1 4744 0274 3 (webready PDF)
ISBN 978 1 4744 1350 3 (epub)

The right of the contributors to be identified as authors of this work has been asserted in accordance with the Copyright, Designs and Patents Act 1988 and the Copyright and Related Rights Regulations 2003 (SI No. 2498).

Contents

List of Figures and Tables vii
Acknowledgements ix
Foreword xi
Thomas M. Devine

Introduction   A Global Force: War, Identities and Scotland's Diaspora 1
David Forsyth and Wendy Ugolini

PART 1

1 Military Scotland in the Age of Proto-globalisation, c. 1690 to c. 1815   13
   Andrew Mackillop
2 Forging Nationhood: Scottish Imperial Identity and the Construction
   of Nationhood in the Dominions, 1880–1914   32
   Edward M. Spiers
3 The Scottish Soldier and Scotland, 1914–1918   53
   Hew Strachan

PART 2

4 Performing Scottishness in England: Forming and Dressing the
   London Scottish Volunteer Rifles   73
   Stuart Allan
5 Canada, Military Scottishness and the First World War   93
   Jeff Noakes
6 'A military fervour akin to religious fanaticism': Scottish Military
   Identity in the Australian Imperial Force   128
   Craig Tibbitts
7 South Africa and Scotland in the First World War   150
   Jonathan Hyslop

8   *Ngāti Tūmatauenga* and the Kilties: New Zealand's Ethnic Military
    Traditions   168
    Seán Brosnahan
9   Scottish Ethnic Associationalism, Military Identity and Diaspora
    Connections in the Late Nineteenth and Early Twentieth Centuries   193
    Tanja Bueltmann

Notes on the Contributors   211
Index   214

Figures and Tables

Figures

1.1	John Campbell, fourth earl of Loudoun, commander in chief in North America	21
1.2	Highland bagpipes said to have belonged to Piper MacCorquodale	21
1.3	Lieutenant Robert Hamilton-Buchanan of the Royal Scots Fusiliers	27
1.4	Dirk and miniature of Captain David Aytone of the 74th Regiment of Foot	27
2.1	*The Storming of Tel el-Kebir* (detail) by Alphonse Marie de Neuville	37
3.1	*Highland Soldier by a Cross*, 1914–18	64
4.1	Original sketch proposing a kilted grey uniform for the London Scottish, 1859	83
4.2	Robert Hepburn, founder member of the Caledonian Society of London	87
5.1	'The Happy Man Today is the Man at the Front'	102
5.2	'5th Royal Highlanders of Canada – Black Watch – 2nd Reinforcing Company'	103
5.3	'Join the 236th Kilties Battalion'	105
5.4	Frank Lucien Nicolet, 'Doing My Bit', 1918	106
5.5	'Heroes of St Julien and Festubert', 1916	107
5.6	'Hoot Mon, the Kilties are Here! British Recruiting Week July 16–21', 1917	110
5.7	'The British Commonwealth in Arms'	112
6.1	Lieutenant Thomas Fowler Gordon MM	145
6.2	Melbourne, Australia, 25 April 1943: the Pipe Band of the 5th Battalion (Victorian Scottish Regiment)	146
6.3	Canberra, Australia, 25 April 1951: the Canberra Pipe Band leading in the ex-servicemen	146

7.1	Sporran worn by the noted poet Charles Murray, a founding officer of the Transvaal Scottish Regiment	155
7.2	Scottish military 'Balmoral' bonnet worn by Captain M. L. Norton of the 4th South African Infantry	155
7.3	Two kilted soldiers of the 4th South African Infantry share a match on a wintry Western Front	157
8.1	The Dunedin Highland Rifles pose with rifles and kitbags in central Dunedin	179
8.2	Inscribed pipe band from the Dunedin Scottish Societies' bagpipes recovered from the battlefield at Gallipoli	180
8.3	Cap badge of the New Zealand Scottish Regiment	180

Tables

1.1	East India Company Cadets, 1806	19
1.2	Lieutenant Colonel James Stuart's Patronage Network, Madras, 1775–83	22

Acknowledgements

This edited volume is the final output of the Royal Society of Edinburgh/ Scottish Government Research Workshop *'Wha Bears a Blade for Scotland'*: *the construction of Scottish diasporic military identities, c. 1880–present day*. Sincere thanks are due to both of these organisations for the grant which made this joint project between the Scottish Centre for Diaspora Studies, the University of Edinburgh and National Museums Scotland possible. The project ranged from an international workshop held at University of Edinburgh in March 2012 through to a public symposium held at the National Museum of Scotland in September 2012 and we would like to thank all those who participated.

Both now retired, Ms Jane Carmichael, formerly Director of Collections at National Museums Scotland, and Dr Alex Murdoch, late of the School of History, Classics and Archaeology at the University of Edinburgh, merit a mention as a great source of encouragement and assistance in the early phase of the project.

The editors are particularly grateful to Stuart Allan, National Museums Scotland, for sharing his specialist knowledge of military history. His suggestions for images have also enhanced this volume. Maggie Wilson of the Photo Library at National Museums Scotland was unswerving and efficient in her help with the technical aspects of the book's images. Kerry Allan, also of National Museums Scotland, eased the burden of procuring some of the images.

Foreword

Thomas M. Devine

Over the last two decades or so the subject of Scottish emigration across the globe has blossomed as a core focus of research for modern historians. Broad studies have been published in addition to some on more specific themes such as return migration, the Scottish military, Scots and slavery, and the Scottish factor in empire, to name but a few of the topics which have resulted in important contributions. It could even be argued that there might now be something of a 'diasporic turn' in modern Scottish historical studies. If so, it is all to the good. For far too long students of Scottish history have concentrated exclusively on the homeland and failed to take account of the broader Scotland, the 'Scotland' originating from the vast migrations over the centuries which left imprints on Europe, England, Ireland, the Americas, the colonial Caribbean, Africa, Australasia, Asia and many other places across the globe.

Looking outwards can also provide manifest intellectual benefits for historians of small nations. As they pursue the study of the people who have gone away, so they may become more familiar with the potential pitfalls of introspection, parochialism and filiopietism, and the multiple connections of transnationalism and internationalism. But even then, rigorous contextualisation, allied with comparative analysis, must also surely be added to the mix. Until recent years numerous books on the Scots abroad since the nineteenth century have been replete with boosterism and ethnic conceit. Undeniably that genre may have leavened the pride in the identity of Scots living both at home and abroad. Nevertheless it marred the possibilities of a truly realistic and convincing perspective which was sensitive to historiographical balance and regard for both the lighter and darker aspects of the remarkable global migrations of the Scottish people.

A Global Force adds to the more sophisticated studies which have been plotting the worldwide significance of the Scottish diaspora. This scholarly and richly referenced volume adds a novel and intriguing dimension to existing contributions by focusing on countries in the Empire, dominions and commonwealth which have adopted Scottish regimental styles in their military formations. The authors all demonstrate the vital allure of Highlandism. When overseas countries configured Scots titles and uniforms they looked to the famous Highland regiments as principal exemplars. Kilts and pipe bands were central to these visible and musical identities.

The contributors to the book also go further by addressing the reasons why the dominions were enamoured of 'the kilties' but also why some countries, notably Australia, soon renounced their love affair with Highlandism in favour of a military with its own strong national identity devoid of ethnic migrant traditions. This is a volume which contains much of interest, appeal and fascination on Scottish military history, the diaspora of the Scots and the migration of national identities across frontiers.

Introduction
A Global Force: War, Identities and Scotland's Diaspora

David Forsyth and Wendy Ugolini

This volume emerged from an international research colloquium in 2012, jointly organised by National Museums Scotland and the Scottish Centre for Diaspora Studies, University of Edinburgh, funded by the Scottish Government and administered by the Royal Society of Edinburgh. Historians and museum curators from Australia, Canada, New Zealand and South Africa were invited to join with their Scottish counterparts to consider the functioning, and the meaning, of 'military Scottishness' in different Commonwealth countries and in Britain from the late Victorian period to the present day, with a particular focus on the impact of the First World War.[1] Another key objective was to throw light on the 'hidden' culture of social networking which potentially operated behind local regiments and military units among Scotland's global diaspora.[2] This edited collection, therefore, provides a comparative overview of the nineteenth-century emergence of military Scottishness and explores how the construction and performance of Scottish military identity has evolved in different Commonwealth countries over the late nineteenth and twentieth centuries.[3] In particular, it looks at the ways in which Scottish volunteer regiments in Commonwealth countries variously sought to draw upon, align themselves with or, at certain key moments, redefine the assertions of martial identity which the Highland regiments represented.

Between the 1820s and 1914 over two million people emigrated from Scotland, settling primarily in North America, Australia, New Zealand and South Africa.[4] Emigration and outward migration have been constant features of the Scottish demographic experience. The official population statistics reveal a massive haemorrhage of people from Scotland, which placed Scotland as one of Europe's top three 'exporters' of people, second only to Ireland.[5] Indeed, despite the comparatively small size of its population there is a general impression of the Scots numbering 'among the most migration-prone of all European peoples'.[6] According to Graeme Morton, such was the fundamental effect of demographic mobility on Scottish society 'that emigration – both permanent and temporary – became an experience common to many Scots'.[7] One of the means of identifying a diaspora is the fact that it 'tends to occur over an extended period of time, incorporating second, third and future generations'.[8] Here the Scottish diaspora scores rather highly, for one of the most significant characteristic features of the Scottish experience is not just its relative scale but also the prolonged nature of the nation's migratory experience. This was a process which began in earnest during the late medieval period and continued right down, and not insignificantly, until the late twentieth century.[9]

The work of Tanja Bueltmann, Andrew Hinson and Graeme Morton underlines how the concept of diaspora needs to be understood as 'capturing diasporic actions' which form part of a wider 'diasporic consciousness'.[10] They identify a core element of Scottish diasporic identity construction as being the ways in which Scottish migrants 'prioritise their ethnicity through an orientation to home', thus 'sustaining a relationship with the homeland'.[11] In turn, while this strong connection to their homeland was experienced by many migrants and next-generation Scots, it was 'expressions of a Scottish identity overseas' which 'facilitated the maintenance of that connection, promoting a global Scottish World'.[12] Building upon the insights of scholars such as John MacKenzie, this volume focuses on one of the most distinctive ways in which the influence and identity of the Scottish diaspora in the Dominions expressed itself: the formation of military units which adhered to outwardly Scottish regimental forms.[13] In the 1880s, in particular, the colonial world witnessed 'a wave of manifestations of Scottish identity' most visibly represented by the establishment of regiments such as the New South Wales Scottish Rifles, the 48th Highlanders of Canada and the Cape Town Highlanders, in Australia, Canada and South Africa respectively.[14] Central to this phenomenon of a globally translated identity was the adoption of recognised Scottish military dress, insignia and music. Jonathan Hyslop has identified this as the 'global politics of military Scottishness', while still acknowledging the complex interplay between class, ethnic and national identity formation which lay behind the diasporic adoption of Highland warrior imagery in the various countries of settlement.[15] From the closing decades of the nineteenth century onwards, Commonwealth nations certainly displayed a willingness to absorb notions of Scottishness to represent their own military participation in imperial conflicts.[16] This complements the work of Katie Pickles, whose study of the Imperial Order Daughters of the Empire in Canada underlines the significance of the imperial experience in shaping the identity of British Canadians and demonstrates how imperial agencies often attempted 'to mimic a revered British core'.[17] However, this volume will also highlight the ways in which expressions of military Scottishness were often complex, how its adoption, composition and deployment varied across different Commonwealth countries at different historical periods and, indeed, in some cases was often subsumed or actively discouraged.

This edited collection uses military service and engagement, particularly in times of war, as the prism through which to explore a neglected dimension of the 'diasporic consciousness' of Scots near and far.[18] The first half of the book addresses the physical export of 'Scottishness' in terms of the origins and evolution of Scottish overseas military service, starting with the seventeenth-century mercenary in the midst of European conflict and the demographic dynamic of the Scottish experience of the eighteenth century which propelled Scots to new destinations, primarily North America. The end of the Seven Years War (1756–63), a successful British campaign which dislodged the French from North America, had acted as a catalyst to further encourage Scots to settle in North America.[19] This was heightened by the number of Scottish soldiers, who had been recruited to serve in the conflict and who in turn became eloquent advocates for the settlement of America.[20] Andrew Mackillop reviews patterns of Scottish military service overseas during the long eighteenth century and underlines the extent of Scotland's involvement in global imperialism. He demonstrates the multiple ways in which the age of proto-globalisation 'reconfigured and perpetuated Scotland's economy of military entrepreneurship', at the same time underlining the need to be aware of the 'continuous interaction' with the local when analysing the global dimensions of Scotland's history in this period.

Addressing the late nineteenth century, Edward Spiers' chapter delineates how Highland regiments achieved an 'immense impact' in the colonial wars of the late nineteenth century, creating a powerful image that resonated among the English-speaking communities of the Dominions. He argues that 'Highlandism' prospered in the Dominions because, fundamentally, it was rooted in loyalty and service to the colonial governments; even at a time of growing national self-consciousness in the respective countries, this military form of imperial Scottishness was able to endure. In the final chapter of this section, Hew Strachan addresses Scotland's response to the First World War, highlighting how the notion of active service with one of the 'famous Scottish regiments' enabled Scottish society more widely to re-acquire 'a patina of militarism', reinforced by post-war memorialisation and the construction of national identity within 'martial trappings'. In particular, military service disseminated the idea of 'Highlandism' throughout the Lowlands, masking the mixed ethnic reality in the ranks.[21]

These opening chapters establish the importance of martial imagery to Scotland's sense of self, notions which were continually disseminated and absorbed among its diasporic communities overseas. The book then moves on to address the phenomenon of military Scottishness in four key nations: Australia, Canada, South Africa and New Zealand, as well as the often neglected 'near diaspora' of England. Tracing the evolution of military Scottishness since the Volunteer movement of the mid-Victorian era, these chapters focus primarily on the First World War, reflecting upon the impact of this conflict on both the interconnections and the competing relationships between national and imperial identities. Many of the chapters highlight the significance of the South African war of 1899–1902 as triggering a transnational response from both individual members of Scotland's diaspora and members of the newly formed Scottish volunteer units. This was seen most clearly in the establishment of the Scottish Horse in South Africa, a cavalry formation raised by the 8th Marquess of Tullibardine, which recruited from Scotland, England and South Africa, as well as a regiment of Scots-Australians.

While these chapters collectively highlight the potency and successful export of the Highland warrior imagery as the cornerstone of Scottish martial identity since the latter half of the nineteenth century, they also explore how the outward expression of military Scottishness related to competing national and cultural identities within the new areas of settlement. In particular, this volume examines the extent to which the First World War served to 'denationalise' the Scottish diaspora units, not only in terms of uniform and personnel but also in significance. Stuart Allan notes that, among the Dominions, only Canada and South Africa sent Scottish battalions to the Western Front as part of their expeditionary forces.[22] Canada still displayed a willingness to embrace 'a specifically Scottish patriotism',[23] entering the conflict with Scottish-named military battalions such as 'The Royal Highlanders of Canada' and often utilising the inspirational narrative of Highland martial valour to strengthen regimental morale.[24] However, it is also apparent that the expression of a separate Scottish military identity did not always sit easily with the need for Dominion governments to forge a new sense of national belonging, with the First World War providing the opportunity, in Australia and New Zealand for example, to suppress overt manifestations of Scottishness. Allan also argues that the deployment of units such as the London Scottish and the 4th South African Infantry on the Western Front, in 1914 and 1916 respectively, can largely be attributed to 'happenstance' and the pragmatism of war mobilisation needs rather than the expression of any 'pan-Caledonian sentiment'.[25]

There is, however, an increasing recognition that imperial identities remained a powerful element in post-war Dominion societies, coalescing with other newer forms of belonging. In relation to Canada, for example, David Mackenzie counters the traditional notion that the Great War signified 'a major catalyst of transformation' acting as the midwife for the birth of Canadian nationalism.[26] This viewpoint is confirmed by Australian scholars such as David Lowe and Joan Beaumont who note that imperial sentiments, and an identification with Britain, remained robust in inter-war Australia.[27] Overall, this volume aims to contribute to the recent literature which qualifies the idea of the First World War as straightforwardly signalling the birth of 'nationhood' within certain Dominion nations and instead views Scottishness as one of many 'multiple layers' of imperial and national identities functioning in Commonwealth countries in the first half of the twentieth century.[28]

Focusing on Canada, Jeff Noakes's chapter outlines the ways in which, since the late nineteenth century, Scottish military identity was constructed and negotiated within both national and imperial frameworks in Canadian society and also as an expression of 'anti-modern sentiment'. In particular, Noakes analyses the visual culture of First World War recruitment posters to explore the ways in which military Scottishness was utilised in early twentieth-century Canada. For example, Scottish imagery was often deployed in posters for broad patriotic and fundraising purposes: the Highland soldier symbolising a 'powerful antimodern image'. Although the war changed Canada's relationship with Britain, it did not mark the end of imperialism in Canada, argues Noakes. Nor did it bring an end to a sense of connection to the British Empire, especially in light of the substantial wave of Scottish immigration in the 1920s which reinforced the earlier influx of almost 170,000 Scots who had arrived between 1910 and 1914.[29] Indeed, Noakes suggests that First World War experiences 'contributed to the spread of tartanism and the continued foregrounding of Scottish identity in parts of Canadian civilian life'.

Craig Tibbitts's chapter focuses on the perceived dominant Scottish influence within a small number of Australian infantry battalions during the First World War. This includes the 56th Australian Infantry Battalion, one of a limited number of units where a larger proportion of officers and men were of Scottish descent, or had pre-war service in militia units with Scottish heritage and identity. Within these units the links to Scottish heritage were generally seen as a positive factor yet, as Tibbitts acknowledges, their presence was also contested by the insistence of the Australian military and parliament during the First World War that units needed to identify exclusively as Australian within the Australian Imperial Force (AIF). In the post-war era, opposition to the idea of military Scottishness appears to have been rooted in the widespread notion that 'the proud traditions created by the AIF in the Great War' had superseded the need to acknowledge Scottish ethnicities. However, the reappearance of a Scottish regiment in 1935, re-formed in Sydney as the 30th Battalion, NSW Scottish Regiment, highlights the resilience of military Scottishness or, rather more prosaically, as Tibbitts suggests, 'the ongoing appeal of Scottish pipe bands' and martial identity.

Acknowledging that the key South African contribution to the First World War primarily occurred 'on the scrublands of South West Africa and on the savannahs of Tanganyika', Jonathan Hyslop examines why the South African government's memorialisation of the nation's wartime role still 'took an oddly Scottish turn'. Post-war commemoration focused on activities of the South African Brigade at Delville Wood in 1916, which included the kilted 4th South African Infantry. His chapter highlights the complexity of the South African relationship to Scottish military tradition and reveals the 'remarkable density of social networks and connections between Scotland and southern Africa' which were intensified during the First World War. Indeed, Stuart Allan and David Forsyth note that the 4th South African Infantry is the only unit which actively incorporates the identities of both the new and diasporic nations: the African Springbok cap badge with the bilingual motto 'Union is Strength', the presence of the Nancy the Springbok doe mascot and even the appropriation of a form of black African identity through the performance of their versions of Zulu war dances. Collectively, these could signify to onlookers that 'these apparently Scottish soldiers were a hybrid'.[30] Ultimately, as Hyslop demonstrates, the role of 'the kilted warriors' was overshadowed by the two 'most powerful political narratives of modern South Africa', representing the experiences of Afrikaners and African nationalists.

Seán Brosnahan's chapter on New Zealand's First World War expeditionary force provides another example of an Antipodean rejection of Scottish military traditions. His chapter makes a unique contribution to the historiography by examining the relative influence of Scottish and Maori traditions on the development of New Zealand's military forces before, during and after the First World War. His chapter traces how, throughout the first half of the twentieth century, an indigenous Maori warrior tradition steadily increased in significance within the New Zealand military, eclipsing earlier manifestations of military Scottishness in the process. Brosnahan suggests that the failure of military Scottishness to 'embed' itself in the military narrative of New Zealand expeditionary forces of the two world wars has 'arguably doomed it to long-term irrelevance'.

Clearly, the meaning and reception of military Scottishness evolved over time as Scottish diasporic communities reached their second, third and fourth generation of settlement. Wendy Ugolini highlights the fluid, shifting and 'inclusive' nature of military Scottishness, particularly over the extended period of diasporic settlement, including its necessary embrace of non-Scots within its regiments.[31] Bueltmann, Hinson and Morton confirm that within the nations of settlement, there were often 'Affinity Scots' who identified with Scotland 'for reasons of cultural or fortuitous choice rather than lineage'.[32] This 'affinity' phenomenon can also be evidenced in the 'near diaspora' of England with, for example, the creation of four battalions of the Tyneside Scottish during the First World War. This was the result of a successful recruitment campaign which drew men, most with no direct Scottish links, from Newcastle and its coal-mining hinterland.[33] Yet it also needs to be acknowledged that the assertion of military Scottishness in the Dominions could also serve to exclude or marginalise other ethnic groups within the nations of settlement. The chapters on Canada and South Africa, for example, touch upon the ways in which, while military Scottishness was an accepted, and often lauded, expression of identity, indigenous ethnicities, such as Aboriginal Peoples or black people, were often sidelined or discriminated against within military spheres.

The creation of a near diaspora through the migration of Scots within the United Kingdom, particularly those who headed south of the border to England and to a lesser extent Wales, has often been overlooked in diaspora literature. Yet figures reveal that between 1841 and 1931 this internal exodus numbered 748,577 Scots who opted to head south, or even west to Ireland, and after 1921 Northern Ireland, in search of a new life.[34] Stuart Allan's chapter addresses the phenomenon of military Scottishness among the near diaspora in England, examining, via a case study of the London Scottish Volunteer Rifles in the Victorian era, 'the interaction of expatriate Scottish associational culture with the volunteer military ethos'. He also briefly alludes to how the First World War signified 'a coming of age' for the London Scottish with its early deployment as a Territorial

Force battalion on active service on the Western Front in 1914, and its subsequent action at Messines in October that year.

One of the more recent and innovative approaches to the history of the Scottish diaspora has been to examine the phenomenon through the prism of associational culture.[35] Indeed, the way in which diasporic associationalism was formed in the host society, and how this influenced a wider public and defined roles or identity for their individual members makes this approach a particularly useful means of 'measuring' Scottishness.[36] David Forsyth stresses the links between diasporic military Scottishness and associationalism in the late nineteenth-century context: in Canada, for example, where military associationalism was most vivid, successions of kilted, Volunteer units over the course of the late nineteenth and early twentieth centuries served to re-energise 'enthusiasm for the Scottish military tradition'.[37] However, Forsyth also points out that very public expressions of Scottishness in Commonwealth counties were not necessarily the sign of a confident community. Rather, 'it was the performance of a community in search of ethnic cohesion in the face of new waves of emigration from other nationalities which the Scots perceived as being in direct competition to themselves'.[38] The challenge for Scottish communities was to preserve their distinctive traditions, while simultaneously making a full contribution to the emergent culture of their new homeland. Tanja Bueltmann's chapter in this volume critically analyses the links between Scottish ethnic associations and military identity, noting how diasporic links with Scotland were particularly strengthened during the First World War through 'a sustained form of transnational charity' undertaken via Scottish diasporic networks.

As many of the chapters within this collection suggest, in the aftermath of the First World War, Scottish associationalism arguably functioned as a form of life support, artificially sustaining and, at times, resuscitating a flagging military Scottish identity. This is evidenced by the recrudescence of diasporic Scottish military units in the late 1930s. Ben Wilkie shows how, in inter-war Australia, the Victorian Scottish Regiment, for example, was deeply interlinked with the Scottish associational culture of Melbourne and Victoria and remained an 'important institution for the maintenance and perpetuation of Scottish culture and heritage'.[39] It could therefore be argued that, in the twentieth century, Scottish military identity endured, even beyond the Second World War, because it remained closely allied to Scottish associationalism and notions of Scottish ethnic exceptionalism. Indeed, from the late nineteenth century to the present day, a unique feature of the Scots, compared to other diasporic groups, is the potency and appeal of military associationalism as a key element of Scottish diasporic identity.

Notes

1. Jonathan Hyslop, 'Cape Town Highlanders, Transvaal Scottish: Military "Scottishness" and Social Power in Nineteenth and Twentieth Century South Africa', *South African Historical Journal*, vol. 47, no. 1 (2002), pp. 96–114, at p. 97.
2. Tanja Bueltmann, Andrew Hinson and Graeme Morton (eds), *Ties of Bluid, Kinn and Countrie: Scottish Associational Culture in the Diaspora* (Guelph: Centre for Scottish Studies, 2009).
3. Hyslop, 'Cape Town'. See also Stuart Allan and David Forsyth, *Common Cause. Commonwealth Scots and the Great War* (Edinburgh: National Museums Scotland, 2014) and Wendy Ugolini, 'Scottish Commonwealth Regiments', in Jeremy Crang, Edward Spiers and Matthew Strickland (eds), *A Military History of Scotland* (Edinburgh: Edinburgh University Press, 2012), pp. 485–505.
4. Thomas M. Devine, *The Scottish Nation 1700–2000* (London: Penguin, 2000), p. 468. See also Tom Brooking and Jennie Coleman (eds), *The Heather and the Fern: Scottish Migration and New Zealand Settlement* (Dunedin: University of Otago Press, 2003); Tanja Bueltmann, *Scottish Ethnicity and the Making of New Zealand Society, 1850–1930* (Edinburgh: Edinburgh University Press, 2011); Tanja Bueltmann, Andrew Hinson and Graeme Morton, *The Scottish Diaspora* (Edinburgh: Edinburgh University Press, 2013); Thomas M. Devine, *To the Ends of the Earth: Scotland's Global Diaspora, 1750–2010* (London: Allen Lane, 2011); Thomas M. Devine (ed.), *Scottish Emigration and Society* (Edinburgh: John Donald, 1992), Thomas M. Devine, 'Soldiers of Empire', in John M. MacKenzie and Thomas M. Devine (eds), *Scotland and the British Empire* (Oxford: Oxford University Press, 2011), pp. 176–95; Marjory Harper, *Adventurers and Exiles: The Great Scottish Exodus* (London: Profile Books, 2003); Marjory Harper, *Scotland No More? The Scots Who Left Scotland in the Twentieth Century* (Edinburgh: Luath Press, 2012); Angela McCarthy, 'Scottish Migrant Identity in the British Empire since the Nineteenth Century', in Devine and MacKenzie, *Scotland and the British Empire*, pp. 118–46; John M. MacKenzie with Nigel R. Dalziel, *The Scots in South Africa: Ethnicity, Identity, Gender and Race, 1772–1914* (Manchester: Manchester University Press, 2007); Malcolm Prentis, *The Scots in Australia* (Sydney: University of New South Wales Press, 2008).
5. Michael Flinn (ed.), *Scottish Population History from the 17th Century to the 1930s* (Cambridge: Cambridge University Press, 1977), p. 448.
6. Christopher Smout, 'The Culture of Migration: Scots as Europeans 1500–1800', *History Workshop Journal*, no. 40 (1995), pp. 106–17.
7. Graeme Morton, *Ourselves and Others: Scotland, 1832–1914* (Edinburgh: Edinburgh University Press, 2012), p. 148.
8. Bueltmann, Hinson and Morton, *Ties of Bluid*, p. 4.
9. Devine, *To the Ends of the Earth*, p. 289.
10. Bueltmann, Hinson and Morton, *Scottish Diaspora*, p. 18.
11. Ibid. p. 18.
12. Ibid. p. 3.
13. MacKenzie with Dalziel, *The Scots in South Africa*.
14. Hyslop, 'Cape Town', p. 102.
15. Ibid. p. 97.
16. Ugolini, 'Scottish Commonwealth Regiments'.
17. Katie Pickles, *Female Imperialism and National Identity: Imperial Order Daughters of the Empire* (Manchester: Manchester University Press, 2009).

18. See also Allan and Forsyth, *Common Cause*; Ugolini, 'Scottish Commonwealth Regiments'.
19. Alexander Murdoch, *Scotland and America, c. 1600–c. 1800* (Basingstoke: Palgrave Macmillan, 2010), p. 52.
20. Ibid.
21. Devine also develops this point in *Clanship to Crofters' War: The Social Transformation of the Scottish Highlands* (Manchester: Manchester University Press, 1994), pp. 92–3. See also Heather Streets, 'Identity in the Highland regiments in the nineteenth century: soldier, region, nation', in S. Murdoch and A. Mackillop (eds), *Fighting for Identity. Scottish Military Experience c. 1550–1900* (Leiden: Brill, 2002), pp. 213–36.
22. Stuart Allan, 'Mobilisation, Memory and Material Culture', in Allan and Forsyth, *Common Cause*, pp. 21–48, at p. 27.
23. Hyslop, 'Cape Town', p. 106.
24. Ugolini, 'Scottish Commonwealth Regiments', p. 500.
25. Allan, 'Mobilisation', p. 34.
26. David Mackenzie, 'Introduction: Myth, Memory, and the Transformation of Canadian Society', in David Mackenzie (ed.), *Canada and the First World War. Essays in Honour of Robert Craig Brown* (Toronto: University of Toronto Press, 2005), pp. 3–14, at p. 13.
27. David Lowe, 'Australia in the World', in Joan Beaumont (ed.), *Australia's War 1914–18* (St Leonards: Allen & Unwin, 1995), pp. 125–48; Joan Beaumont, 'Australia's War', in Beaumont, *Australia's War*, pp. 1–34.
28. Ben Wilkie, 'Warriors of Empire: Popular Imperialism and the Victorian Scottish Regiment, 1898–1938', *Victorian Historical Journal*, 85:1 (2014), pp. 73–96, at p. 85.
29. Flinn (ed.), *Scottish Population History*, p. 450; Harper, *Scotland No More*, p. 12.
30. Stuart Allan, 'South Africans', in Allan and Forsyth, *Common Cause*, pp. 81–93, at pp. 84–5.
31. Ugolini, 'Scottish Commonwealth Regiments', p. 487.
32. Bueltmann, Hinson and Morton, *Scottish Diaspora*, p. 26.
33. Allan and Forsyth, *Common Cause*, p. 124.
34. Flinn (ed.), *Scottish Population History*, p. 442.
35. See particularly Bueltmann, Hinson and Morton, *Ties of Bluid*.
36. David Forsyth, 'The Global Reach of the Scottish Diaspora', in Allan and Forsyth (eds), *Common Cause*, pp. 1–20, at p. 12.
37. George F. Stanley, 'The Scottish Military Tradition', in Stanford W. Reid, *The Scottish Tradition in Canada* (Toronto: McClelland and Stewart, 1988), pp. 137–60, at p. 150. Noakes's chapter in this volume also acknowledges the plethora of Scottish militia units which appeared in this period, many through the 'lobbying' of local Scottish interest groups.
38. Forsyth, 'Global Reach', p. 14.
39. Wilkie, 'Warriors of Empire', p. 87.

Part 1

1

Military Scotland in the Age of Proto-globalisation, c. 1690 to c. 1815

Andrew Mackillop

On 23 September 1781 Alexander Macleod of Ullinish in Skye informed his kinsman, John Macpherson, a senior figure on the English East India Company's [thereafter EIC] supreme council in Bengal, of the death of his son, Lieutenant Roderick Macleod, while campaigning with the 71st Highland regiment against American patriots in the Carolinas. Ullinish asked Macpherson to extend his protection to his two other sons, Norman and Alexander, officers in the Company's Madras and Bengal armies respectively, and to tell them '. . . to come home wt [sic] whatever acquisitions they have made'.[1] Death in battle in North America and the need to secure profits acquired through military service in Asia speak to the continuities in motivation and radical changes in geography that marked out Scottish society's experience of warfare in the long eighteenth century.

The example of this one, relatively obscure, Skye family fits a much wider pattern. Service in distinctive units of the British army such as Fraser's 71st Highlanders and in the less well-known context of the EIC's military complex chimes with established understandings of Scotland's history in this period. Long acknowledged as a major exporter of manpower – to Ireland in the sixteenth century and the Dutch Republic and Sweden in the seventeenth centuries – changing patterns of military employment are held to have mirrored Scotland's constitutional trajectory. The established European avenues of service gave way to an increasingly Anglo- and then British framework from the 1690s onwards.[2] This is of course a well-known argument and has formed the basis of Linda Colley's cogent conception of military service, along with Protestantism and empire, as one of the fundamental building blocks of Britain and Britishness.[3] Although the work of Stephen Conway, with its revisionist emphasis on the enduring importance of Continental connections, offers an important corrective, the model of British integration remains the widely accepted orthodoxy.[4] The result has been the consolidation of a particular reading of military Scotland in the century or so after 1707. John Cookson and Hew Strachan have emphasised the essentially 'British' nature of the country's post-union military ethos and identity.⁵ While regimental cultures and modes of militarism – especially the cult of Highlandism – undoubtedly modernised aspects of Scotland's centuries-old martial identity, these were deliberately ambiguous acts of representation designed to complement rather than compete with the pronounced British ethos of the army as an institution.

This emphasis on the British character of Scottish service can be tied back into wider debates on the nature of emerging national identities and Scotland's subordinate economic position within the union.⁶ Assessments of Scottish militarism during the crucial eighteenth-century period stress the marginality and material poverty of the Highlands, the region which contributed most conspicuously to the post-union forms of Scottish involvement in British military service. Eric Richards has argued for the fundamentally dualistic nature of Scotland's engagement with the Atlantic empire between c. 1700 and c. 1800. While the dynamic west coast and Glasgow specialised in remunerative imports and re-exports of high-value colonial produce, the Highlands were reduced to a satellite economic zone specialising in the one-way export of primary produce in the shape of civil and military emigrants or cattle, sheep and fish.⁷ Viewed in this light, large-scale involvement in the army is concrete proof of the Highlands' chronic lack of economic development and diversity. As noted by Hew Strachan, 'the fragile foundations on which Scotland's newly established military identity rested . . . was not on the progressive and dynamic sectors of Scotland, on the Lowland cities, but on its backward and primitive regions'.⁸

Scots now fought for the most advanced fiscal-military state in Europe, but many of the socio-cultural attitudes and economic motives that sustained post-union military entrepreneurship would, it seems, have been recognisable to sixteenth-century redshanks (part-time mercenary soldiers, often from the West Highland seaboard) or Scots in the armies of Gustav II Adolf. The country's militarism, at least as it evolved in the Highlands, emerges as a deeply conservative phenomenon. In this analysis it is a manifestation of cultural continuity and enduring economic underdevelopment which contrasts sharply against that other Scotland – Lowland, enlightened, commercial and improving. As an explanation of how, why and with what success Britishness was inculcated across Scotland after 1707, this distinction has much to commend it. However, with its focus very much on Britain's own internal development and that of its empire, the model takes little cognisance of debates over the nature of globalisation in this period and its effects on those regions specialising in or reliant upon military service.

An era of 'proto-globalisation'

Through their simultaneous involvement in the eastern and western hemispheres of Britain's worldwide empire, the Macleods of Ullinish exemplify in microcosm the global nature of the wars fought in the hundred or so years after the 1707 union. Understanding this era of Scotland's military history involves moving beyond debates on the emerging nature of Britishness and remaining sensitive to key dynamics operating across the planet as a whole. The eighteenth century has been re-envisaged as falling within an era of 'proto-globalisation', a distinct phase of development between c. 1600 and c. 1800 marked by relatively simple but genuinely global trading systems. Intensifying overlap between the Atlantic and Asian economic worlds facilitated greater capital flows, commodity transfers, the enslavement of millions of Africans and the conquest of equally large numbers of Asians by aggressive mercantile corporations from northwest Europe.[9] Regulation of this much greater volume of profitable commerce facilitated increasing government command of key financial resources and the development of what has been described as the 'fiscal-military state'.[10] There have been suggestions that proto-globalisation involved phases of particularly intense development – the 1760s, for example, are described as '. . . a globalizing decade'.[11] However, a striking feature of interpretations of this particular age of historic globalisation is the degree of emphasis placed on continuities. The new did not suppress the old, but co-opted, adapted and redeployed pre-existing political, economic, social and cultural systems to drive forward radically new forms of global interactions. While a definite quickening of planetary-wide exchange in goods and capital was well underway, the world's great states remained overwhelmingly agrarian in their modes of production and resultant political and military structures.[12] These early modern polities were only ever partially centralised and sustained substantial internal socio-economic diversity. As a result, a range of functions was farmed out to hereditary and semi-autonomous nobilities, religious interests or mercantile corporations. This was true even of the most putatively 'modern' states like England, and after 1707 Britain, which used institutions such as the EIC and Hudson's Bay Company to regulate and rule whole swathes of its overseas empire and international economy.[13] State formation in this period did not entail an uncontested process of fiscal-military centralisation but progressed through a constantly adjusting balance between the power of the centre and a host of different ethnic, religious, legalistic and corporate groupings. Each of these 'estates' related to the state in different ways. Among the many productive insights afforded by the idea of proto-globalisation is that empires and states are recast as 'multi-ethnic conglomerates', with ongoing if increasingly regulated diversity a defining aspect of their character and operation.[14]

In economics the emphasis shifts from the modernity of 'industrial revolution' to the concept of 'an industrious revolution', where rural populations engaged in new modes of productivity and began migrating in patterns that generated increasingly capitalist forms of profit.[15] These new forms of human mobility ranged from the extremes of transatlantic slavery and mass colonisation of the New World by socially aspiring emigrants to state service in naval and military machines or their corporate offshoots like the EIC. A key feature of proto-global economics was that their influence did not induce assimilation and homogeneity but rather an interactive dynamic by which nations, regions and localities were influenced by wider trends but often adjusted to these on their own terms and 'fed off' the process to create new forms of difference.[16]

This heightened awareness of the non-industrial and early modern nature of much of Europe's expansion before c. 1800 has found expression in a British context in the form of the 'gentlemanly capitalism' thesis. First articulated by Peter Cain and Anthony Hopkins over twenty years ago, the idea has been met with a curious indifference from Scottish historical studies. This is both unfortunate and surprising given the numerous lines of interpretation it offers to historians of Scotland. The theory re-institutes London as the political and economic engine for English and British imperialism. The fundamental basis of this gentlemanly order was an alliance between the rentier capitalism of the landed and aristocratic classes, who dominated the political and state system, and the financial and service sectors of London. In this formulation, pre-industrial forms of wealth were allied to notions of social credit and an ethos of honourable and genteel forms of state employment to generate what amounted in effect to Britain's version of proto-globalisation.[17]

Understanding Scotland's military economy

These frameworks for rethinking the nature of the pre-1815 British Empire have profound implications for how Scotland's military economy in the long eighteenth century can be reconsidered and best be understood. If proto-globalisation constituted the redeployment of pre-existing political, economic and social conditions for radically new ends, then arguments that rely on the 'backward' and 'primitive' nature of the Highlands begin to look like a major misreading of the basis upon which the region and the rest of Scotland responded to new global pressures. Moreover, viewed from the perspective of the gentlemanly capitalism concept, Scotland's military gentry – be they Highland, like the Macleods of Ullinish, or Lowland – become active players in the latest trends in state and financial development. What they were not were the marginalised representatives of an outdated political, socio-economic order.

That the forces working across Britain's global empire and beyond utilised rather than overturned pre-existing conditions helps to explain the obvious mixture of continuity and change that marked out military Scotland's first hundred years of union. The continuities included the social composition of the leadership corps and ongoing regional reliance on military employment. The new factors at work ranged from clear alternations in organisation, with a shift from proprietary to state-sanctioned regiments, to the geographic spread of combat destinations. The volume of Scots employed as soldiers almost certainly dropped in comparison to the scale of enlistment evident during the previous two centuries. This decline tracked the overall fall in emigration more generally during the eighteenth century.[18] However, the key question is not why Scots may have become less inclined to soldiering but why, given the country's rapid economic and social development from c. 1740 onwards, so many continued to see the army as a viable option. Eighteenth-century Scotland is a telling example of the need to be wary of any simplistic link between ideas of economic 'backwardness' and a conservative reliance on military service. Likewise, the evolution of its military economy illustrates the surprising ways in which the new dynamics unleashed by global empire could maintain and reshape phenomena that might otherwise be rendered obsolete. If the age of 'improvement' seemed poised to negate old, martial Scotland, the age of proto-globalisation did in fact reconfigure and perpetuate its tradition of military entrepreneurship.

It is in this context that patterns of military service between c. 1707 and c. 1815 can best be understood. There is little need to rehearse at length the general characteristics of Scotland's military profile within the British state and empire in this period. Patterns had been set prior to the parliamentary union. Continental observers commented explicitly upon the large number of Scots within the Grand Alliance regiments fighting in the Low Countries and western German kingdoms during the Nine Years War of 1688 to 1697.[19] One-third of Marlborough's staff were Scots – including individuals from the top and secondary ranks of the aristocracy such as John Campbell, second duke of Argyll and George Hamilton, first earl of Orkney.[20] These men fit exactly the definition of 'gentlemanly capitalists', using as they did their political and social power to acquire high-status state offices for themselves and their extended networks of kin and regional associates. Yet expanding opportunities in British employment did not immediately displace older, established avenues of service. Until the 1750s, the Scots brigade in the service of the Dutch Republic remained a significant option for scions of gentry lacking the resources or connections in London. Indeed, the number of its regiments and commissioned personnel reached a new zenith as late as 1747, with the authorisation in July that year of a new regiment under the command of James Douglas, Lord Drumlanrig.[21] The additional fifty-four officer posts represented a major enhancement in the pool of available genteel patronage and underscored the enduringly transnational basis of Scotland's military economy during the age of proto-globalisation.

A range of facts and figures shows that Scotland was just as militarised in 1800 as it had been in 1600 and 1700. Warfare was endemic, with worldwide conflicts between 1702 and 1713, 1739 to 1748, 1756 to 1763, 1775 to 1783, 1793 to 1802 and 1803 to 1815. When not actively engaged in such wars, the country was usually preparing for a renewal of hostilities, invariably against France and Spain. Although subject to rapid expansion and contraction, Britain's military machine evolved continually with each successive conflict.[22] The figures for Scottish participation in this process are best comprehended against Scotland's demographic weight within the British-Irish Isles. In 1707 Scotland had approximately 20 per cent of the population of England and Wales. The ratio fell steadily over the course of the rest of the eighteenth century and beyond. By 1800 this declining share of population meant that Scots constituted only around 12 per cent of the total population of the British-Irish union. Set against these trends, the acquisition of commissioned posts was impressive, although far less than the wholly disproportionate share of military offices secured by Ireland's Protestant aristocracy and gentry.[23] Between 1714 and 1763, approximately 25 per cent of staff appointments went to Scots, as did around one in five offices at the rank of regimental colonel.[24] Scots comprised no less than 207 (31.5 per cent) of the 654 officers commanding Britain's 14,126-strong force of regulars in North America in mid-1757.[25] This large percentage share remained consistently high. The most systematic study of the armed forces during the global conflicts of the French Revolutionary and Napoleonic era has demonstrated that Scots acquired around 25 per cent of the enormous c. 15,000-strong British army officer corps generated between 1793 and 1815.[26] This was approximately twice the rate that might be reasonably expected given Scotland's share of population.

Less well appreciated is just how truly global the involvement of Scotland's military gentry became. It is not surprising that a society with an acute sense of its martial history and the kudos associated with soldiering should commit so noticeably to the British army.[27] But as a world power Britain developed a range of military machines including the rapidly expanding commercial-fiscal-military complex of the EIC.[28] Even as Scots secured over one-quarter of officers' positions in British America, on the other side of the world they made up 21 per cent of commissioned personnel in the Madras presidency army in 1762.[29] Death rates meant a high turnover of personnel in the Company's armies of Bengal, Madras and Bombay, and so resulted in a constant stream of replacements heading to Asia.[30] The scale of appointments can be illustrated by the example of the 437 cadets authorised by the corporation's directorate just for the year 1806. Usually aged between fifteen and twenty-two, cadets were destined for commissioned positions in the EIC's European and sepoy regiments.[31] Although the number sanctioned in that year was especially large, the social composition and regional backgrounds of the Scottish cadets provide a valuable insight into how Scottish society participated in one of the most expansive areas of Britain's global military effort. No fewer than eighty-two Scots (19 per cent) obtained posts – equivalent to the officer establishment of well over two entire battalions. Their general characteristics are summarised in Table 1.1.

Not only was the acquisition of commissioned posts impressive, the regional background of this elite warns against viewing Scotland's post-union military experience primarily through the prism of the Highlands. The figures demonstrate that urban, modernising Scotland committed substantial numbers to the booming export market for military officers in South Asia. However much the Highland regiments point to a military economy driven by regional underdevelopment, patterns of officer enlistment demonstrate conclusively that all of Scotland participated in the expanding fiscal-military complex in Asia. Regions not usually associated with a reliance on martial activity, such as the national capital, the Lothians, and the central shires of Fife and Perth, provided substantial numbers. The sons of the country's middling orders, the clergy, the legal establishment and merchant classes provided almost 50 per cent of personnel. The potential for social mobility through global forms of military entrepreneurship can be seen clearly in the fact that the scions of Highland tacksmen such as William, son of John Macdonald of Greshornish in Skye, or Robert Fernie, son of John, tenant of Sythrum in Markinch, Fife, acquired commissions.[32] If the officer ranks of the British army remained a

Table 1.1 East India Company Cadets, 1806

Totals	Region *	Social Origins
437	Edinburgh/Lothians = 16	Unknown = 18
Scots = 82 (19%)	Central = 15	Clergy/Legal = 17
	Borders = 13	Landed gentry = 11
	NE = 13	Merchant/Military = 11
	Highlands = 13	Tacksman/Tenant = 9
	West Central = 10	Government/Municipal = 6
	India = 1	Miscellaneous = 10
	North America = 1	

* The counties are grouped into the following regions: Edinburgh/Lothians = Mid Lothian/Edinburgh, Haddington, Linlithgow; Central = Clackmannan, Stirling, Kinross, Fife, Perth; Borders = Wigton, Kirkcudbright, Dumfries, Peebles, Selkirk, Roxburgh, Berwick; NE = Angus, Kincardine, Aberdeen, Banff; Highlands = Moray, Nairn, Caithness, Ross, Cromarty, Inverness, Argyll, Bute; West Central = Ayr, Renfrew, Lanark, Dunbarton.

(Source: India Office Records, L/MIL/9/115/Parts 1-4/1-437)

bastion of aristocratic and landed privilege, not least through the need to purchase commissions, the EIC's three armies offered an avenue of real upward social mobility.[33]

The nature and extent of Britain's worldwide expansion did not just produce separate clusters of Scots officers in North America, the West Indies or Asia. A number had truly global careers, serving in multiple theatres and acquiring a genuine sense of the empire as an inter-related whole.[34] Individuals like James Stuart of Torrance and Castlemilk in Lanarkshire, a former Scots-Dutch officer, and Archibald Campbell of Inverneil in Argyll cut their teeth in North America and the West Indies in the 1750s to early 1760s before serving in Asia in the 1770s and 1780s.[35] Inverneil was posted back and forth between the two hemispheres over the course of his long career. He served first in the Atlantic, then Bengal in the late 1760s to early 1770s, fought again in North America and Jamaica from the late 1770s to 1783, before returning a final time to South Asia and command of the Madras government and army in the mid- to late 1780s.[36] These patterns of mobility reveal how soldiers as well as merchants led key aspects of Britain's experience of proto-globalisation, a development in which Scotland's military gentlemanly capitalists were very much to the fore. What is remarkable is that the country's tradition of military migration not only persisted but expanded into multiple imperial theatres simultaneously. This was not simply the case for individuals holding field rank like Inverneil or Stuart. Even relatively lowly commissioned personnel found that warfare took them across the globe. While the Macdonald of Kingsborough family are a well-known example of the flight of former clan gentry to North America in the 1760s and 1770s, their adjustment to new socio-economic realities went much further.[37] As they established themselves in North Carolina and then fought for the British during the American Revolutionary War, the family also sent a scion, Charles, into the Bengal army.[38] Like their near neighbours in Skye, the Macleods of Ullinish, the Macdonalds became involved in both wings of the empire in ways that typify the dynamic reaction of erstwhile clan gentry to the opportunities afforded by proto-globalisation.

As horizons broadened it became possible to mobilise networks of patronage and professional and financial association in ways that connected Scottish localities to the furthest reaches of British imperialism. The result was a strong mutual reliance and close affiliation among Scots officers in the Atlantic and Asia hemispheres. John Campbell, fourth earl of Loudon's tenure as commander in chief in North America in the mid-1750s was undermined by accusations of blatant favouritism towards his own countrymen. There were even suggestions that he ran the army as little more than a 'Scotch expedition'.[39] Anti-Scottish sentiment was a recurrent feature of post-1745 British and Irish society, and so such charges should not be accepted uncritically. All senior commanders, regardless of their nationality, used their powers to dispense offices and favours to relations, political clients and associates.[40] There is little reason to believe that Scots were particularly more inclined to nepotism and cronyism than their Irish, Welsh or English counterparts. However, the appointment of a Scot to a senior command could herald a spike in appointments. When Lieutenant Colonel James Stuart of Torrance and Castlemilk obtained command of the Madras army in the early 1780s, he acted as patron to a wide web of local, regional and national interests. Table 1.2 shows the nature of his connections and the heavy concentration on the west central shires where he and his brother, Andrew Stuart, MP for Lanarkshire, naturally sought to enhance their influence. However, his links spread out beyond the local and regional and encompassed large swathes of the rest of Scotland. These individuals received military commissions, army contracts or posts for relatives and associates.

This was gentlemanly capitalism through imperial service. The cumulative value of the commissions, salaries and other allowances dispersed through the connections shown above was substantial and constitutes a typical example of how Scotland's military economy exploited Britain's proto-globalisation.

Patterns of enlistment

If involvement in the officer ranks proved to be both disproportionate and evident across the whole empire, then patterns of enlistment at the level of rank and file suggest a far more complex and regionally diverse picture. The emergence of the Highland regiments, particularly during the Seven Years War (1756–63), has dominated perceptions. The apparently dramatic volte-face from truculent, rebellious region to a source of reliable, cheap and relatively plentiful manpower gives the Highland dimension a distinctive aura which can eclipse other crucially important facets of the country's engagement with the British military.[41] In fact, Scots served throughout the army, often in regiments with little or no

MILITARY SCOTLAND IN THE AGE OF PROTO-GLOBALISATION | 21

Figure 1.1 John Campbell, fourth earl of Loudoun, commander in chief in North America, 1756–7. Allan Ramsay, c. 1747. © National Museums Scotland. Courtesy of The Bute Collection at Mount Stuart.

Figure 1.2 Highland bagpipes said to have belonged to Piper MacCorquodale who played at the raising of the 74th Regiment of Foot for service in the American War of Independence, 1778. © National Museums Scotland.

Table 1.2 Lieutenant Colonel James Stuart's Patronage Network, Madras, 1775–83

Local/Regional	National
Lts Andrew & George Cochrane; Basil Cochrane (Dundonald)	Col. Charles Stuart (Bute)
	Capt. William Murray (Atholl)
	John Maitland (Lauderdale)
Hamilton of Stobbs	Maxwell of Annan
Hamilton of Monkland	Dalziell of Anstruther
John Campbell (Renfrew)	Maj. Maclellan (Stirlingshire)
John Wallace (Ayr)	Col. Donald Macleod (Argyll)
Col. Moses Crawford (Ayr)	Byres of Tonley (Aberdeen)
Lt. Napier (Renfrew)	
Lt. Thomas Boyes (Hamilton)	
Lt. William Stuart (Lanark)	
Lt. James Orr (Glasgow)	
Lt. James Spens (Renfrew)	

(Source: National Library of Scotland, Stuart-Stevenson Papers, MSS 8250-57, 8326-30)

association with Scotland. A breakdown of the army at Halifax, Nova Scotia commanded by Loudon in 1757 confirms the need to move beyond obviously Scottish units and consider the dispersed nature of Scotland's contribution in officers and men.[42] The Royal Scots were commanded by Lieutenant-Colonel James St Clair; eighteen of its forty-one (43.9 per cent) commissioned personnel were Scots, one less than the Irish total; meanwhile, 462 (41 per cent) of its 1,124 rank and file were Scots. Yet any suggestion that a high percentage of Scots officers in a given unit led automatically to a similarly prominent Scottish presence in the rank and file is disproved by the example of the 55th regiment. Only six out of its thirty-two-strong officer corps were Scots, while 427 (54.3 per cent) of the soldiers hailed from north of the border. They had been raised across various Scottish shires in 1756 by means of the Impressment Act.[43] These men were conscripts in an army supposedly comprised of volunteers. The dispersal of Scots throughout the British army is important in rethinking the emphases and consequences of the eighteenth-century era. The overall amount entering units that were not linked in some way with the Lowlands must have been substantial over the course of the century, and their history remains to be written.

However, no assessment of Scotland's increasing role in British global expansion can be complete without considering the Highland regiments. These units undoubtedly suffer from overexposure and risk being used as a shorthand metaphor for military Scotland more generally. If contrasted against wider patterns of Scottish enlistment, what stands out about the Highland units raised prior to 1793 is less their Gaelic nature or their uniforms and music – hugely important as these well-known characteristics undoubtedly are. The composition of their manpower is equally significant and constitutes a neglected reason why they have come to dominate, in some ways unfairly, representations of Scotland's contribution to the British army. While many eighteenth-century regiments often had a preponderance of English or Irish officers or men, the normal state of affairs involved a leavening effect by which all the various British and Irish nationalities were represented to a greater or lesser extent.[44] Regiments therefore constituted melting pots in micro, bringing English, Irish, Scots and Welsh personnel together. As a mosaic of nationalities they reflected the diversity of the British-Irish Isles themselves. The contrast with the early Highland regiments was a stark one. Historians have already noted that a stand-out feature of units such as the 42nd Black Watch, or Fraser's and Montgomery's Highlanders, sent to North America in 1756–7, or Seaforth's 78th (later 72nd) Highlanders deployed to India in 1778, is the overwhelmingly Scottish origins of both the officers and men. Returns for Montgomery's show all the officers were Scots, as were the mass of the men, dividing unequally into 1,001 Highland and fifty-nine Lowland.[45] All 1,059 men and forty-six officers of the two battalions of the Black Watch in North America in 1757 were Scots. Similarly, when the 89th Highland regiment departed for India in 1759, every one of its twenty-nine officers and a substantial majority of its 834 men came from north of the border.[46] The result could be conspicuous concentrations of Scottish manpower in particular imperial theatres in ways that belied the much larger but evenly spread quantities of men from England and Ireland. By late 1757, with additional companies added to each of the three Highland regiments, the number of men from the north of Scotland serving in North America came to 5,493.[47] This total was only slightly below that in the main Jacobite army towards the latter stages of the 1745 rising.

The importance of this highly concentrated pattern of enlistment has not been sufficiently factored into assessments of how ideas of Scotland and Scottishness were maintained and even amplified through army service in this period. By creating such obvious clusters of Scottish or Highland manpower, the early Highland regiments reinforced the sense among contemporary commentators that Scotland punched above its weight. William Pitt the Elder's oft-quoted statement in 1766 about mobilising Highland valour and the memorable personification of martial Scotland in the form of the Seven Years War veteran, Lieutenant Obadiah Lismahago in Tobias Smollett's 1771 novel *The Expedition of Humphry Clinker*, reveal just how closely Scots were automatically linked with soldiering.[48] It mattered not that by the mid-1790s the country's limited human reserves were exhausted in ways that left nominally Scottish and Highland units heavily reliant on recruits from elsewhere in Britain and Ireland. Scotland's status as the poor demographic cousin of both England and Ireland eventually resulted in five regiments having in 1809 to abandon kilts and other Scottish accoutrements in order to better reflect the origins of their recruits.[49] By that date, cultural perceptions that associated Scotland with soldiering had solidified not just in Scotland but across the rest of the British-Irish Isles. The impression created by the wholly Scottish-manned regiments raised in the 1750s, in the 1770s and in

1793 persisted until the outbreak of the First World War and beyond, as examined by other chapters within this volume.

This reputation as a font of soldiers was to some extent justified. However, it has not been properly tested against the realities of Britain's global efforts. One of the most important characteristics of Scotland's experience of the eighteenth-century era of warfare was that the country continued to supply officers at a disproportionate rate, but not rank and file manpower. The traditional focus on the wars in North America has disguised the reality that, in some key areas, the Scottish contribution was actually below what might be expected, and indeed marginal when compared to the much larger Irish presence. Nowhere is this more obvious than in recruitment to the EIC's European regiments.[50] Although maintaining a much smaller size of military force comprised of British and Irish nationals, mortality rates in South Asia forced the London-based corporation into a constant search for men in order to maintain the garrison force of British and Irish nationals used to supplement and if necessary police the large number of sepoys. In this context Scotland was not a fertile recruiting ground. Embarkation lists prove conclusively that in marked contrast to the attractiveness of Asia to the military gentry, ordinary Scots avoided the eastern hemisphere of the empire. Ship rolls for the years between 1775 and 1781 reveal a total of 4,949 men sent east: only 170 (3.4 per cent) were Scots.[51] The top-heavy nature of Scottish military migration to Asia is captured perfectly in the example of the EIC ship, the *Besborough*, which departed for Bombay in 1776 with a total of forty-three military personnel onboard: eight cadets and thirty-five rank and file. While three of the junior officers (37.55 per cent) were Scots, there was not a single Scottish soldier among the enlisted men.[52] This example fits a much wider and telling pattern where ship after ship departing to India contained more Scottish officers than ordinary Scots soldiers.

The marked differences in how Scots interacted with the different spheres of British imperialism warn against a one-dimensional reading of the country's post-union military experience. A holistic assessment involves juxtaposing the well-known examples of involvement in conflicts overseas with far more mundane but equally important domestic developments. In a seminal analysis of martial Scotland, John Cookson rightly stresses the process by which Scottish manpower became increasingly responsible for the country's defence. Not least as a consequence of fears over Jacobitism, post-union Scotland had been largely garrisoned by non-Scottish regiments from 1707 until the American War of Independence. This changed dramatically in the 1790s with the advent of a militia and mass volunteering.[53] These innovations constituted a major renewal of the country's sense of its own martial tradition and inculcated a new level of confidence regarding Scotland's place within the union. Only by factoring in this crucial change at home can the eighteenth- and early nineteenth-century phase of military history be properly comprehended. The conventional emphasis upon the country's lack of a militia throughout most of the century and on the high-profile Highland regiments means it is easy to forget just how popular parish and county-based defence service became during the 1790s.[54] Compared to the volume of manpower in the regular line regiments, unglamorous part-time soldiering for purely local purposes attracted huge numbers. In 1797, with over 26,200 enrolled, Scotland supplied 36 per cent of the UK's entire volunteer strength.[55] By 1805 the Scottish total stood at 47,583, with a further 7,900 in the militia.[56] A noticeable feature of this upsurge in community soldiering was the way state incomes were used quite deliberately to diversify the financial basis of rural economies. This explains why it was often in areas like the Highlands, far removed from the likely seat of invasion, where volunteering proved most popular. In an important example of how agrarian communities 'cannibalised' and 'fed off' the latest trends in state development, landlords, gentry and tenantry used national defence imperatives to service their own domestic socio-economic needs.[57] By 1805 no fewer than 500 men were enlisted as volunteers in Skye alone, providing much-needed income and slowing down the rate of emigration.[58] In many ways this alignment of soldiering and local economy represented the sort of martial activity that the bulk of Scots related to and found most palatable. The dramatic deeds in exotic locations of the regular regiments may be how Scotland's martial past is commonly represented. Yet for the vast majority of eighteenth-century Scots soldiering took the form of weekly training within the parish. This part-time, prosaic and community-orientated version of service constitutes as important a part of the history of military Scotland as the exploits of the Black Watch at Ticonderoga or the Camerons at Waterloo. To fully comprehend the global dimensions of Scotland's history in this period it is vital to remain aware of the enduring and even growing role of the local experience.

Eighteenth-century Scotland did not possess a single military economy but rather several distinct, if inter-related, export streams in manpower. As a society it deployed a range of military emigrants, from gentlemanly capitalist officers like Stuart to large numbers of ordinary soldiers. Meanwhile, by the 1790s, there also developed a popular and widespread culture of part-time defence service. This diversity facilitated an acute sensitivity and responsiveness to the wide range of opportunities offered by Britain's global empire while broadening access to state earnings. Material and financial gain was evident through the whole social hierarchy and across the whole country, not just the Highlands. Within their own terms of reference these new economies of manpower and military entrepreneurship proved decidedly profitable. Once connected to the empire in North America between c. 1740 and c. 1780 it was possible to deploy thousands of ordinary rank and file – disproportionately Highlanders. However, this does not mean Richards's characterisation of the region's transatlantic militarism as dependent and underdeveloped in comparison to that of Lowland Scotland is correct.[59] It certainly did not produce large financial profits equivalent to Glasgow's tobacco or sugar trades; but the capacity of the Highland elite to mobilise reserves of manpower still brought tangible returns in the form of hundreds of regular army commissions – the highest per capita within any region of the British-Irish Isles – while confirming their status as honourable gentlemen.

For ordinary soldiers too, the profits could be substantial. Within five months in 1784 Highland soldiers demobilised upon the peace with the Americans were granted a total of 54,300 acres in Nova Scotia and Upper Quebec.[60] In the age of proto-globalisation, where agrarian resources and the material and cultural kudos arising from secure access to land remained an enduring characteristic of all societies, the new transatlantic military economy delivered massive upward social mobility. Soldiering also drove the oceanic expansion of the Highlands, Scotland's poorest and supposedly most commercially 'backward' region, to the furthest reaches of the empire.

Profits from Asia were in many ways more conventional in that they came in the form of financial gain. The EIC's expansion across South Asia represented the continuation of the predatory plunder economies that had characterised Spain's conquest of the New World in the early sixteenth century. In this sense it conforms to the concept of proto-globalisation as a persistence of older forms of activity within new frameworks. Cultures of military entrepreneurship were no different. Soldiering in Asia constituted a high-risk, high-return form of military emigration.[61] Mortality rates were extremely high for officers and men alike. But the potential rewards for officers and the material security afforded to the Company's ordinary soldiers made even this most dangerous of career options attractive. To stable and predictable rates of pay could be added the proceeds of plunder and prize money. As late as 1799, when the EIC's forces stormed Srirangapatna, the capital of the southern Indian kingdom of Mysore, the scale of the monies taken amounted to £1,259,500.[62] The high profile of Scots in the officer corps ensured the country benefited disproportionately from such events. 'Nabob' generals like Sir Hector Munro of Novar profited from earlier phases of expansion in the 1750s and 1770s and invested tens of thousands worth of plunder from India back into their home locales.[63] When he acquired command of the Madras army, Stuart of Torrance and Castlemilk received a salary of £3,200 per annum. This amount can be put into context by a contrast against his elder brother's estate, just south of Glasgow, with a rent of £787 per annum.[64] In the high-risk, high-return environment of Asia, soldiering could bring financial gain to more than just the elite; it percolated down the social hierarchy. In 1789 Sergeant Robert Brockie of the Madras army died and left his belongings to his two brothers and one sister in Midlothian.[65] Although it amounted to only £176 – a world away from the fortunes made by the likes of Munro of Novar or Stuart of Torrance and Castlemilk – it was only one of many examples of financial remuneration acquired by those at the lower reaches of the military machine.[66]

Reviewing Scotland's military experience during the long eighteenth century underlines the extent of the country's precocious involvement in global imperialism. There is no doubting the sophistication, diversity and effectiveness of engagement with Britain's military complex from the 1690s onwards. It is hard to sustain the conventional conclusion that Scotland's militarism within the British state and union was evidence of relative backwardness and underdevelopment. Here was an economy of state service which responded effectively to the

Figure 1.3 Lieutenant Robert Hamilton-Buchanan of the Royal Scots Fusiliers. Studio of David Allan, c. 1779. © National Museums Scotland.

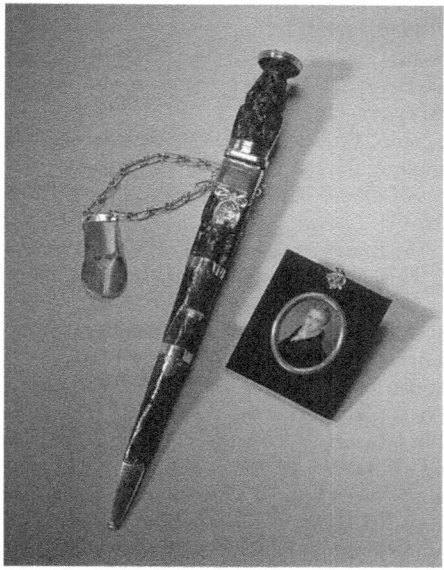

Figure 1.4 Dirk and miniature of Captain David Aytone of the 74th Regiment of Foot. Aytone was wounded at Srirangapatna (Seringapatam) on 26 April 1799. © National Museums Scotland, courtesy of the earl of Lindsay.

opportunities of proto-globalisation by redeploying older cultures of soldiering in new ways and to radically different geographies. Military Scotland constantly adapted and re-utilised local, regional and national resources, be these surplus manpower or social networks of gentlemanly capitalist patronage. The overriding hallmark of this hugely important era in Scotland's long military history is its complexity, efficiency and, above all, the intimate and continuous interaction of the global and the local.

Notes

1. British Library (BL), India Office Records (IOR), Papers of Sir John Macpherson, Mss Eur F291/119/7-21.
2. Hugh Dunthorne, 'Scots in the Wars of the Low Countries, 1572–1648', in Grant C. Simpson (ed.), *Scotland and the Low Countries, 1124–1994* (East Linton: Tuckwell, 1996), pp. 104–21; Steve Murdoch, *Scotland and the Thirty Years War* (Leiden: Brill, 2001), pp. 9–20; Alexia Grosjean, *An Unofficial Alliance: Scotland and Sweden, 1569–1654* (Leiden: Brill, 2003), p. 106; Jochem Miggelbrink, 'The End of the Scots-Dutch Brigade', in Steve Murdoch and Andrew Mackillop (eds), *Fighting for Identity: The Scottish Military Experience, c. 1550–1900* (Leiden: Brill, 2002), pp. 83–103; Allan Carswell, '"Mercenaries": the Scottish Soldier in Foreign Service, 1568–1860', in Edward M. Spiers, Jeremy A. Crang and Matthew J. Strickland (eds), *A Military History of Scotland* (Edinburgh: Edinburgh University Press, 2012), pp. 248–70; Keith M. Brown, 'From Scottish lords to British officers: State building, elite Integration and the army in seventeenth century Scotland', in Norman Macdougall (ed.), *Scotland and War AD 79–1918* (Edinburgh: John Donald, 1990), pp. 133–69, at pp. 145–9.
3. Linda Colley, *Britons: Forging the Nation, 1707–1832* (London: Pimlico, 1992), pp. 126–9; Victoria Henshaw, *Scotland and the British Army, 1700–1750* (London: Bloomsbury, 2014), pp. 35–51.
4. Stephen Conway, 'Scots, Britons and Europeans: Scottish military service, c. 1739–1783', *Historical Research*, 82, no. 215 (2009), pp. 114–30; Stephen Conway, *Britain, Ireland and Continental Europe in the Eighteenth Century* (Oxford: Oxford University Press, 2011), pp. 267–75.
5. John E. Cookson, *The British Armed Nation, 1793–1815* (Oxford: Clarendon Press, 1997), pp. 126–52; Hew Strachan, 'Scotland's Military Identity', *Scottish Historical Review*, vol. 85, no. 2 (2006), pp. 315–25.
6. Andrew Mackillop, *'More fruitful than the soil'; Army, Empire and the Scottish Highlands, 1715–1815* (East Linton: Tuckwell, 2000), passim.
7. Eric Richards, 'Scotland and the Uses of the Atlantic Empire', in Bernard Bailyn and P. D. Morgan (eds), *Strangers within the Realm: Cultural Margins of the First British Empire* (Chapel Hill: Johns Hopkins University Press, 1991), pp. 92–111.
8. Strachan, 'Scotland's Military Identity', p. 324.
9. Anthony G. Hopkins, 'Introduction: Globalization – An Agenda for Historians', in Anthony G. Hopkins (ed.), *Globalization in World History* (London: Pimlico, 2002), pp. 1–10, at pp. 5–6; Felicity A. Nussbaum, 'Introduction', in Felicity A. Nussbaum (ed.), *The Global Eighteenth Century* (Baltimore: Johns Hopkins University Press, 2003), pp. 1–18, at p. 12.
10. John Brewer, *The Sinews of Power: War, Money and the English State, 1688–1783* (London: Routledge, 1989), passim; John Brewer, 'The Eighteenth-Century British

State: Contexts and issues', in Lawrence Stone (ed.), *An Imperial State at War: Britain from 1689–1815* (London: Routledge, 1994), pp. 52–71.
11. Tony Ballantyne, 'Empire, Knowledge, and Culture: From Proto-Globalization to Modern Globalization', in Hopkins, *Globalization in World History*, pp. 115–40, at pp. 117–18.
12. Christopher A. Bayly, *The Making of the Modern World, 1780–1914* (Oxford: Blackwell, 2004), pp. 27–48.
13. Peter J. Marshall, 'The eighteenth-century empire', in Peter J. Marshall, *'A Free though Conquering People': Eighteenth-century Britain and its Empire* (Aldershot: Ashgate, 2003), pp. 177–200, at pp. 181–3; Philip J. Stern, *The Company State: Corporate Sovereignty and the Early Modern Foundations of the British Empire in India* (Oxford: Oxford University Press, 2011), pp. 9–12.
14. Anthony G. Hopkins, 'The History of Globalization – and the Globalization of History?', in Hopkins, *Globalization in World History*, pp. 11–46, at pp. 24–6.
15. Jan de Vries, 'The Industrial and the Industrious Revolution', *Journal of Economic History*, vol. 54, no. 2 (1994), pp. 249–57; Bayly, *The Birth of the Modern World*, pp. 51–64.
16. Christopher A. Bayly, '"Archaic" and "Modern" Globalization in the Eurasian and African Arena, c. 1750–1850', in Hopkins, *Globalization in World History*, pp. 47–73, at p. 50.
17. Peter J. Cain and Anthony G. Hopkins, *British Imperialism: Innovation and Expansion, 1688–1914* (London: Longman, 1993), pp. 53–104.
18. T. Christopher Smout, Ned C. Landsman and Thomas M. Devine, 'Scottish Emigration in the Seventeenth and Eighteenth Centuries', in Nicholas Canny (ed.), *Europeans on the Move: Studies on European Migration, 1500–1800* (Oxford: Oxford University Press, 1994), pp. 76–95; David Armitage, 'The Scottish Diaspora', in Jenny Wormald (ed.), *Scotland: A History* (Oxford: Oxford University Press, 2005), pp. 272–303, at pp. 278, 287–8; Steve Murdoch and Esther Mijers, 'Migrant Destinations, 1500–1750', in Thomas M. Devine and Jenny Wormald (eds), *The Oxford Handbook of Modern Scottish History* (Oxford: Oxford University Press, 2012), pp. 320–7, at pp. 323–6.
19. *Scots Magazine*, 6 (1744), p. 39.
20. Brown, 'From Scottish lords to British officers', pp. 148–9.
21. *Scots Magazine*, 9 (1747), pp. 350–1.
22. Brewer, *The Sinews of Power*, pp. 29–45.
23. Sean J. Connolly, *Divided Kingdom: Ireland, 1630–1800* (Oxford: Oxford University Press, 2008), p. 164; David Allan, *Scotland in the Eighteenth Century* (Harlow: Pearson, 2002), pp. 81–2; Toby Barnard, *A New Anatomy of Ireland: The Irish Protestants, 1649–1770* (New Haven: Yale University Press, 2003), p. 178.
24. James Hayes, 'Scottish Officers in the British Army, 1714–1763', *Scottish Historical Review*, vol. 37, no. 123 (1958), pp. 23–33.
25. Stephen Brumwell, *Redcoats: The British Soldier and the War in the Americas, 1755–1763* (Cambridge: Cambridge University Press, 2006), p. 319.
26. Cookson, *The British Armed Nation*, p. 127.
27. The eighteenth century produced striking examples of literature that celebrated Scottish society's historic and ongoing commitment to military service. See Patrick Abercromby, *The martial achievements of the Scots nation. Being an account of the lives, characters, and memorable actions, of such Scotsmen as have signaliz'd themselves by the sword at home and abroad . . .* vols I–II (Edinburgh: Robert Freebairn, 1711); Tobias Smollett, *The Expedition of Humphry Clinker* (Ware: Wordsworth, 1995), p. 191.

28. Gerry J. Bryant, 'The East India Company and its army, 1600–1778', PhD thesis, University of London, 1975, pp. 328–30; Raymond Callahan, *The East India Company and Army Reform, 1783–1798* (Cambridge, MA: Harvard University Press, 1972), pp. 5–15.
29. IOR, L/MIL/11/109: 'Roll of the Hon. Company's Troops on the Coast of Cormondel, 1762.'
30. As early as September 1769 the Court of Directors approved an annual appointment of 200 cadets. See IOR, B/85, pp. 220–1.
31. Gerry J. Bryant, 'Officers of the East India Company's Army in the Days of Clive and Hastings', *Journal of Imperial and Commonwealth History*, vol. 6, no. 3 (1978), pp. 203–27, at p. 206.
32. IOR, L/MIL/9/115/Parts 1-4/171 and 178.
33. Peter E. Razzell, 'Social Origins of Officers in the Indian and British Home Army: 1758–1962', *The British Journal of Sociology*, vol. 14, no. 3 (1963), pp. 248–60.
34. Huw V. Bowen, 'British Conceptions of Global Empire, 1756–1763', *Journal of Imperial and Commonwealth History*, 26, no. 3 (1998), pp. 1–20.
35. National Records of Scotland (NRS), Campbell of Inverneil Muniments, RH 4/121/7: Fort William, 3 December 1772: Archibald Campbell to Council of Bengal; 'Memorial of Lieutenant-Colonel Archibald Campbell to Viscount Barrington'; National Library of Scotland (NLS), Melville Papers, Ms 3837, fo. 4; NLS, Stuart-Stevenson Papers, Ms 8250, fo. 40; IOR, B/98, pp. 700, 730.
36. E. Irving Carlyle, 'Stuart, James (d. 1793)', rev. Michael Fry, *Oxford Dictionary of National Biography*, Oxford University Press, 2004, http://www.oxforddnb.com/view/article/26709 (last accessed 15 May 2015); Andrew Mackillop, 'Fashioning a "British Empire": Sir Archibald Campbell of Inverneil and Madras, 1785–1789', in Andrew Mackillop and Steve Murdoch (eds), *Military Governors and Imperial Frontiers: A study of Scotland and empires, 1600–1800* (Leiden: Brill, 2003), pp. 205–31.
37. NLS, Mackenzie of Delvine Papers, MS 1306, fos. 5–76.
38. Vernon C. P. Hodson, *List of the Officers of the Bengal Army, 1758–1834*, III (London: Constable, 1927), pp. 119–20.
39. The National Archives (TNA), Chatham Papers, PRO 30/8/96, fo. 30.
40. Paul Langford, 'South Britons' Reception of North Britons, 1707–1820', in T. C. Smout (ed.), *Anglo-Scottish Relations from 1603 to 1900* (Oxford: Oxford University Press, 2005), pp. 143–69; Ronald M. Sunter, *Patronage and Politics in Scotland 1707–1832* (Edinburgh: John Donald, 2003), pp. 42–60.
41. Stuart Allan and Allan Carswell, *The Thin Red Line: War, Empire and Visions of Scotland* (Edinburgh: NMSE, 2004), pp. 5–30; Charles J. Esdaile, 'The French Revolutionary and Napoleonic Wars, 1793–1815', in Spiers, Crang and Strickland (eds), *A Military History of Scotland*, pp. 407–35, at pp. 407–9.
42. Brumwell, *Redcoats*, p. 74.
43. Huntington Library, Pasadena, CA (HL), Loudon (American) Collection: LO 3936(1): Return of the 55th Regt, 13 July 1757; NLS, Fletcher of Saltoun Papers, MS 17505, fos. 97–8; TNA, WO 1/972, fo. 305; WO 1/974, fo. 485.
44. For regiments in North America staffed largely with English or Irish officers and men, respectively see HL, Loudon (American) Collection: LO 1683 (1): Returns of the 40th Regt, 7 July 1757; LO 4012(1): Returns of the 27th Regt Inniskillen, 13 July 1757.
45. Peter J. Marshall, 'A nation defined by Empire', in Alexander Grant and Keith J. Stringer (eds), *Uniting the Kingdom? The Making of British History* (London: Routledge, 1995), pp. 208–22, at p. 210.

46. Brumwell, *Redcoats*, pp. 318–19; IOR, L/MIL/9/85: Embarkation lists, 1753–63 [1759], p. 133.
47. BL, Newcastle MSS, Add MS 33047, fo. 215.
48. Thomas M. Devine, *Scotland's Empire, 1600–1815* (London: Penguin, 2003), p. 311; Smollett, *The Expedition of Humphry Clinker*, p. 176.
49. Cookson, *British Armed Nation*, pp. 128–30, 136.
50. Andrew Mackillop, 'Locality, Nation and Empire: Scots and the Empire in Asia, c. 1695–c.1813', in John M. MacKenzie and Thomas M. Devine (eds), *The Oxford History of the British Empire: Scotland and the British Empire* (Oxford: Oxford University Press, 2011), pp. 54–83, at pp. 68–9.
51. IOR, L/MIL/9/90: Embarkation Lists, 1775–84, pp. 1–229.
52. IOR, L/MIL/9/90, pp. 39–40.
53. Cookson, *British Armed Nation*, pp. 144–5.
54. John Robertson, *The Scottish Enlightenment and the Militia Issue* (Edinburgh: John Donald, 1985), pp. 106–12.
55. NRS, Irvine-Robertson Series, GD1/53/104; Colley, *Britons*, pp. 382–4; Cookson, *British Armed Nation*, pp. 140–1.
56. NRS, Hope of Luffness Muniments, GD364/1/1160/7, 'Return of forces in arms in North Britain, 17 August 1805'.
57. Mackillop, *'More fruitful than the soil'*, pp. 225–33.
58. NRS, Seafield Muniments, GD248/1534, pp. 36–9, 240.
59. Richards, 'Scotland and the Uses of the Atlantic Empire', pp. 92–111.
60. BL, Haldimand Papers, Add MS 21828, fos. 29–151.
61. Gerry J. Bryant, 'Scots in India in the Eighteenth Century', *Scottish Historical Review*, vol. 64 (1985), pp. 22–41, at pp. 23–7; Thomas M. Devine, *Scotland's Empire, 1600–1815* (London: Allen Lane, 2003), pp. 250–70.
62. IOR, L/MIL/5/159: Correspondence relating to Seringapatam prize money, 1800, pp. 360–3.
63. Andrew Mackillop, 'The Highlands and the Returning Nabob: Sir Hector Munro of Novar, 1760–1807', in Marjory Harper (ed.), *Emigrant Homecomings: The Return Movement of Emigrants, 1600–2000* (Manchester: Manchester University Press, 2005), pp. 233–62, at p. 245.
64. NLS, Stuart-Stevenson Papers, MS 8257, fo. 45; MS 8207, fo. 15e.
65. IOR, L/AG/34/29/193: Madras Wills 1791, pp. 1040–2.
66. For the property affairs of ordinary enlisted Scots in India, see IOR, P/328/62: Madras Mayor Court Wills [1763], pp. 67–8; [1765], pp. 8–9.

2

Forging Nationhood: Scottish Imperial Identity and the Construction of Nationhood in the Dominions, 1880–1914

Edward M. Spiers

On the morning of 1 September 1880, as the column from Kabul breakfasted near Kandahar, Major Ashe, who served on the staff of Major-General Sir (later Lord) Frederick S. Roberts, observed that:

> It was impossible not to be struck with the splendid appearance and peculiarly fine physique of the Highland regiments: their chest measurement, muscular development, and the bronzed hues of sun and wind giving them a martial appearance beyond all the other corps.[1]

Thereafter in the ensuing battle of Kandahar, the 72nd (later the 1st Battalion, Seaforth Highlanders) and the 92nd Gordon Highlanders would win fresh laurels in the first of a series of military triumphs, and some tragedies, over the next twenty years that would confirm the worldwide reputation of the Scottish soldier. That reputation had been forged since the Nine Years War (1688–97) and the War of the Spanish Succession (1701–14) as a loyal and resolute servant of the British Crown. It was tested by the response to Jacobite risings, or rebellions, of 1715 and 1745–6, bolstered by imperial service in North America, India and throughout the empire; and enhanced by engagement with the French Revolutionary and Napoleonic forces.[2] Yet as the empire approached its zenith in the late nineteenth century, the fighting reputation of the Scottish soldier attained fresh heights in achievement, reportage and imagery. This imagery firmly associated the Scottish soldier with a distinctive concept of Scottish identity, expressed within the British army and imbued with an imperial purpose. The Scottish diaspora responded by creating Highland regiments, as 'a wave of manifestations of Scottish identity' swept through the colonial world in the 1880s, largely stimulated by the formation of Caledonian societies.[3]

Scottish regiments and 'Highlandism'

In 1881 the recently elected Liberal government established the context within which the Scottish, and in particular the kilted, soldier would thrive. By endorsing the regimental reforms of Hugh Childers, the secretary of state for war (1880–2), it established nine double-battalion and one single-battalion Scottish regiments (six of which had Highland status and five were kilted). The ten Scottish regiments represented some 14 per cent of the seventy double-battalion regiments and one single-battalion regiment formed across the United Kingdom. This represented a huge concession to 'the particularisms of Highland regiments and their popular following',[4] as Scottish recruiting had already fallen significantly below its 10 per cent share of the United Kingdom's population[5] and would remain below its proportionate share until the onset of the Great War.[6] As these reforms codified the localisation of the new regiments, with permanent depots and local militia and volunteer units attached in specific territorial districts, they perpetuated a further myth, namely that the Highland regiments could recruit within their dedicated Highland districts. However, the Clearances, emigration to North America and internal migration in search of better-paid employment had ensured that Scottish infantry regiments had to recruit predominantly within the industrial belt of central Scotland. They competed thereby with the Scots Guards and Scotland's only cavalry regiment, the Royal Scots Greys – regiments that could recruit across the United Kingdom as a whole – as well as with the specialist attractions of the Royal Artillery, Royal Engineers and Royal Marines. As some Scots chose to serve in English or Irish regiments, or joined the Royal Navy, Scottish infantry regiments had to find additional recruits from England and to a lesser extent Ireland. By 'the late nineteenth century', as Heather Streets observes, 'the men who enlisted in the Highland regiments were increasingly urban and from the lower working classes, in contrast to the rural, clan-based Highland-born warriors of popular legend'.[7]

So why did the War Office authorities 'pander' to the Scots and treat them more generously than, say, Yorkshire, England's largest county by area, which received only six double-battalion regiments?[8] Many senior officers shared the popular perspective that the Highland regiments were exceptional fighting units. Sir Garnet J. Wolseley, who was one of the few senior officers willing to promote army reform, had set aside the 1st West India Regiment in his planning for the Asante campaign (1873–4) in favour of 'a Regiment with such fine traditions and in so fine a state of discipline as Her Majesty's 42nd Highlanders'.[9] Similarly, in India, Wolseley's great rival, Roberts, heaped accolades on the 72nd and 92nd after the victory of Kandahar: 'you beat them at Cabul [sic, Kabul], you have beaten them at Candahar [sic, Kandahar], and you can now leave the country, feeling assured that the very last troops the Afghans wish to meet in the field are Highlanders and Goorkhas [sic]. You have made a name for yourselves in Afghanistan.'[10] Sir Colin Campbell and Henry Havelock expressed similar sentiments after commanding Highland regiments during the Crimean War (1854–6) and Indian Mutiny (1857–9),[11] and these tributes reinforced romanticised perceptions of the Highland warrior.

These notions underpinned the belief that Highland soldiers, by being drawn from a remote, austere and unspoiled landscape, possessed moral and physical attributes that were lacking in their undersized, urban slum-bred counterparts.

These supposedly innate qualities of resolve, courage, endurance and stoicism resonated among Scottish communities overseas, especially where the taming of the wilderness loomed large in their collective consciousness. Scots had been all too prominent in this process: Mungo Park, David Livingstone and James Bruce *inter alia* in Africa, John McDouall Stuart, who had led several explorations of inland Australia, and Charles Edward Douglas, who was still exploring the west coast of New Zealand in the 1880s. Exploring, surveying, trading, and spreading the Gospel reflected the Romanticist tenet that 'the wild could be physically and culturally tamed'.[12] In Canada, where the environmental and climatic conditions were particularly challenging, Alexander Mackenzie, Simon Fraser, John Howison, Robert Campbell, John Rae and John McLeod had undertaken some remarkable expeditions. By the late nineteenth century, as Jenni Calder writes, 'there was a growing regret at the loss of the wilderness', but also 'a growing nostalgia for the skills and fortitude that brought about that loss'.[13]

The personal attributes associated with the Highland soldier were bolstered by the belief that he came from a martial culture, based upon loyalty to the hereditary clan chief, and that this loyalty had been transposed into loyal service of the Crown. From the novels of Sir Walter Scott (1771–1832), the cultural musings of Major General David Stewart of Garth (1772–1829), and their choreographing of the Highland festival for George IV, when he visited Edinburgh as the first Hanoverian monarch in 1822,[14] 'Highlandism' had emerged. It would be sustained in the mid-Victorian era by the Romantic writings of James Grant (1822–87), by the Highland gentry in their memorable reception for Queen Victoria on her first visit to the Highlands in 1842, and by the proliferation of Highland societies, both across the UK and the empire, until the costume and tartans associated with Highlanders became accepted by outsiders and Lowlanders alike as emblematic of Scotland.[15]

Of all these factors, none was more important than the queen's fascination for Scotland and its people. If rooted in her early reading of Sir Walter Scott's writings, and so pre-dating the tour of 1842, she found this passion enhanced by her first sight of Balmoral in 1848, and her long and frequent visits thereafter. Her ensuing set of beliefs about Scottish identity, sometimes dubbed as 'Balmorality', may have been 'a romantic, backward-looking vision of Scotland as a society ... characterized by clan-based hierarchical loyalties and distinctive Highland rituals'[16] but they were nonetheless profound, and often focused upon the Highland regiments. She took a close interest in her Highland guards of honour, asked after individual soldiers, bestowed a royal title upon the 79th Highlanders in 1873 (whereupon it became the Queen's Own Cameron Highlanders), and regularly presented regimental colours to Highland regiments at Balmoral.[17] She also lobbied directly on behalf of the kilted regiments, opposing earlier versions of the reforms ultimately approved by Childers. In 1877 she informed her first cousin, Prince George, the second duke of Cambridge, who was the field marshal commanding in chief, that 'to direct the 42nd to wear the Cameron Tartan, or my own Cameron Highlanders to wear that of the Black Watch, would create great dissatisfaction, and would be unmeaning'.[18] She again objected to a proposal in 1880 to clothe all the Highland regiments in the Royal Hunting tartan, and pressed for the 72nd to be 'rewarded for their services in Afghanistan by being given the kilt as their dress instead of the trews'.[19] While the queen welcomed a concession that the old numbers and special designations of the single-battalion regiments would be preserved, she insisted successfully that the kilted regiments could not be forced into a single tartan. 'These are', she wrote, 'most of them representatives of old Clans, and even in the present proposals *new* clan names are suggested. To take from them their clan tartans would be a great mistake . . .'[20]

Facing such opposition, Childers capitulated and preserved the five kilted regiments by forcing four single-battalion regiments, which had lost the kilt in 1809,[21] to join four kilted single-battalion regiments, leaving the Cameron Highlanders as the sole single-battalion regiment (but it received a second battalion in 1897 with all of Scotland as its recruiting area).[22] The reform created, or confirmed, the new names of the Highland regiments: the Black Watch (Royal Highland Regiment), the Highland Light Infantry which wore trews, Seaforth Highlanders, Gordon Highlanders, Queen's Own Cameron Highlanders, and the Argyll and Sutherland Highlanders. In addition, the War Office imposed forms of Highland dress and semi-Highland accoutrements upon the Lowland regiments, namely tartan trews, kilted pipers (where pipe bands did not exist), doublets and basket-hilted broadswords.[23] This imposition of a Highland form of Scottish identity upon the Lowland regiments, the Royal Scots, the Royal Scots Fusiliers, the King's Own Scottish Borderers (as it became in 1887) and the Cameronians – all senior to their Highland counterparts in the army's hierarchy – ensured, as Tom Devine observes, that 'the victory of Highlandism was complete'.[24]

The new regiments earned legendary renown over the next two decades and a reputation that received accolades across the empire. They exploited opportunities in colonial campaigns across Africa and the north-west frontier of India. If few of these were quite as controversial as the Second Anglo-Afghan War (1878–81), which William E. Gladstone denounced in his famous Midlothian campaign,[25] the African campaigns in Egypt (1882) and the Sudan, including the ill-fated expedition to relieve Major General Charles 'Chinese' Gordon in Khartoum (1884–5), all had a high political profile in the United Kingdom and ensured an extensive coverage in the printed and illustrated press. More distant campaigns in the late 1880s and 1890s, whether in Burma or the tribal regions of northern India or again in the Sudan (1896–8), required newspapers to consider whether to send their own correspondents or rely upon reports from the central news agencies or pay for reports from local sources, including military correspondents. There were always some reporters available, even if they were military personnel, such as Winston S. Churchill, then a second lieutenant in the 4th Hussars, and the Younghusband brothers, artists and sketchers like Corporal John Farquharson (Cameron Highlanders) and Lieutenant Angus McNeill (Seaforth Highlanders), or photographers like Captain Edward A. Stanton (Egyptian Army) and Colonel Francis 'Frank' A. Rhodes (formerly 1st Royal Dragoons).[26]

The iconography of battlefield triumphs

Scots were prominent, too, in the major engagements of this era. Following their success at Kandahar, the Seaforths led the assault on the south side of the Sweetwater Canal in the battle of Tel-el-Kebir (13 September 1882), while a Highland Brigade (1st Battalions, Black Watch and Gordon Highlanders, 2nd Battalion, Highland Light Infantry and the Queen's Own Cameron Highlanders) attacked the Egyptian fortifications north of the canal. Both the Black Watch and the Gordons fought at El Teb (29 February 1884) and at Tamai (13 March 1884) in the Eastern Sudan, while the Black Watch, alongside the South Staffordshire Regiment, fought the Mahdists again at Kirbekan (10 February 1885). Subsequently, the Cameron Highlanders engaged the Mahdists at Ginnis (30 December 1885), where British forces fought in red for the last time. On the north-west frontier, the 1st Battalion, Gordon Highlanders, operating alongside the 2nd Battalion, King's Own Scottish Borderers (and the 60th King's Royal Rifle Corps), stormed the Malakand Pass (3 April 1895). In a subsequent campaign, the 1st Gordons seized the Dargai Heights (20 October 1897) after the Gurkhas and two English regiments had failed to do so. Finally, the Camerons and Seaforths fought together again in the battles of the Atbara (8 April 1898) and Omdurman (2 September 1898) where Mahdist forces were routed. In all these victories, and in the defeats of Majuba Hill (27 February 1881) and Magersfontein (12 December 1899), where Boer firepower overwhelmed Highland units, Scots provided ample material for the accompanying corps of correspondents, artists and photographers.[27]

Of all these battles none approached the international impact of Dargai. The spectacle of the Gordons ascending precipitous heights, and scattering a more numerous enemy, while a lone, injured piper sat under fire, playing them on, created a sensation in Britain and across the empire. Tributes poured into the regiment, including telegrams from Queen Victoria, and from London, India, Ceylon, and the Caledonian societies in Johannesburg, Cape Town, Durban and even the United States. At a ball of the Highland Society in Johannesburg, Dr Munro, the chief, called upon the company to drink to the health of the Gordon Highlanders and proposed three cheers for the regiment and its 'brave piper'.[28] The correct name of that piper was not known for a couple of months as none of the correspondents were near the battle, and it required a letter from the principal piper, Lance Corporal Patrick Milne, to his brother in Vancouver to clarify that it was Piper George F. Findlater who deserved the accolades and would eventually win the Victoria Cross. Lauded in poetry and prose, including verse composed in Montreal, Canada,[29] Findlater became an imperial icon. His image was captured in photographs, prints, cards, and subsequently reproduced as the central figure of at least four paintings of the charge by Stanley Berkeley, Vereker Hamilton, R. Caton Woodville and Edward M. Hale.[30] He received public subscriptions on account of his gallantry and injury, including one from Scotsmen in Cape Colony, and was reportedly offered a hand in marriage from a wealthy lady in Indian

THE CONSTRUCTION OF NATIONHOOD IN THE DOMINIONS | 37

Figure 2.1 *The Storming of Tel el-Kebir* (detail) by Alphonse Marie de Neuville. This painting depicts an attack by the 1st Battalion, The Black Watch during the 1882 Egypt campaign. © National Museums Scotland.

society. He became a celebrity, playing his pipes in the music halls, but then lost public esteem over a breach of promise suit. He nonetheless toured North America, before retiring to live in a croft at Turriff, Aberdeenshire.[31]

Inevitably the campaigns, which involved major engagements, received much more reportage and commentary than those that were either bloodless or bereft of set-piece battles. While the latter in Zululand and the Black Mountain expeditions (1888 and 1891) provided evocative images,[32] they hardly represented the tests of courage, will and fortitude associated with battlefield triumphs. Moreover, in battle, Highland units served repeatedly as the spear point of the empire, often engaging the enemy in advance of other units. They either pressed ahead of other corps (as the Highland Brigade did at Tel-el-Kebir) or advanced somewhat recklessly (as the Black Watch did at Tamai, leaving a gap in their square) or dictated the whole pace of the advance (as the Camerons did at the Atbara). None of this was new: Campbell had had to restrain the eagerness of the 93rd Highlanders at Balaclava (1854),[33] and the 42nd (Black Watch) had pressed ahead in the Asante War (1873–4), enabling the accompanying correspondent, Winwood Reade, to 'scoop' his rivals as the 42nd entered Kumase, the Asante capital, first.[34] Melton Prior of the *Illustrated London News* resolved thereafter always to follow the tartan, and so when his rival, Frederic Villiers of the *Graphic*, decided to throw in his 'lot' with the

Highland Brigade at Tel-el-Kebir, he encountered Prior already following the Highlanders.[35]

In a golden age of war reporting, the 'special' correspondents provided not only the first histories of the campaigns but also vivid and dramatic accounts of the major battles. Most, if not all,[36] correspondents were staunchly patriotic, identified with the army (sometimes fighting alongside it), and shared the 'proudly ethnocentric imperial and racial beliefs' of the officers with whom they messed.[37] In this era Bennet Burleigh of the *Daily Telegraph* and John Cameron of the *Standard* were prominent Scottish correspondents but most reporters and artists, irrespective of their nationality, celebrated the services of the Scottish soldier. George Warrington Steevens, arguably the doyen of war correspondents, wrote of the advance at the Atbara that 'the bullets were swishing and lashing now like rain on a pond. But the line of khaki and purple tartan never bent or swayed; it just went slowly forward like a ruler.' Once inside the Mahdist stockade, there 'was a wild confusion of Highlanders, purple tartan and black-green, too, for the Seaforths had brought their perfect columns through the teeth of the fire, and were charging in at the gap'.[38]

The work of correspondents and artists was not confined to their employers' newspapers; it was often reproduced, with or without permission, in other newspapers, or in despatches as 'instant' histories, such as Churchill's *The Story of the Malakand Field Force* (1898), which was well reviewed in Britain and India.[39] Some reporters spoke on lecture circuits, wrote reviews for magazines and journals, and published their memoirs as both Prior and Villiers did. Meanwhile, artists used their sketches to illustrate novels, juvenile fiction, popular histories, textbooks and encyclopedias, as well as advertising and packaging, while the more famous, such as Robert Caton Woodville, used them as sources for battle paintings, many of which were then reproduced as prints and engravings for display in schools, clubs, messes and public houses.[40]

Military Scottishness and the Dominions

Given the strong support for the empire within the English-speaking communities of the Dominions, much of this material found its way overseas, reinforcing the cultural and ideological ties that bound these communities to the mother country. Several volunteers in Canada's second contingent during the South African War acknowledged their childhood inspirations from the writings of G. A. Henty and R. M. Ballantyne.[41] When correspondents from the Dominions began reporting Britain's wars, as several did during the South African War (1899–1902), many of them dwelled upon the actions and images associated with Scottish identity. Sent by the Melbourne *Argus*, Donald A. Macdonald was the first Australian to reach the war zone, where he found himself beleaguered in the siege of Ladysmith (1899–1900). Forced to return home after the siege with dysentery, he arrived in Australia at the same time as his despatches. The latter caused a sensation and were reprinted as *How We Kept the Flag Flying* (1900), before Macdonald embarked on a lecture tour in Australia, New Zealand and Britain.[42]

Despite over 12,000 troops being invested in Ladysmith, Macdonald focused overwhelmingly on the exploits of the 2nd Battalion, Gordon Highlanders. In the 'brilliant fight' at Elandslaagte (21 October 1899) he described how the bayonet charge of the Gordons had caused panic among the burghers, and prompted their flight. During the investment he recalled how they boosted morale on 'a braw Scotch necht' when celebrating St Andrew's Night, with pipers playing 'Highland airs, and there was much enthusiasm'. He described, too, how the Gordons were 'extremely anxious' to mount a night attack on the enemy guns after other attacks had succeeded, albeit at a cost that Sir George White, the commanding officer, was unwilling to repeat. In his account of the major Boer assault upon Caesar's Camp (6 January 1900), Macdonald lamented the death of a famous Gordon, Colonel W. H. Dick-Cunyngham, VC, claiming that 'no regimental commander in the British army was better loved'. He lauded the efforts of several Scots, including the thrice-wounded Captain the Hon. Robert Francis Carnegie of the Gordons, who stayed with his men, and led them on, 'fighting nobly, until the enemy were finally driven off the hill'. Although Macdonald acknowledged that the Devons turned the tide of this battle in a 'last grand charge', he saved his final plaudits for another Scot (and former Gordon Highlander), Colonel Ian S. M. Hamilton: he 'held my fancy more than any other man in Ladysmith, as the very *beau-ideal* of a soldier'. This was not because Macdonald knew Hamilton but on account of Hamilton's overall command at Caesar's Camp 'during that desperate seventeen hours of fighting'.[43]

Andrew Barton 'Banjo' Paterson, arguably the most renowned of the Australian commentators, arrived in South Africa with the first volunteers to leave New South Wales. Engaged to send reports and photographs by the *Sydney Morning Herald*, the *Sydney Mail* and the Melbourne *Argus*, Paterson joined the relief force that eventually liberated Kimberley on 15 February 1900. He published about twenty poems, including two Scottish verses, one about a Scottish civil engineer who lost his life on an armoured train and another, 'Jock', that celebrated the Scottish soldier:

> There's a soldier that's been doing of his share
> In the fighting up and down and round about.
> He's continually marching here and there
> And he's fighting, morning in and morning out.
>
> The Boer, you see, he generally runs;
> But sometimes when he hides behind a rock,
> And we can't make no impression with the guns,
> Oh, then you'll hear the order, 'Send for Jock!'
>
> Yes—it's Jock—Scotch Jock.
> He's the fellow that can give or take a knock.
> For he's hairy and he's hard,
> And his feet are by the yard,

And his face is like the face what's on a clock.
But when the bullets fly you will mostly hear the cry—
'Send for Jock!'

The Cavalry have gun and sword and lance,
Before they choose their weapon, why, they're dead.
The Mounted Foot are hampered in advance
By holding of their helmets on their head.

And when the Boer has dug himself a trench
And placed his Maxim gun behind a rock,
These mounted heroes—pets of Johnny French—
They have to sit and wait and send for Jock!
Yes, the Jocks—Scotch Jocks,
With their music that'd terrify an ox!
When the bullets kick the sand
You can hear the sharp command—
'Forty-Second! At the double! Charge the rocks!'
And the charge is like a flood
When they've warmed the Highland blood
Of the Jocks![44]

Written in a Kiplingesque idiom, the poem has been dismissed as one that celebrates 'heroic and warlike Scots' in 'trite and conventional tones', but even this critic admits that the poetry is in 'keeping with the literary conventions of empire'.[45] After the skirmish of Retief's Nek on 23–24 July 1900, Paterson commended the Highlanders as 'the finest troops I have ever seen. They are much more intelligent-looking than the ordinary Tommies.' They might have failed at Magersfontein (11 December 1899), and in the first assault on Paardeberg (18February 1900), but Paterson claimed (incorrectly as regards Paardeberg) that 'no other troops have been asked to do such tasks'. No one, he affirmed, 'could fail to be struck by the bearing and appearance of the Highlanders, or the "Jocks", as they are always called in the army . . .'[46]

Compounding the effects of the wartime reporting was the deepening of the cultural and heritage ties shared between Britain and the Dominions during this period. Many of the great battle paintings involving Scots commemorated past glories, including Robert Gibb's trilogy on the Crimean War. In *Comrades* (1878) he captured the close personal bonds within Highland regiments, and, in *The Thin Red Line* (1881), the resolute defiance of the 93rd Sutherland Highlanders at Balaclava. In *Alma: Forward the 42nd* (1889), he depicted the steady advance of the Black Watch under Campbell's leadership. In two paintings completed in 1900, artist Richard Simkin celebrated the early ties that bound Lowland regiments – the Royal Scots at Steenkirke (1692) and the Cameronians at Blenheim (1704) – to the Protestant succession. In 1896 William Skeoch Cumming represented the heroism of the Black Watch at Fontenoy (1745) in its first battle fought for the Hanoverian cause. Lady Elizabeth Butler, who described the kilted troops as 'so essentially pictorial',[47] commemorated one of the great events of Waterloo, namely the charge of the Scots Greys, in *Scotland For Ever!* (1881). William Lockhart Bogle also used Waterloo in 1893 to capture both the golden thread of regimental tradition, and the bravery of the piper, by portraying Piper Kenneth Mackay of the 79th Cameron Highlanders piping outside the square. Another studio-based artist, Stanley Berkeley, dramatised one of the great myths of Waterloo, namely Gordons clinging to the stirrups of charging Scots Greys, by painting *Gordons And Greys to The Front* (1898). All these works were reproduced in prints, engravings, cards and textbooks, so ensuring the widest possible dispersal of the derivative works. The shared imagery found its reflection in cultural understandings within the Dominions during the South African War, where the Canadian poet and staunch Tory, William Wilfred Campbell, wrote about 'Our Bit of "The Thin Red Line"'. He thereby identified the Canadian forces with the resolve demonstrated by the Sutherland Highlanders at the battle of Balaclava and immortalised thereafter in the painting by Gibb.[48]

These decades also sustained the imagery of the Scots in battle through the emergence of new, battle-scarred commanders. Sir Archibald Alison, who lost an arm at the relief of Lucknow, commanded a Highland Brigade for the last time at Tel-el-Kebir. Ian Hamilton incurred a severe wound at Majuba, which left his left hand almost useless, but garnered medals and honours on the north-west frontier and in South Africa. Andrew Gilbert Wauchope, though one of the richest men in Scotland, continued to serve in the Black Watch despite suffering severe wounds in the Asante War, at El Teb and Kirbekan. He later commanded a brigade at Omdurman and died at the head of the Highland Brigade at Magersfontein, an event that plunged Scotland into national mourning. The 'most grievous loss of all', intoned the *Scotsman*, 'is that of the gallant and well-loved commander of the Brigade, General Wauchope'.[49]

None of these commanders, though, matched the adulation accorded to Hector A. Macdonald. Born in 1853, the son of a crofter, he rose by his own merit and professionalism through the ranks of the Gordon Highlanders to become a major general, a remarkable achievement in the late nineteenth century. Popularly known as 'Fighting Mac', he was offered either a Victoria Cross or a commission after his services in the Anglo-Afghan War, and chose the latter. He served with distinction at Majuba and in the Sudan; was awarded a Distinguished Service Order after the battle of Toski in 1889; and earned commendations for his command of a Sudanese brigade at Omdurman. On his return home, Macdonald undertook a tour of Scotland, receiving plaudits and ecstatic receptions all across the country. The tour began with an extraordinary banquet held by the Highland societies of London in Hotel Cecil under the chairmanship of John Stewart-Murray, the seventh duke of Atholl. Amid a glittering array of Scottish nobility, parliamentarians, senior officers and representatives of literary, religious and cultural associations were the agents-general of New South Wales, South Australia, Western Australia, Queensland, Nova Scotia,

British Columbia, New Brunswick, Natal and the Cape of Good Hope. The gathering toasted Macdonald and presented him with a sword of honour. Macdonald was knighted subsequently for his services in the South African War, which included command of the Highland Brigade after Wauchope's demise, but he later incurred allegations of homosexual practices in Ceylon and shot himself in Paris. Nevertheless, he remained a popular hero in Scotland, where monuments were erected in his honour, and across the empire. Robert William Service, the British-Canadian poet, composed a famous poem in tribute: 'Fighting Mac'. It began 'A pistol shot rings round and round the world; in pitiful defeat a warrior lies . . .', and in two evocative verses described Macdonald's imperial service:

> He sees the sullen pass, high-crowned with snow,
> Where Afghans cower with eyes of gleaming hate.
> He hurls himself against the hidden foe.
> They try to rally – ah, too late, too late!
> Again, defenseless, with fierce eyes that wait
> For death, he stands, like baited bull at bay,
> And flouts the Boers, that mad Majuba day.
>
> He sees again the murderous Soudan,
> Blood-slaked and rapine-swept. He seems to stand
> Upon the gory plain of Omdurman.
> Then Magersfontein, and supreme command
> Over his Highlanders. To shake his hand
> A King is proud, and princes call him friend.
> And glory crowns his life – and now the end.[50]

Finally, Scottish consciousness in the Dominions[51] identified with the Scottish military during times of crisis, as over the fate of General Gordon and the ensuing Russo-British scare over Penjdeh (1885), or shared military service within the empire. As the British government had withdrawn its garrisons from Australia and New Zealand in 1870, and from Canada in 1871 (save for imperial bases in Halifax and Esquimalt), these Dominions became more self-reliant and sent forces overseas. The first Canadians to serve abroad were the 386 voyageurs employed on the ill-fated Nile expedition, and, after Gordon's death, the first Australians arrived in Suakin on 29 March 1885. Sent by the government of New South Wales, these volunteers included an infantry battalion of twenty-four officers and 522 men, and an artillery battery of 212 men. The infantry saw little action, working mainly on the construction of a railway line, but some served in a few sorties with an improvised camel corps. The artillery saw even less action and mainly drilled; both units left within two months when the operation was aborted in the wake of the Penjdeh scare. This commitment, nonetheless, had demonstrated both an enduring link with Britain and the development of colonial self-confidence.[52]

Military action and a growing Scottish presence were more immediate factors in southern Africa. The 2nd Battalion, Gordon Highlanders received a hearty welcome on 30 January 1881, when they arrived in Durban as the first kilted soldiers to be seen in Natal. The subsequent defeat on Majuba Hill in which the three companies of Gordons suffered 121 casualties barely diminished their popularity, as most accounts blamed the deceased commanding officer, Sir George Pomeroy Colley, for attempting to hold the summit with only 405 officers and men, and without any artillery or Gatling guns.[53] By the 1880s Scots, lured by the mineral boom whether in the Boer republics or the Crown colonies, were steadily growing in number. Their rate of immigration was far higher than their proportionate share of the UK's population and they lacked any significant competition from Irish migrants.[54] Manifestations of Scottishness found reflection in the proliferation of Caledonian societies and other distinctively Scottish associations, including the formation of the first 'Highland' regiment in the southern hemisphere in 1885, namely the Cape Town Highlanders. It adopted the Gordon tartan for its kilt and the sporran, spats and hose of the Sutherland Highlanders, imported a stag as a regimental mascot, and offered classes in Gaelic. The 'Highlander' designation, coupled with the costly and prestigious uniform, may have served social purposes, too, bolstering the social status and self-esteem of the officer corps.[55]

Distinctively Scottish volunteer units were also formed in the self-governing colonies of New Zealand and Australia, the most durable of which were the Dunedin Highland Rifles and the New South Wales (NSW) Scottish Rifles, both formed in 1885. All these units were raised during imperial crises and, as imperial military activity reached a crescendo towards the end of the 1890s, the Victorian Scottish Regiment (VSR) was created in 1898 and the South Australia Scottish Company in 1899. This martial enthusiasm served as a backdrop to the Antipodean engagement in the South African War. New Zealand began the process, when its parliament, as distinct from the colonial executives, was the first to proffer assistance to Britain. So popular was the cause that by 21 October 1899 the first New Zealand contingent had set sail, and it proved the first of ten contingents, involving 315 officers and 6,192 men,[56] as volunteering across the empire, as in Britain, surged after the British reverses of 'Black Week' (10–15 December 1899). More 'Highland' rifle units were established in New Zealand, at Wanganui, Wellington, Canterbury and Auckland, during 1900.[57]

Nearly all the Australian colonies sent volunteers, and ultimately some 16,000 Australian officers and men served in the war, including eight Commonwealth Horse battalions raised by the federal authorities after 1901. Colonial Scots joined many of the units despatched from New Zealand and Australia, and subsequently some Victorian Scots-Australians joined the second contingent of the Lovat Scouts. Another 250 Scots-Australians joined the second battalion of the Scottish Horse, a body of Scots mounted riflemen raised by John Stewart-Murray, the eighth marquess of Tullibardine, from Scots at home and those in South Africa.[58]

Of all the colonial Scottish formations, only the Cape Town Highlanders served as a unit in the South African War. It had already seen action with the First City Regiment of Grahamstown in the suppression of a rebellion in Bechuanaland (1896–7), and now undertook a range of garrison and support duties. It suffered a notable reverse at Jacobsdal (25 October 1900) when the Boers, having infiltrated the town overnight, attacked the garrison at dawn, killing fourteen and wounding another thirteen, nearly all Cape Town Highlanders. Otherwise the unit discharged its garrison duties successfully, while detachments later patrolled blockhouse lines or guarded lines of communication.[59] Scots, who were resident in South Africa, provided the nucleus for the new formation, the Scottish Horse, which eventually comprised two regiments, numbering 3,252 NCOs and men, of whom 1,250 enlisted in Britain. This unique imperial unit, based on the 'spirit of Scottish nationality', earned an excellent reputation for its riding, tenacity and gallantry, with only one officer and twenty-two men taken prisoner in its first year. In promoting its re-creation after the war, the marquess of Tullibardine raised both a Yeomanry (and later Territorial) regiment in Scotland and, with the assistance of the Caledonian Society of Johannesburg, a volunteer mounted regiment for the Transvaal army. Although the latter would be disbanded in 1907 in favour of the Transvaal Imperial Light Horse, the Caledonian Society also assisted in selecting men for what would become the Transvaal Scottish. This infantry unit was given permission by the marquess's father, the duke of Atholl, to wear the Murray of Atholl tartan and use the regimental march 'The Atholl Highlanders'. Other groups, such as the First City Volunteers of Grahamstown, sought to exploit the passion for Scottish military tradition by re-inventing themselves as a Scottish regiment, adopting the Graham of Montrose tartan, and forming a Highland company and pipe band.[60]

In Canada, where the Militia Acts of 1858 and 1859 had provided for the formation of Volunteer regiments, Scots formed the 48th Highlanders in Toronto in 1891 and the 91st Highlanders (later the Argyll and Sutherland Highlanders) in Hamilton in 1903, redesignated as the 91st Canadian Highlanders in 1904. The 5th Battalion, Royal Light Infantry, first raised in Montreal in 1862 and redesignated as the 5th Battalion, Royal Scots of Canada in 1884, became the Royal Highlanders of Canada (Black Watch) in 1907.[61] Canadian-Scottish volunteers duly served in the South African War after the Canadian government succumbed to agitation from the English-speaking Canadians and agreed to support the British cause.[62] Nevertheless, Frederick Borden, the minister of militia and defense, insisted that these units should fight as Canadian forces, with the first contingent, chosen from a representative body of volunteers from all across Canada, serving under its own officers, and organised and clothed to emphasise its distinctive identity. When the Royal Canadian Regiment of Infantry reached Table Bay, they were greeted with cheers from another incoming vessel, carrying the kilted soldiers of the 1st Battalion, Gordon Highlanders, and the Canadians cheered them in return. They were then marched off to a base at Green Point Common, headed by the pipers of the Cape Town Highlanders.[63]

Although relations between British and imperial troops were at times quite fraught,[64] Lord Roberts heaped praise upon the Canadians for their role and sacrifices at Paardeberg, and the Canadians were mightily impressed by the bayonet charge of the Gordons uphill at the battle of Doornkop on 29 May 1900. On the following day, as the Highlanders, led by their pipers, marched past, Sergeant Hart-McHarg recalled that 'every Canadian jumped to their feet and hurrahed till he was hoarse. It was the heartiest and most spontaneous thing I witnessed during the whole campaign.' The Gordon officers expressed their appreciation as they had suffered ninety-seven casualties in the battle, and a couple of months later a Gordon sergeant thanked one of the Canadians for 'the cheer you fellows gave us after Doornkop'.[65] As set-piece battles became increasingly rare, ending with the Boer defeat at Bergendal (25–27 August 1900), and a protracted guerrilla war set in, Highland battalions were never seen in action again. During the counter-guerrilla operations, many battalions were split into companies or sections and even smaller groups, garrisoning the blockhouses that protected the railway, and many served, as the colonials did, as mounted riflemen.

Military service in South Africa represented an important stepping-stone for the Dominions. It was their first major experience of war, nourishing feelings of national pride, particularly among the overseas forces, and instilling a greater sense of self-confidence and independent military identity. In the aftermath of the war, Canadian militias received higher estimates, more training facilities, more serviceable uniforms, higher standards of training and promotion, and re-equipment with new rifles and guns. Although the accolades heaped on the returning Canadians were often complemented by criticisms of the British army's performance on the veld, positive memories of the Scots endured. As early as 1905 the local Scottish community in Winnipeg, led by the St Andrew's Society, began lobbying the government to raise a Highland regiment. When granted permission in 1909 to raise Western Canada's first Highland regiment, prospective officers formed committees to deal with finances, uniforms and the band. They found an additional $25,000 to import accoutrements from Scotland and, on 1 February 1910, raised the 79th Cameron Highlanders of Canada. On 9 October 1910 the regiment received its first stand of colours from Mrs D. C. Cameron, wife of the honorary lieutenant colonel. Later in the same year, Vancouverites of Scottish descent raised the 72nd Highlanders of Canada, which was re-designated as the '72nd Regiment The Seaforth Highlanders of Canada' in 1912. Both of these regiments secured alliances with their Scottish counterparts, following the earliest official alliance between the 48th Toronto Regiment and the Gordon Highlanders in 1904, followed by the 91st Canadian Highlanders and its affiliation with the Argyll and Sutherland Highlanders in 1905.

Like the western Canadians, Hamiltonians had struggled to raise the 91st Canadian Highlanders even with the support of local clan and Scottish societies, notably the St Andrew's Society and the Sons of Scotland. James Chisholm and William Alexander Logie, two prominent lawyers and members of the Liberal Party, had to organise a campaign, lobby Members of Parliament in Ottawa, and send a petition to Borden. Although the group was able to recruit above its quota, and raise sufficient funds for Highland dress, Chisholm and Logie had to argue that the proposed 'officers are a fine lot of fellows and of good standing and large influence in the community', and that the men were 'a particularly fine class drawn chiefly from the better class of Scotchmen who own their own homes and have a stake in the community . . .' With community support, political backing, astute lobbying and adequate finances, Chisholm and Logie prevailed, despite the reluctance of Borden to endorse a uniform so costly and divergent from the national kit.[66]

Much of the early enthusiasm exhibited by Canadian-Scots for Highland dress, bagpipe music and ceremony accorded with Alfred Vagts's concept of militarism, whereby the customs, prestige and ceremonies associated with military units transcended their 'true military purposes'.[67] In an elegant officers' mess, officers could socialise after weekly parades and at full mess dinners, special functions, balls or annual Scottish celebrations. This Highland militarism was closely entwined with Canada's militia myth, namely, a conviction that the country's defences could rely on a trained citizen army of sharpshooters in preference to a professional army, a view reinforced by the reported performance of Canadian forces in South Africa.[68] Conversely, in New Zealand, where a Defence Act of 1909 provided for the creation of a Territorial Force from 1910, and a system of compulsory military training, all Volunteer units were transferred into the Territorial Force in 1911. In 1911, too, Australia announced the formation of a new Citizens' Army based upon compulsory service, and when all existing units were absorbed in 1912, the Scottish formations lost the kilt.[69]

Britain itself had embarked upon wide-ranging army reforms during and after the South African War. Following the findings of a royal commission into the war, a small War Office (Reconstitution) Committee (1904), chaired by Lord Esher, advocated the creation of an army council and a general staff, headed by a chief of the general staff with a seat on the army council, and the abolition of the office of commander in chief.[70] The self-governing colonies largely followed suit, removing British-held appointments such as general officer commanding the militia in Canada by a chief of the general staff from 1904 onwards, and the general officer commanding, Australian Military Forces by a military board (1905–8) and, in 1909, by a chief of the general staff. Military developments, though, progressed unevenly within the Dominions – in South Africa the process had to wait upon the creation of a Union Defence Force (1912) – and had to take account of differing priorities among the self-governing colonies. New Zealand and South Africa were much more supportive of imperial defence than Canada or Australia. Prime Minister Wilfrid Laurier opposed the creation of any centralised authority in Canada, or any prior commitment of Canada's militia other than in self-defence, so retarding the development of imperial defence.[71]

Richard Burdon Haldane, the Scottish Liberal secretary of state for war (1905–12), knew the Liberal leadership of Canada personally and was quite prepared to indulge their sensibilities.[72] In promoting the cause of an imperial general staff he supported cautious and incremental change, and described such a body as purely advisory and without any powers of command. At successive colonial conferences he secured agreement on an exchange of general staff officers to secure uniformity in military thought, organisation and weaponry; agreement on the principles of organising imperial forces while preserving complete Dominion autonomy; and acceptance of British inspections of overseas forces (Lord Kitchener in Australia and New Zealand in 1909 and Sir John French in Canada in 1910). He gained acceptance, too, of the appointment of a chief of the imperial general staff, and the principle of mutual assistance in defence but without interfering with the powers of the local chiefs of Dominion forces or the responsibilities of their governments.[73]

Although some reforms in organisation and training followed these limited measures,[74] Dominion self-confidence and defence autonomy had grown since the South African War. Imperial bonds endured despite the absence of major wars and found reflection in Dominion participation, including some members of their Highland regiments,[75] in the coronation of King George V on 22 June 1911, and in the continuing interest in the activities of Scottish regiments. During Britain's national railway strike of 1911, when several regiments were deployed at railway stations, it was the despatch of 600 Gordon Highlanders to protect the railway in Sheffield that became imperial news.[76] Ironically, in South Africa, after volunteers from the Transvaal Scottish had contributed to the suppression of the Bambatha rebellion (1906), the regiment participated in the newly formed Union Defence Force, which crushed the Rand strike of 1914.[77]

So the Highland regiments, preserved in such large numbers by the indulgence of an English secretary of state for war, had achieved an immense impact in the colonial wars of the late nineteenth century, and a powerful image that resonated among the English-speaking communities of the Dominions. All the qualities that the Highland soldier seemed to embody appealed not only to emigrant Scots by birth or descent but also to those who revered the bonds of empire and the values required to tame the wilderness and defeat internal foes. The readiness of Scottish emigrants to raise Highland regiments in response to imperial crises, or to volunteer for overseas service after the reverses of 'Black Week', demonstrated the powerful ties of kinship, even if the ensuing military service enhanced a sense of national self-worth. Just as the Highland regiments reflected an entwining of Scottish and British identities, focused on an imperial purpose, so 'Highlandism' in the Dominions prospered at a time of growing national self-consciousness, and did so because it always presumed loyalty and service to the colonial governments.

Notes

1. Quoted in Lieutenant Colonel Charles Greenhill Gardyne, *The Life of A Regiment: The History of the Gordon Highlanders from 1816 to 1898 including an Account of the 75th Regiment from 1787 to 1881*, 8 vols (London: The Medici Society, 1903, reprinted 1929), vol. 2, p. 148.

2. Victoria Henshaw, *Scotland and the British Army, 1700–1750: Defending the Union* (London: Bloomsbury, 2014); John C. R. Childs, 'Marlborough's Wars and the Act of Union, 1702–1714', Stephen Brumwell, 'The Scottish Military Experience in North America, 1756–83' and Edward M. Spiers, 'Scots and the Wars of Empire, 1815–1914', in Edward M. Spiers, Jeremy A. Crang and Matthew J. Strickland (eds), *A Military History of Scotland* (Edinburgh: Edinburgh University Press, 2012), pp. 326–47, 383–406, 458–84; John E. Cookson, *The British Armed Nation, 1793–1815* (Oxford: Oxford University Press, 1997) and Stephen Conway, 'The Scots Brigade in the Eighteenth Century', *Northern Scotland*, vol. 1, no.1 (2010), pp. 30–41.
3. Thomas M. Devine, *The Scottish Nation 1700–2000* (London: Allen Lane Penguin Press, 2000), p. 468; see also Wendy Ugolini, 'Scottish Commonwealth Regiments', in Spiers, Crang and Strickland (eds), *Military History of Scotland*, pp. 485–505.
4. Hew Strachan, *The Politics of the British Army* (Oxford: Clarendon Press, 1997), p. 205.
5. By 1870 Scotland, possessing 10.5 per cent of the UK population, provided only 8 per cent of the army: Harold J. Hanham, 'Religion and Nationality in the Mid-Victorian Army', in Michael R. D. Foot (ed.), *War and Society* (London: Paul Elek, 1973), pp. 159–81, at p. 163.
6. Parliamentary Papers (PP), *The General Annual Report on the British Army for the year ending 30th September 1913*, Cd. 7252 (1914), LII, p. 92; see also Edward M. Spiers, *The Scottish Soldier and Empire, 1854–1902* (Edinburgh: Edinburgh University Press, 2006), p. 210.
7. Heather Streets, *Military Races: The Military, Race and Masculinity in British Imperial Culture, 1857–1914* (Manchester: Manchester University Press, 2004), p. 177; see also Diana Henderson, *Highland Soldier: A Social Study of the Highland Regiments, 1820–1920* (Edinburgh: John Donald, 1989), pp. 26–30.
8. The Prince of Wales's Own (West Yorkshire) Regiment, the East Yorkshire Regiment, Alexandra Princess of Wales's Own Yorkshire Regiment, Duke of Wellington's (West Riding) Regiment, King's Own Yorkshire Light Infantry and the York and Lancaster Regiment.
9. The National Archives (TNA), WO 33/26, Sir Garnet Wolseley to the War Office, 18 December 1873; see also Halik Kochanski, *Sir Garnet Wolseley: Victorian Hero* (London: The Hambledon Press, 1999), pp. 65, 112–13, and Garnet J. Wolseley, 'Long and Short Service', *Nineteenth Century*, vol. 9 (1881), pp. 558–72.
10. 'General Roberts and the 72nd Highlanders', *Huntly Express*, 9 October 1880, p. 8.
11. Spiers, *Scottish Soldier*, pp. 6–9; Streets, *Martial Races*, pp. 55–9.
12. John M. MacKenzie with Nigel R. Dalziel, *The Scots in South Africa: Ethnicity, identity, gender and race, 1772–1914* (Manchester: Manchester University Press, 2007), p. 206; see also John M. MacKenzie, *Empires of Nature and the Nature of Empires: Imperialism, Scotland and the Environment* (East Linton: Tuckwell, 1997), pp. 38–42.
13. Jenni Calder, *Lost in the Backwoods: Scots and the North American Wilderness* (Edinburgh: Edinburgh University Press, 2013), p. 208.
14. Hugh Trevor-Roper, 'The invention of tradition: The Highland tradition of Scotland', in Eric Hobsbawn and Terence Ranger (eds), *The Invention of Tradition* (Cambridge: Cambridge University Press, 1983), pp. 15–41; Charles Withers, 'The historical creation of the Scottish highlands', in Ian L. Donnachie and Christopher A. Whatley (eds), *The Manufacture of Scottish History* (Edinburgh: Polygon, 1992), pp. 143–56; Robert Clyde, *From Rebel to Hero. The Image of the Highlander, 1745–1830* (East Linton: Tuckwell, 1995); Henshaw, *Scotland and the British Army*, pp. 3–6.
15. Thomas M. Devine, *Clanship to Crofters' War: The Social Transformation of the Scottish Highlands* (Manchester: Manchester University Press, 1994), pp. 92–3;

John E. Cookson, 'The Napoleonic Wars, military Scotland and Tory Highlandism', *Scottish Historical Review*, vol. 78, no. 205 (1999), pp. 60–75; Joan W. M. Hichberger, *Images of the Army: The Military in British Art, 1815–1914* (Manchester: Manchester University Press, 1988), p. 108; Alex Tyrrell, 'The Queen's "Little Trip": The Royal Visit to Scotland in 1842', *Scottish Historical Review*, vol. 82, no. 213 (2003), pp. 47–73; MacKenzie, *Scots in South Africa*, p. 245.

16. Tyrell, 'Queen's "Little Trip"', p. 65.
17. Spiers, *Scottish Soldier*, p. 4; David Duff (ed.), *Queen Victoria's Highland Journals* (Exeter: Webb & Bower, 1980), pp. 25, 47, 161.
18. Queen Victoria to the duke of Cambridge, 25 April 1897, in Colonel William Willoughby Verner, *The Military Life of H. R. H. George, Duke of Cambridge*, 2 vols (London: John Murray, 1905), vol. 2, pp. 201–2, at p. 202.
19. Sir Henry Ponsonby to the duke of Cambridge, 20 December 1880, in Verner, *Military Life*, vol. 2, p. 213. The 72nd (Duke of Albany's Own) Highlanders would become the 1st Battalion, Seaforth Highlanders, and regain the kilt as a result of these reforms.
20. Queen Victoria to Hugh Childers, 21 December 1880, in Verner, *Military Life*, vol. 2, p. 216.
21. Apart from the 72nd (see n. 19), the new kilted regiments were the 73rd (Perthshire) Regiment, the 75th (Stirlingshire) Regiment and the 91st, which had worn trews as the Argyllshire Highlanders: Henderson, *Highland Soldier*, p. 8.
22. Once again the queen and influential Highlanders prevented the Cameron Highlanders from being converted into a 3rd Battalion of the Scots Guards, scotching such rumours in 1887 and 1893. Lieutenant Colonel Angus Fairrie, *"Cuidich 'N Righ": A History of the Queen's Own Highlanders (Seaforth and Camerons)* (Inverness: Regimental HQ, Queen's Own Highlanders, 1983), p. 51.
23. Just as the linking of disparate regiments, and the loss of historic regimental numbers, caused widespread resentment, so the Royal Scots Fusiliers 'raised strong objections and the Scots Guards categorically refused' to wear Highland costume: John Buchan, *The History of the Royal Scots Fusiliers (1678–1918)* (London: Thomas Nelson, 1925), p. 228; see also Allan Carswell, 'Scottish Military Dress', in Spiers, Crang and Strickland (eds), *Military History of Scotland*, pp. 627–47, at pp. 640–1; Hew Strachan, 'Scotland's Military Identity', *Scottish Historical Review*, vol. 85, no. 220 (2006), pp. 315–32, at p. 327.
24. Devine, *Clanship to Crofter's War*, p. 93.
25. Robert Kelly, 'Midlothian: A Study in Politics and Ideas', *Victorian Studies*, vol. 4, no. 2 (1960), pp. 119–40, at pp. 127, 137.
26. Robert J. Wilkinson-Latham, *From our Special Correspondent: Victorian War Correspondents and their Campaigns* (London: Hodder & Stoughton, 1979), Ch. 6; Peter Harrington, 'Images and Perceptions: Visualising the Sudan Campaign', in Edward M. Spiers (ed.), *Sudan: The Reconquest Reappraised* (London: Frank Cass, 1998), pp. 82–101.
27. Spiers, *Scottish Soldier*, passim.
28. Gordon Highlanders Museum (GM), PB 1215, field telegrams on Dargai, 1897; 'Honour for the Gordons in South Africa', 'The Gordon Highlanders on the Frontier' and 'The Gordon Highlanders', *Aberdeen Journal*, 23 November 1897, p. 6; 30 November 1897, p. 5; 7 December 1897, p. 5; Greenhill Gardyne, *Life of a Regiment*, vol. 2, p. 294.
29. 'The Gordon Highlanders at Dargai' (by John McDonald, Montreal, Canada), *Aberdeen Evening Express*, 12 December 1897, p. 4.
30. Spiers, *Scottish Soldier*, pp. 126–7.

31. 'The Wounded from India', *Navy and Army Illustrated*, 30 April 1898, pp. 135–6; 'The Dargai Charge', *Inverness Courier*, 21 January 1898, p. 3; 'Piper Findlater', *Ross-shire Journal*, 27 May 1898, p. 7 and generally Edward M. Spiers, 'Findlater, George Frederick', http://www.oxforddnb.com/view/article/96873 (last accessed 12 September 2014).
32. See the photographs of the Royal Scots in Zululand and the Seaforths on the Black Mountains in Spiers, 'Scots and the Wars of Empire', in Spiers, Crang and Strickland (eds), *Military History of Scotland*, p. 471 and Michael Barthorp, *Afghan Wars and the North-West Frontier 1839–1947* (London: Cassell, 1982), pp. 95, 97.
33. William Howard Russell, *My Diary in India, in the Year 1858–9*, 2 vols (London: Routledge, Warne & Routledge, 1860), vol. 1, pp. 211, 394; see also Patrick Mileham, *Fighting Highlanders! The History of the Argyll and Sutherland Highlanders* (London: Arms & Armour Press, 1993), p. 53.
34. William Reade, *The Story of the Ashantee Campaign* (London: Smith Elder & Co., 1874), pp. 312–13, 317–19.
35. Frederic Villiers, *Villiers: His Five Decades of Adventure*, 2 vols (London: Hutchinson, 1921), vol. 1, p. 266; Melton Prior, *Campaigns of a War Correspondent* (London: Edward Arnold, 1912), pp. 174–6.
36. The radical Ernest Bennett of the *Westminster Gazette* criticised Kitchener after Omdurman: Hugh Cecil, 'British Correspondents and the Sudan Campaign of 1896–98', in Spiers (ed.), *Sudan: Reconquest Reappraised*, pp. 102–27, at pp. 120–2.
37. Roger Stearn, 'War correspondents and colonial war, c. 1870–1900', in John M. MacKenzie (ed.), *Popular Imperialism and the Military, 1850–1950* (Manchester: Manchester University Press, 1992), pp. 139–61, at p. 149.
38. George Warrington Steevens, *With Kitchener to Khartum* (Edinburgh: Blackwood, 1898), pp. 146–7.
39. Winston Spencer Churchill, *My Early Life: A Roving Commission* (London: Odhams Press, 1947), pp. 153–4.
40. Stearn, 'War correspondents and colonial war', p. 157.
41. Carman Miller, *Painting the Map Red: Canada and the South African War, 1899–1902* (Montreal and Kingston: Canadian War Museum and McGill-Queen's University Press, 1993), p. 460, n. 3.
42. Hugh Anderson, 'Donald Alaster Macdonald (1859–1932)', *Australian Dictionary of Biography*, http://adb.anu.edu.au/biography/macdonald-donald-alaster-7335 (last accessed 10 September 2014).
43. Donald A. Macdonald, *How We Kept The Flag Flying: The Story of the Siege of Ladysmith* (London: Ward, Lock & Co., 1900), pp. 22, 28, 109, 136, 176, 185–6, 284.
44. A. B. Paterson, *Rio Grande's Last Race and Other Verses* (London: Macmillan, 1904), pp. 175–6.
45. Peter Stanley, 'With Banjo to Kimberley: Banjo Paterson's South African War Verse as History', in Peter Dennis and Jeffery Grey (eds), *The Boer War Army, Nation and Empire, the 1999 Chief of Army/Australian War Memorial Military History Conference* (Canberra: Army History Unit, 2000), pp. 162–72, at p. 165.
46. 'The Battle of Retief's Nek', *Sydney Morning Herald*, 6 September 1900, in Clement Semmler (ed.), *The World of 'Banjo' Paterson: His Stories, Travels, War Reports, and Advice to Racegoers* (Sydney: Angus & Robertson, 1967), pp. 243–9, at p. 245.
47. Elizabeth Butler, *An Autobiography* (London: Constable, 1922), p. 99.
48. *Ottawa Journal*, 22 February 1900, p. 7; Miller, *Painting the Map Red*, p. 19.
49. *Scotsman*, 14 December 1899, p. 6; Spiers, *Scottish Soldier*, pp. 162–4.
50. Robert William Service, 'Fighting Mac', *Spell of the Yukon and Other Verses* (New York:

Barse & Hopkins, 1907), p. 79; on Macdonald, see Trevor Royle, *Fighting Mac: The Downfall of Major-General Sir Hector Macdonald* (Edinburgh: Mainstream Publishing, 2003).
51. The term is being used here to refer to Australia, New Zealand, Canada and South Africa, each of which had significant Scottish communities. Only Canada had achieved 'Dominion' status in 1867; New Zealand was a self-governing colony (but achieved 'Dominion' status in 1907), while Australia remained a collection of colonies until united in a federation in 1901. The South Africa Act (1909) created the union of Cape Colony, Natal, the Transvaal and the Orange River Colony in 1910.
52. Australian War Memorial, 'Sudan (New South Wales Contingent) March–June 1885', http://www.awm.gov.au/atwar/sudan/ (last accessed 14 September 2014).
53. Greenhill Gardyne, *Life of a Regiment*, vol. 2, pp. 162–3, 174; Spiers, *Scottish Soldier*, pp. 57–60; Joseph H. Lehman, *The Boer War* (London: Buchan & Enright, 1985), p. 260.
54. Christopher Harvie, *Scotland and Nationalism: Scottish Society and Politics 1707–1977* (London: George Allen & Unwin, 1977), p. 94; Jonathan Hyslop, 'Cape Town Highlanders, Transvaal Scottish: Military "Scottishness" and Social Power in Nineteenth and Twentieth Century South Africa', *South African Historical Journal*, vol. 47, no. 1 (2002), pp. 96–114; MacKenzie, *Scots in South Africa*, pp. 161–2.
55. Neil Orpen, *The Cape Town Highlanders 1885–1970* (Cape Town: Cape Town Highlanders History Committee, 1970), pp. 4–7; Hyslop, 'Cape Town Highlanders, Transvaal Scottish', p. 103.
56. John Crawford with Ellen Ellis, *To Fight for The Empire: An Illustrated History of New Zealand and the South African War, 1899–1902* (Auckland: Reed Books, 1999), p. 109.
57. Malcolm Prentis, *The Scots in Australia* (Sydney: University of New South Wales Press, 2008), p. 144; Ugolini, 'Scottish Commonwealth Regiments', p. 488.
58. Denis Judd and Keith Surridge, *The Boer War* (London: John Murray, 2002), pp. 78–81; Prentis, *Scots in Australia*, p. 145.
59. Orpen, *Cape Town Highlanders*, Ch. 2 and pp. 50–2, 54, 56–7.
60. PP. *Report of Her Majesty's Commissioners Appointed to Inquire into Military Preparations and other matters connected with the War in South Africa*, C. 1789 (1904), XL, pp. 75–6; Spiers, *Scottish Soldier*, p. 192; Hubert Calla Juta, *The History of The Transvaal Scottish* (Johannesburg: Hortors Ltd, 1933), pp. 4–7; Hyslop, 'Cape Town Highlanders, Transvaal Scottish', pp. 103–4.
61. Ugolini, 'Scottish Commonwealth Regiments', p. 488. In Nova Scotia, the Victoria Provisional Battalion of Infantry, established in 1871, added 'Highland' to its title in 1879, and after several further name changes became the '90th Victoria Regiment, Argyll Highlanders' in 1900 (and the Cape Breton Highlanders in 1920).
62. Richard Clippingdale, *The Power of the Pen: The Politics, Nationalism, and Influence of Sir John Willison* (Toronto: Dundurn, 2012), pp. 136–9.
63. William Hart-McHarg, *From Quebec to Pretoria With the Royal Canadian Regiment* (Toronto: William Briggs, 1902), p. 56; on the raising of the regiment, see Miller, *Painting the Map Red*, Ch. 4.
64. Carman Miller, 'The Unhappy Warriors: Conflict and Nationality among Canadian Troops during the South African War', *The Journal of Imperial and Commonwealth History*, vol. 23, no. 1 (1995), pp. 77–104.
65. Hart-McHarg, *From Quebec to Pretoria*, pp. 215–16; on the charge of the Gordons, 'a sad but memorable day', see Lieutenant Colonel Lachlan Gordon-Duff, *With the Gordon*

Highlanders to the Boer War and Beyond (Staplehurst: Spellmount, 1997), pp. 100–2; the number of casualties is taken from the regimental history, Greenhill Gardyne, *Life of a Regiment*, vol. 3, p. 488.
66. Robert L. Fraser, 'The Regimental Foundation of The Argyll and Sutherland Highlanders of Canada', http://www.argylls.ca/history (last accessed on 17 September 2014).
67. Alfred Vagts, *A History of Militarism: Civilian and Military* (New York: The Free Press, 1937), pp. 13, 21–2.
68. Miller, *Painting the Map Red*, p. 439.
69. 'Dunedin Highland Rifles', *Otago Daily Times*, 22 July 1911, p. 12; 'Highland Rifles', (*Wellington*) *Evening Post*, 30 May 1912, p. 2; 'Garrison Band Recital', *Wanganui Chronicle*, 5 August 1912, p. 8; Prentis, *Scots in Australia*, p. 146.
70. John Gooch, *The Plans of War: The General Staff and British Military Strategy, c. 1900–1916* (London: Routledge & Kegan Paul, 1978), Ch. 2.
71. Ibid. pp. 154–7.
72. Ibid. pp. 132–3, 140, 145; National Library of Scotland (NLS), Haldane Mss., Ms. 5,905, f. 215, Sir Wilfrid Laurier to Richard B. Haldane, 12 July 1902 and Ms. 5,976, ff. 116–17, Richard B. Haldane to his mother, 12 October 1906.
73. Edward M. Spiers, *Haldane: An Army Reformer* (Edinburgh: Edinburgh University Press, 1980), pp. 125–34.
74. George F. G. Stanley, *Canada's Soldiers: The Military History of an Unmilitary People* (Toronto: Macmillan, 1960), pp. 304–9.
75. 'Coronation Celebrations', *North Otago Times*, 24 June 1911, p. 4; Orpen, *Cape Town Highlanders*, pp. 69–70; 'The Queen's Own Cameron Highlanders: A Brief History' (St Andrew's Society of Winnipeg), http://standrews-wpg.ca/history/queens-highlanders.cfm (last accessed 19 September 2014).
76. 'Rioting at Sheffield', *The Times*, 18 August 1911, p. 9; 'Turbulence at Sheffield', *Sydney Morning Herald*, 19 August 1911, p. 15; 'The Labour War', *The (Canterbury) Press*, 19 August 1911, p. 9; 'General Railway Strike Ordered', *The Colonist (Nelson, New Zealand)*, 19 August 1911, p. 2.
77. Juta, *History of the Transvaal Scottish*, pp. 18, 68–71; Hyslop, 'Cape Town Highlanders, Transvaal Scottish', p. 108.

3

The Scottish Soldier and Scotland, 1914–1918

Hew Strachan

The First World War transformed Scotland's relationship with military service, reversing the trends of the previous hundred years and reconnecting with those of the eighteenth century and earlier. The emergency of 1914–18, while traumatic, was transitory, but it also left a national legacy. Scottish society, learned and industrious, thrifty and devout – at least in the stereotypes – re-acquired a patina of militarism which it has subsequently proved reluctant wholly to shed. Here, Scotland compares less with its southern neighbour, England, which by the early twenty-first century has become remarkably distant from its military legacy, and more with the Dominions of the pre-1914 British Empire. The constitutions of Australia, New Zealand and Canada all pre-date the First World War, but the first two nations have increasingly linked their identities with the Gallipoli campaign of 1915, as Canada has done with the more successful, but also more bloody, battle of Vimy in 1917. The 'white' Dominions entered the war as self-conscious members of the British Empire, but emerged with an enhanced sense of their own distinctiveness. Today Australia in particular, by invoking the 'Anzac spirit', venerates its accomplishments in war, despite its commitment to democracy, international order and other liberal values.[1] Its capital, Canberra, is dominated by war memorials, and by the Australian War Memorial in particular, as it looks across to parliament. Scotland confronts comparable paradoxes. It is sceptical of war's utility and yet vests a surprisingly large element of its national identity in martial trappings.

During the eighteenth century, the leading figures of the Scottish enlightenment rejected Scotland's reputation as an exporter of soldiers, arguing that fit, able-bodied men should devote their energies to more productive pastimes. During the Seven Years War (1756–63) Scotland stood aloof from the English debate on compulsory service in the militia for this reason, and thereafter its leading economic theorist, Adam Smith, used his argument for the division of labour to favour a professional army rather than universal military service.[2] Recruiting in the Highlands plummeted, as much because of the rural depopulation following the Clearances – another symptom of the drive for economic growth – as because of a high-minded aversion to the profession of arms. As early as 1809, just as the Peninsular War was getting under way, five previously kilted regiments lost their Scottish trappings because they were no longer able to enlist sufficient Highlanders.[3] From the 1830s onwards, recruiting across Scotland, and not just in the Highlands, declined, both in absolute numbers and in relation to the Scottish population. By 1913 Scots made up 10 per cent of the United Kingdom's population but provided only 7.6 per cent of its soldiers.[4]

The imbalance between delivery and expectation had been institutionalised in 1881. Single-battalion infantry regiments were paired to create new regiments with territorial, not numbered, titles. Given that there were five kilted infantry regiments before 1881, there should have been 2.5 new Highland regiments thereafter. Instead the government retained five, even if one was a single-battalion regiment, the Cameron Highlanders. All five – the others were the Black Watch, the Seaforth Highlanders, the Gordon Highlanders and the Argyll and Sutherland Highlanders – quickly became household names. Late Victorian society, and Queen Victoria herself, made the Scottish soldier the *beau idéal* of imperial defence, and after 1881 even the Lowland regiments had to adopt the trappings of 'Highlandism': tartan trews, broadswords and bonnets. To match their post-1881 establishments, Highland regiments drew about half their numbers from the Lowlands, and the Lowland regiments in turn filled their ranks by recruiting from south of the border.[5]

Scotland may increasingly have turned its back on full-time military service, but its martial spirit was sustained in another way, through the part-time Volunteers raised to meet the threat of French invasion in 1859–60. Lanarkshire formed more units than any other county in Britain, although their absolute numbers or their strength in relation to population size have still to be established.[6] In 1908 the Volunteers were swept up with the Militia in the re-organisation of the auxiliary forces undertaken by the Scottish secretary of state for war, Richard Burdon Haldane. The result, the Territorial Force, or later Army, struggled to recruit to its establishment before the First World War, but by 1914 its drill halls gave it a physical presence throughout the country.

The First World War

When the First World War broke out, Lord Kitchener, newly installed as secretary of state for war, set about the creation of a mass army similar in size to those of mainland Europe, but raised through voluntary enlistment rather than through conscription. By the end of 1915 he had secured 2.4 million men, with 20 per cent of the British male labour force joining up by July 1915. Scotland reversed the pre-war pattern, contributing disproportionately to the total: 24 per cent of its men of military age enlisted, as opposed to 22 per cent in the next ranking regions, the south-east and south-west of England.[7] These figures may actually under-represent the numbers of Scots joining up, because, as with the nineteenth-century numbers, they are based on place of enlistment rather than ethnic identity or place of birth. It is reasonable to assume that more

Scots, who had migrated south in pursuit of work, joined up in England than Englishmen enlisted in Scotland. That said, the Scottish figures include many Irish immigrants from the industrial west of Scotland.[8]

The absolute numbers came from the big cities. The war immediately boosted unemployment by 10 per cent, as industries ran short of imported raw materials and businesses engaged in non-essential production suffered from falling demand. Many men may have enlisted for patriotic reasons, but others sought job security: nine out of ten unemployed were in uniform by the end of September 1914. South of the border, communities formed 'Pals' battalions for Kitchener's New Armies, so that they could serve alongside workmates or neighbours. In Scotland, 'Pals' battalions were fewer. The phenomenon proved strongest in Glasgow: the 15th, 16th and 17th battalions of the Highland Light Infantry were drawn from the Glasgow Tramways, the Boys' Brigade and the city's Chamber of Commerce. On the other side of the country, in Edinburgh, Sir George McCrae built the 16th Battalion, Royal Scots around the Heart of Midlothian Football Club.[9] Scotland's response to the call for men also differed from England's in another respect. It was high across all sectors of society, not just among middle-class and white-collar occupations, but also in agriculture, which elsewhere was low.

The recruiting rate in rural areas reflected the role of the Territorial Force in enabling enlistment, not just because of its widespread distribution but also because of the queues and processing logjams at regular army recruiting offices. In several remoter areas enlistment rose to over 60 per cent of the population of military age.[10] Kitchener had resisted building his recruiting drive around the Territorials, for several good reasons. They had struggled to recruit to establishment before the war; they were administered by county associations and not centrally by the War Office; and, most importantly, they were not liable for overseas service unless they had taken the imperial service obligation, a commitment entered into by only five units before the war.[11] The Territorial Army could be seen as a way out of the war, not into it.

Anybody who actually joined the Territorials in order to avoid going overseas was likely to be disappointed. On 21 August 1914 those units in which 80 per cent volunteered were permitted to complete to their war establishment. By the end of the war, 318 battalions and twenty-three infantry divisions of the Territorial Army had served overseas. The first Territorial infantry battalion to arrive in France, on 16 September, the 1/14 London Regiment, better known as the London Scottish, was by the beginning of November holding the line on the Messines ridge south of Ypres. Scotland sent two Territorial divisions overseas. The 52nd Lowland Division arrived on the Gallipoli peninsula in June 1915, while possibly the most famous of them all, the 51st Highland Division, was blooded on the Somme in 1916.

By then, the first of Scotland's New Army divisions, the 9th Scottish and 15th Scottish, were battle-hardened. Both fought at Loos, the major British offensive of 1915, and as a result Scotland suffered then in ways that the rest of the United Kingdom was not to experience until the following summer. On

25 September 1915 one-third of the attacking battalions and a half of all casualties were Scots. The battle continued for another three weeks, until 16 October. One-third of those commemorated on the memorial to the missing bear Scottish surnames and, of the twelve British battalions which suffered more than 500 casualties in the battle, eight were Scottish. The 6th and 7th Battalions of the Cameron Highlanders each lost about 700 missing, wounded and killed from original strengths of just over 900. Five commanding officers of Scottish battalions died in action. The domestic impact was made clear by the local press, the *Inverness Courier* urging its fit and young readers to fill the depleted ranks of the Camerons.[12] Scots were awarded five of the Victoria Crosses won in the offensive, one going to Piper Daniel Laidlaw of the 7th Battalion, King's Own Scottish Borderers. The attack was preceded by the discharge of gas, which then blew back to the British lines, disrupting the advance. Laidlaw mounted the parapet and played his company forward, despite the risk of inhaling gas-corrupted air.

Writing Scotland's war

One reason for the Scottish identification with Loos was a best-selling book, *The First Hundred Thousand*, published at the end of the same year and written by John Hay Beith under the pseudonym of Ian Hay. Hay was born in Manchester to parents of Scottish descent who sent their son to Fettes College in Edinburgh. He had proved less successful in his chosen career as a schoolmaster, than as a writer of school stories. In 1912 he was adopted as a Unionist candidate but on the outbreak of war, already a Territorial, he joined the 10th Service (New Army) Battalion, the Argyll and Sutherland Highlanders. He described its training and social life in a series of humorous articles published in the Edinburgh-based *Blackwood's Magazine*: 'War is hell and all that, but it has a good deal to recommend it. It wipes out all the small nuisances of peace-time', Captain Wagstaffe declares. 'Such as – ?', comes the response. 'Well, Suffragettes, and Futurism, and – and – ', Wagstaffe answers. Bernard Shaw, the Tango, party politics and golf maniacs are duly added to the list.[13]

The articles were not written as propaganda, but the book version which followed was supported by Wellington House, the home of the War Propaganda Bureau, which recognised its sales potential and also saw to its publication in the United States and France. However, it should not be condemned on those grounds. Cyril Falls, an official historian and later professor of the history of war at Oxford, opined in 1930 that Hay 'was about the first in the field, he shared the enthusiasm of the men whom he depicted, and he brought out not only for readers of that day, but, we believe, also for posterity, the spirit which animated the first volunteers'.[14]

The battle of Loos forms the culmination of *The First Hundred Thousand*. Hay and his battalion were in the fight with the 9th Division and its historian subsequently described Hay's book as 'the best account of [its] life and training'.[15] The history of its partner, the 15th Division, was co-written by another Scottish author and Unionist politician, John Buchan. A son of the manse, educated in

Glasgow but with strong Peeblesshire links through his mother's family, Buchan had gone to Oxford. In the autumn of 1914, neither young nor fit enough to be a soldier, he began the writing of a history of the war published by the Edinburgh-based firm of Thomas Nelson which eventually extended to twenty-four volumes. The first of Buchan's Richard Hannay novels, *The Thirty-Nine Steps*, was itself published in September 1915, the month in which the attack at Loos was launched, and had sold 33,000 copies by the end of the year. Because Buchan had been accredited as one of five journalists attached to the British army in May 1915, he witnessed the fighting at Loos for himself. His war poetry too was shaped disproportionately by the battle and by the experiences of the Scottish Service battalions within it. In 'On Leave', written in 1916 and published in 1917, a Borderer returns home, to find his infant son dead. He climbs a nearby hill to reflect on Loos, life and religious faith:

> I clamb the Lammerlaw
>   And sat me doun on the cairn; –
> The best o' my freends were deid,
>   And noo I had buried my bairn; –
>
> The stink o' gas in my nose,
>   The colour o' bluid in my ee,
> And the bidden' o' Hell in my lug,
>   To curse my Maker and me.

As he goes on, the soldier recognises that 'Loos and the Lammerlaw, the battle was feucht in baith', and he makes his 'peace wi' God'.[16]

Buchan, like Hay, would become swept up in the propaganda work of the government, and the reputation of his work, like Hay's, has suffered in consequence. Thus two of the best-known writers of 'war books' in their own day do not figure in today's canon of First World War literature. Nor, with the exception of the poet Charles Hamilton Sorley, who was himself killed at Loos serving with the 7th Battalion of the Suffolk Regiment, do many Scots. That is surprising on two counts. One is statistical: given the number of Scots who served and their reputed literacy, Scottish voices ought to be better represented. The other relates to subject matter. Despite the reputations of some as propagandists, the Scots who addressed the war did more than simply reflect jingoistic and patriotic themes. Buchan's wartime poetry deserves greater recognition, and his third Hannay novel, *Mr Standfast*, published in 1919, captured tensions of central importance in 1917–18. Buchan ends the story at the front, but its dominant themes are those of developments at home, of war weariness, of trade unionism and its possible effects on war production, and of the opportunities they provided for pacifists and even German spies. Buchan's choice of title, with its reference to John Bunyan's *Pilgrim's Progress*, makes clear that he did not deny the moral and spiritual challenges of the war, and confronted its costs and losses.

The same could be said of Robert Service. The son of a Scot, born in Preston but educated at Hillhead High School in Glasgow, Service went to Canada. Today he is best known for such doggerel as 'The cremation of Sam McGee' and 'The shooting of Dan McGrew', the latter even being held up as the inspiration for 'Eskimo Nell'. He enjoyed massive commercial success, particularly in Canada. His *Rhymes of a Red-Cross Man*, published in 1916, had been reprinted eight times by 1923. The verses reflect his experiences as a volunteer stretcher-bearer and ambulance driver with the American Red Cross in 1916. They move from the jaunty rhythms of care-free young men to disgust, expressed in a language that owes little to Scotland and much more, as with the characters of the Richard Hannay novels, to a form of imperial cosmopolitanism:

> My stretcher is one scarlet stain,
> And as I tries to scrape it clean,
> I tell you wot – I'm sick with pain
> For all I've 'eard, for all I've seen;
> Around me is the 'ellish night,
> And as the war's red rim I trace.
> I wonder if in 'Eaven's height
> Our God don't turn away 'Is Face.

Acknowledging his move to Paris in 1913, Service's poem 'Tri-colour' took the red, white and blue of the French flag and saw them in the flowers of the battlefield: 'Poppies . . . glowing there in the wheat' are in fact 'blood . . . gleaming wet in the grasses'; cornflowers are 'the dead . . . stark on the dreadful plain, all in their dark-blue blouses, staring up at the skies'; and lilies 'the poor little wooden crosses over their quiet graves'.[17] Service, in the words of one of his titles, sings 'the song of the pacifist'.

Another Scot who, like Hay, captured the enthusiasm of the early Volunteers was Captain R. W. Campbell, author of *Private Spud Tamson*, published in 1915, and of a poetic melodrama, *The Making of Micky McGhee* (1916), whose cadences and content owed not a little to Robert Service. In 1916 Campbell also published *The Mixed Division (T.)*, a fictionalised account of a Territorial unit, formed as Volunteers in Glasgow in 1859–60 and nicknamed 'The Clydeside Kilties'. The Territorials of the Great War, Campbell declared in his introduction, will 'act as an inspiration to those men who will follow the drum in years to come. To banish those regiments would, to a soldier, seem like abolishing the Guards or the Scots Greys.'[18]

Although the book's narrator described himself as a regular with strong links to the Black Watch, in reality Campbell had a background in journalism, having worked for newspapers in Australia and New Zealand. In October 1915 he was inspired by Gallipoli to produce a paean to the Australian soldier, called *The Kangaroo Marines*, a unit of 'bushmen', made up of 'one thousand cheerful toughs', who should be 'sharpshooters on the wallaby, able to live on condensed air and boiled snakes'. Campbell acknowledged that he was a Scot, 'not an Australasian', but 'I am an Imperialist – one filled with admiration for our overseas Dominions and the self-sacrifice of our colonial cousins.'[19] That belief in empire, in its future as a federal organisation, united him with Service and Buchan, both of whom had also broadened their horizons beyond Scotland before the war. Service had worked in the Yukon as a bank clerk, and his verses evoked the toughness of the Klondike gold rush. He dedicated the *Rhymes of a Red-Cross Man* to the memory of his brother, Lieutenant Albert Service, who served with the Canadian infantry and was killed in Belgium in August 1916. Buchan had worked for Lord Milner in South Africa, and went on to include South African characters in his Hannay novels and, after the war, to write the history of the South African Brigade in France, which had coincidentally been placed in the 9th Division, so linking 'the misty land of Scotland with the Dominion that extends from the Cape of Good Hope to the Zambesi'.[20]

The latter stages of the war

All three writers addressed Scotland's early engagement in the First World War with the perspective of distance, looking at their own homeland as outside observers as much as intimate participants. That initial response, with its focus on both army and empire, provided a striking contrast with Scotland's experience of the conflict from 1916 to 1918. At the beginning of 1916 Britain resolved to conscript single men aged eighteen to forty-one, and in May the government removed the protection for married men. Those who claimed exemption, on such grounds as business, family circumstances or conscientious objection, had their cases heard by local boards. The records of the military service tribunals of Lothians and Peeblesshire were one of three sets retained after the war as representative examples, and are to be found in the National Records of Scotland, but the details of the implementation of compulsory military service in Scotland still lack their historian. For the moment we can only draw conclusions from the experience of Northamptonshire, the subject of a study by James McDermott. Here the army's demand for boots meant that in practice many more were granted exemptions from military service than popular perceptions suggest.[21] Those who sat on the tribunals, being drawn from the local community, reflected the needs of local business. The purpose of conscription was not just to get more men for the army but also to ensure a sensible allocation of resources between the armed services and the war production needed both to equip the forces and to sustain Britain's allies. By January 1918 the cabinet committee on national service ranked the manpower demands of the army third, below shipbuilding and naval manning, the first priority, and the manufacture of aeroplanes and tanks, the second.[22]

Scotland, and particularly Glasgow, was home to much of the heavy industry which sustained Britain's war effort, not just shipbuilding but also munitions production. It experienced full employment and, as a result, the recruiting patterns of 1914–15 were not sustained. Scotland contributed more men for the army than was the British national average in the period of voluntary recruiting but then provided fewer in the period of conscription. Scotland raised 320,589 men through voluntary recruiting, 173,055 under the various intermediate steps employed in 1916 in the progression towards full national service, and 63,974 under national service between November 1917 and November 1918. The appearance of decline in the absolute numbers is corroborated by the comparative percentages. The voluntary enlistment figures represented 26.9 per cent of males aged fifteen to forty-nine living in Scotland according to the 1911 census. The comparable figure for England and Wales was 24.2 per cent. But in the era of conscription England and Wales recruited 22.1 per cent of the same cohort, whereas Scotland's contribution fell to 14.6 per cent. For the war as a whole, as opposed to 1914–15 only, England and Wales bore a heavier burden of military service than Scotland: 46.3 per cent of men aged fifteen to forty-nine as opposed to 41.5 per cent.[23]

The idea of the Scottish soldier

Although the popular notion in Scotland that its manpower contribution to the empire's military effort in 1914–18 was disproportionate is unsustainable, the figures do not gainsay the massive impact of the army on Scots: after all, 557,618 served in it. Furthermore, the First World War revivified the idea of the Scottish soldier. Each of the regiments of 1881 expanded through the mechanisms of the Territorial and Service Battalions from bodies with two regular battalions with perhaps one militia and three or four Volunteer battalions to about twenty battalions in all. Men who had no pre-war military calling before 1914 learned to identify with the Royal Scots or the Black Watch during it. In 1916, because of the local impact of the heavy losses sustained by 'Pals' battalions on the Somme, the Adjutant General of the army decided to move away from localised military service. However, the War Office still sought to put Scots into Scottish regiments. By 1918 they lacked the close community identity of McCrae's battalion, which at the close of the opening day of the battle of the Somme found twelve officers out of twenty-one and 573 of 723 other ranks to be missing, but they were still recognisably Scottish in comparison to other units.[24] The Scots Guards became more Scottish during the war, not less.[25]

Of course there were exceptions to these generalisations. Falling enlistment rates in Scotland in the second half of the war meant that many ostensibly Scottish units had to be made up to strength with non-Scots. A famous example is Winston Churchill, whose front-line service in 1915–16 was passed as commanding officer of 6th Battalion, the Royal Scots Fusiliers. One of his company commanders and in due course the adjutant, Andrew Dewar Gibb, wrote in 1924, 'When the news [of Churchill's appointment] spread, a mutinous spirit grew ... Why could not Churchill have gone to the Argylls if he must have a Scottish regiment! We should all have been greatly interested to see him in a kilt.'[26] Churchill took over the battalion after Loos, and gave it up when falling rolls forced the amalgamation of the 6th with the 7th Battalion of the regiment. The new 6/7th Battalion was hit hard again at Arras on 9 April 1917, when one of its fatalities was John Buchan's brother, Alastair. Deneys Reitz joined it in the aftermath of the battle. As discussed in Jonathan Hyslop's chapter in this collection, he had fought as a Boer commando leader in the South African War, and now found himself in a Scottish battalion as one of three South African officers, including the commanding officer.[27] Many who were not in fact Scots by birth or descent adopted fiercely Scottish identities, in an emotional sense, through service with Scottish regiments.

The focus on Scottish infantry regiments leaves far too much out of the historical account. It neglects Scots, like Charles Hamilton Sorley, who joined English regiments; it ignores the growth of other arms within the army through the advent of new technologies: the Royal Artillery, the Royal Engineers, the Royal Army Service Corps, the Royal Army Ordnance Corps and the Royal Flying Corps, all of which employed significant numbers of Scots. Scotland is an archipelago with an abundant coastline in relation to its land mass, and particularly in 1914 many inhabitants made their living by the sea, not least in the Merchant Navy and in the fishing fleet. Scots served in the Royal Navy and the Royal Naval Reserve, and because Scotland sustained the navy's principal wartime bases, Scapa Flow, Invergordon and Rosyth, it also provided the skilled labour which they required.

Before the war, the British empire may have made Scots outward-, rather than inward-, looking, and so disproportionately ready to travel to seek new opportunities. The advent of the war changed this, blocking the normal pattern of migration and even in some cases reversing it, as Scots returned to join up. The disruption to normal migratory patterns in 1914 may in part explain the voluntary recruiting surge of 1914–15.[28] The war took Scots not to transposed communities in Dunedin or Nova Scotia but to new cultures and customs outside the empire. It confronted them with foreign languages: *Punch* had fun with the Scottish soldier who asked for 'twa oofs' and was delighted to be given three, or one more than he had bargained for, his French interlocutor having decided he wanted 'trois'. Not only in France and Flanders but also in Iraq, Egypt and Palestine, the visible Scottish identity that accompanied the Scot was a military one, shaped by bagpipes and kilts.

Perhaps the most important encounter of all was with England, through which the Scottish divisions travelled on their way to the front and where they might also be trained. In late 1914 the 51st Highland Division was based in Bedford, its soldiers perplexed by billets which boasted running water and gas lighting. Their East Anglian hosts were sufficiently worried by the approach of Hogmanay to suggest that they had 'got somewhat confused with the tales of the St Bartholomew's Day Massacre', and accordingly provided a large dinner between Christmas and New Year to line the soldiers' stomachs. They were duly rewarded on the first night of Hogmanay with 'no more than a few wild Highlanders dancing reels, shaking hands, shouting and singing'. By the second night fighting had broken out, but between battalions, not with the local population. More serious was the consequence of the Highlanders' relative isolation from British population centres before the war: having not been exposed to measles in childhood, eighty-five soldiers died of the disease.[29]

In sum, after 1918, as opposed to before 1914, many more Scots had military experience, and much of it had been acquired through wearing the cap badge of a famous Scottish regiment, which in turn ensured that regimental identity became the vessel for national identity. In particular, military service disseminated the idea of 'Highlandism' throughout the Lowlands, not least through patterns of memorialisation. In Glasgow, the 5th Battalion, the Cameron Highlanders, which in 1914 had recruited heavily from the city's university, established a history prize to commemorate those who were killed in the war. In Edinburgh, another educational institution, Fettes College, where Ian Hay both studied and taught, featured a falling Highland, rather than Lowland, officer as its war memorial. Above all, those who had served in other 'Scottish' divisions, the 9th and 15th, which were both Highland and Lowland in regimental composition, or in the 52nd Lowland Division, were irked by the reputation and self-regard generated by the 51st Highland Division, which entered the fight much later than they had. The author of *England, their England*, A. G. Macdonell, who had served with the Royal Field Artillery, writing in 1937, observed that the division possessed a fearsome reputation with the enemy but few of the characteristics of the Highland soldiers of the seventeenth and eighteenth centuries. His explanation was simple: 'The Highland Division was largely composed of Lowlanders.' The Highlands were no better able to sustain mass recruiting in the First World War than they had been in the nineteenth century. But the Highlander was canny: 'He made no attempt to disavow the vicarious glory which his cousins and their English friends so generously brought him . . . The Lowlander was to be allowed to wear the coveted panoply, to stand in the ranks of regiments that bore historic names, to be called a Highlander, and no questions asked. In return he was to do nine-tenths of the fighting, and nine-tenths of the dying, and all the credit was to go to the Highlander, and no stones thrown. Each side made a contribution, the one putting their lives into the common pool, and the other putting glamour. Each side took something out of the common pool, the one an undeserved name and the other an unearned fame.'[30]

Remembering Scotland's war dead

Unsurprisingly, therefore, Scotland's depiction and memorialisation of the war stressed continuities more than change, frequently reaching back to the nation's early history or to the image of the kilted warrior, rather than portraying the war as the dawning of a new era.[31] Futurism and Vorticisim, the pre-war *avant garde* movements which provided the painterly vocabulary for much of the most famous British war art, had little following in Scotland. Muirhead Bone, the first British official war artist and a Glaswegian, produced representational drawings of the western front and of war industries, but despite his prolific output has almost dropped out of public recognition. The same might be said of James McBey, best known for his etchings of the Palestine campaign. James Lavery, an official war artist, and John Duncan Fergusson who was not, but received permission from the Admiralty to paint at Portsmouth, focused on the war at sea. Their subject matter precluded any engagement with the defining aspects of the war, the fighting in

France and Flanders, and so they too barely figure in accounts of war art, however assured their reputations today. Fergusson's partner, Margaret Morris, recalled that he tried to be commissioned as a naval war artist because he so disliked the khaki colour of army uniform.[32]

The reluctance not to shock, but to reassure and to comfort, and to use traditional forms to do so, was also manifest in Scotland's war memorials, not least in the widespread use of the Celtic cross. Just as Australia, New Zealand and Canada found a national identity through the war, so did Scotland, which it expressed, as they did, through the construction of a national war memorial. Public fundraising for the project, which had been initiated in 1917, was launched on 23 June 1922, the anniversary of the battle of Bannockburn, dubbed for this purpose 'Thistle Day'. Scotland created a memorial dedicated to all those who had fallen defending the nation against its enemies, aligning its First World War dead with the warriors of the past, not just Robert the Bruce but also Alexander III and William Wallace. Here the National War Memorial was not alone. In the following year, 1923, Evelyn Beale designed a war memorial for the Lansdowne Church in Glasgow of three gilded and vibrantly coloured panels: it shows Christ in the centre, arms outstretched above the communion table, while from either flank soldiers from the First World War lead a procession of supplicating Scottish warriors, including Wallace and the Bruce. The architect for the National War Memorial was Sir Robert Lorimer, who had been engaged by the Imperial (now Commonwealth) War Graves Commission to design the cemeteries in Italy and Egypt, and he recruited a team of about 200 Scottish craftsmen to help him. Those to whom he was particularly indebted were Douglas Strachan, responsible for the stained glass, and Charles d'Orville Pilkington Jackson, both veterans of the war. The project was dogged by controversy, not least because its chosen site was Edinburgh Castle. Although described as 'a sacred place' – the memorial stood on the rock where King David I had founded the chapel of St Mary – the original design intruded on a familiar and famous skyline.

These were innovations which upset conservationists. *The Scotsman* was opposed and so too was the Cockburn Society. But at one level what is more striking was the memorial's stress on continuity, not just with its references to Scotland's past but also in its rejection of the simplicity and universality of designs like the Cenotaph, developed by Sir Edwin Lutyens for Whitehall in London and replicated for Glasgow's George Square by Sir J. J. Burnet. Lorimer and his associates sought inspiration from a Scottish vernacular tradition, and the memorial's interior organised its roll call of names by regiment, so sustaining the themes of 1914–15. Ian Hay, commissioned to write an introduction to the building in 1931, four years after its completion in 1927, used words he had originally written for *The First Hundred Thousand* to explain why: 'Never a Scottish regiment comes under fire but the whole of Scotland feels it. Scotland is small enough to know all her sons by heart. You may live in Berwickshire, and the man who has died may have come from Skye; but his name is quite familiar to you. Big England's mourning is local; little Scotland's is national.'[33]

Figure 3.1 *Highland Soldier by a Cross*, 1914–18 by Tom Curr. This image was used for a poster for the Scottish National War Memorial. © National Museums Scotland.

The project's driving force was the eighth duke of Atholl, whose commitment proved particularly important when the committee appointed to direct it was riven by the wider public controversy. As mentioned in Edward Spiers's chapter in this collection, the marquess of Tullibardine had raised two regiments of Scottish Horse for service in the South African War, one from Scots living in South Africa, and the other from Australia and Scotland itself. In 1902 Tullibardine raised two new yeomanry regiments in Scotland, also called the Scottish Horse, and in 1914 they were expanded into a yeomanry brigade, which went to Gallipoli under Tullibardine's command. So Atholl's vision, and the memorial itself, marched in step with the sort of aspirations which Buchan, Service and Campbell had expressed in 1915: his was a Scotland whose identity was bound up with empire. At the left of the National War Memorial's entrance a unicorn holds St Andrew's Cross but on the right is a lion with the Union Flag, and the 'tree of Empire' dominates the back wall of the entrance.[34] The memorial commemorates the Scots who served in English, Irish and Welsh units or in the armed forces of the Dominions, specifically identifying those regiments with Scottish titles. It is not a manifestation of Scottish nationalism in a political sense.

That is not to say that the Scottish National War Memorial cannot be interpreted in political terms or that after 1918 the First World War more generally was not used for nationalist purposes. In 1919 the Treaty of Versailles emphasised the principle of national self-determination, at least within Europe. Unlike the Austro-Hungarian, German, Ottoman and Russian empires, the British empire was not shattered by the First World War, but the war did change the relationships within it. Dual identities before the war – the sense of being both Australian (or Canadian or even New Zealander) and British – were redefined by the war. As the commemorations of Anzac and Vimy Ridge showed, the Dominions used the war to differentiate themselves from the United Kingdom. Even John Buchan realised after the war that hopes of international order could no longer be vested in the British Empire, and looked instead to the League of Nations and the expectation that the United States would remain committed to it. For Scotland, the significance of Australia, Canada, New Zealand and South Africa after the war lay less in the promise they offered to emigrants and more in their progression to greater sovereignty. War memorials set in this context not only overseas but also within Britain were manifestations of cultural nationalism. As Sir Lawrence Weaver, its former architectural editor, said in *Country Life* when describing the Scottish National War Memorial in 1927, 'When the Englishman bows his head on Armistice day, the Scot lifts up his voice . . . the Scot watches the cloud shadows chase over the hills and mourns dead chieftains.'[35]

For some the war had fostered Anglophobia, not Unionism. On 28 April 1918 Sergeant Christopher Murray Grieve of the Royal Army Medical Corps wrote from Salonika, 'However loyal I may be to certain ideals bound up in the Allied Cause I was never to say the least an Anglophile – and when I am free of his majesty's uniform again I shall have a very great deal to say and write.'[36] As

Hugh MacDiarmid, he did. He was not necessarily typical. Another Scottish man of letters, Eric Linklater, also a non-commissioned officer in 1918 but with the Black Watch on the western front, found himself caught up in the retreat following the Germans' April offensive. Cut off from his own regiment, he encountered two members of the South Irish Horse, who told him that their war service was a form of training for the future struggle with the English. The senior Irishman, a sergeant, urged Linklater to join them: 'Scotland and Ireland together: we'd knock the bloody English to hell.' But, Linklater protested, 'I haven't got any quarrel with England.'[37]

Scottish home rule had entered the British political agenda before the war, and was resurrected after it. In 1922 *Home rule for Scotland: the case in 90 points*, published by the Scottish Home Rule Association, claimed that the war had reinforced its argument.[38] In 1934 the Scottish National Party was formed, and its chairman between 1936 and 1940 was Andrew Dewar Gibb, who had become Regius Professor of Civil Law at Glasgow in 1934 but was also the man who had served in the Royal Scots Fusiliers under Churchill's command. The party could use the symbols of nationalism which the conflict had promoted, proving a redoubtable advocate of the Scottish regiments, while rejecting wars fought in Britain's name when it did not approve of the outcome.

Scotland's losses in the Great War therefore became a matter of political consequence as well as of national grief. The 1921 census of Scotland reported 74,000 deaths abroad as a result of the war.[39] The census almost certainly underestimated total Scottish military deaths in the war, as it excludes those who died of wounds at home or who succumbed after 1921. The Scottish National War Memorial at its foundation commemorated the names of 85,548 dead from the Scottish infantry regiments alone, but this figure includes those who were born outside Scotland and some who may not even have been Scots; it also contains an element of double counting as those who enlisted in one regiment but died serving with another could appear twice. 'Nationalist propaganda' quickly reached a tally of 110,000 deaths.[40] But this figure pales by comparison with current claims. In 2013 Colin Campbell, a former SNP defence spokesman and the author of a history of the 51st Highland Division in the war, claimed in an otherwise well-informed letter to the press that 26.4 per cent of Scots did not return from the war, and that the Scottish adult male population was depleted by 3.1 per cent, when England's fell by only 1.6 per cent.[41] These figures have become standard in today's Scotland. They are also almost certainly wrong.

Common sense says that, if over the war as a whole England and Wales produced more men proportionately for the armed forces than did Scotland, then Scottish death rates cannot be twice theirs, however brave Scottish soldiers or however allegedly ready their commanders might have been to expend Scottish lives as opposed to English. The latter argument seems particularly perverse given Scotland's representation in the army's senior ranks: after all, the commanders of both the British Expeditionary Force in France from 1915 to 1918 and of the Mediterranean Expeditionary Force sent to Gallipoli in 1915 – Douglas

Haig and Ian Hamilton respectively – were Scots. True, if Scots joined up in greater numbers earlier in the war than did others, more of them were exposed to danger longer, as Loos showed. However, Scottish voluntary recruitment was only 2.7 per cent higher than that of England and Wales, not twice as high. It is also true that those Scots who had emigrated and enlisted outside Scotland are not included in the 1921 census. By including the Scottish diaspora, the Scottish National War Memorial reached a figure by 2005 of 148,218 Scottish deaths, a total which is still being added to.[42] However, if the comparison with England and Wales is to be continued, it would be necessary to include their emigrant populations as well, not simply compare an inflated Scottish figure with a constant figure for other parts of Britain.

The National War Memorial figure is equivalent to that produced by T. M. Devine for what is now regarded as the standard history of modern Scotland, *The Scottish Nation*. He claims that 26.4 per cent of the 557,000 Scots who enlisted in all services lost their lives.[43] Devine is misleading on two counts. First, his total enlistment figure is in fact that for the army only, and ignores the Royal Navy. Jay Winter has estimated total Scottish mobilisation to have been 688,416.[44] Trevor Royle has put total mobilisation at 690,235, although it is not clear how this is calculated: it may include those already serving in both armed forces before the war as well as those recruited during it. Total mobilisation, using Royle's number and if we accept Devine's death rate of 26.4 per cent (the same as that used by Campbell), produces 182,222 Scots dead.[45] This is so high as to be incredible. Devine gives no source for the death rate of 26.4 per cent, but it seems probable that it comes from the work of another Scottish historian. In 1998 Niall Ferguson asserted that 'Scots were (after the Serbs and Turks) the soldiers who suffered the highest death rate of the war'. He too gives 26.4 per cent killed of all Scots mobilised, as opposed to a rate of 11.8 per cent for Britain and Ireland. The latter figure is generally accepted, but it does of course include the Scottish figure within it, a point which the unwary reader may overlook. More importantly, and the most likely source of all Campbell's and Devine's confusion, Ferguson's 26.4 per cent is actually the proportion of Scottish males of military age who volunteered before the end of 1915. It is neither a death rate nor a figure applicable to the war as a whole.[46]

The death rate reported by the 1921 Scottish census of 74,000 is roughly 10 per cent of British military deaths in the war, and is what might be expected because it is proportional to the size of the Scottish population in relation to that of the United Kingdom in 1911. The fact that it was calculated on this basis, rather than on actual deaths, may be a good reason for increasing the total Scottish military dead. But methodological problems multiply once we move beyond the reasonably tight definition of residence provided by the 1911 census. Who is a Scot? If we use an inclusive definition, based on surname and descent, for example, and follow that through the female line as well as the male, we create networks of kinship but not figures that can provide meaningful comparisons, either internationally or domestically. We will certainly end up double-counting.

However, an exclusive definition denies the multiple identities possessed by many throughout the empire in 1914. Recognising the danger of under-reporting in the census, Trevor Royle has proposed a figure as high as 100,000. Michael Anderson considers 100,000 war-related deaths to be an upper figure and reckons the total almost certainly to be less. Scottish census and registration numbers suggest a maximum of 90,000.[47] Finally, any proposed increase in the Scottish totals should be set against the possibility of similar under-reporting in the figures of other national groups, especially if comparisons are to be made. Because the level of military service is comparable, there is little reason to think that Scottish death rates in the war were massively out of line with those of Britain as a whole. This is not to deny either their scale or their impact. However, neither the history of Scotland in general, nor Scottish military history in particular, needs more myths: there are quite enough of them as it is.

Notes

1. See the essays in Marilyn Lake and Henry Reynolds, with Mark McKenna and Joy Damousi, *What's Wrong with Anzac? The Militarisation of Australian History* (Sydney: University of New South Wales Press, 2010); James Brown, *Anzac's Long Shadow: the Cost of our National Obsession* (Collingwood, Vic: Black Inc., 2014).
2. John Robertson, *The Scottish Enlightenment and the Militia Issue* (Edinburgh: John Donald, 1985).
3. J. E. Cookson, *The British Armed Nation 1793–1815* (Oxford: Oxford University Press, 1997), pp. 130, 147; Andrew Mackillop, '*More fruitful than the soil*': *Army, Empire and the Scottish Highlands, 1715–1815* (East Linton: Tuckwell, 2000), pp. 227–8.
4. H. J. Hanham, 'Religion and nationality in the mid-Victorian army', in M. R. D. Foot (ed.), *War and Society: Historical Essays in Memory of J. R. Western, 1928–71* (London: Collins, 1973), pp. 159–81, at pp. 163–6; Ian Beckett, 'The British army, 1914–18: the Illusion of Change', in John Turner (ed.), *Britain and the First World War* (London: Routledge, 1988), pp. 98–116, at p. 105.
5. Hew Strachan, *The Politics of the British Army* (Oxford: Oxford University Press, 1997), pp. 200–6.
6. James Moncrieff Grierson, *The Scottish Volunteer Force, 1859–1908* (Edinburgh: William Blackwood & Sons, 1909) remains the only account; both Hugh Cunningham, *The Volunteer Force: A Social and Political History, 1859–1908* (London: Croom Helm, 1975) and Ian Beckett, *Riflemen Form: a Study of the Rifle Volunteer Movement 1859–1908* (Aldershot: Midas Books, 1982) effectively ignore Scotland.
7. P. E. Dewey, 'Military recruiting and the British labour force during the First World War', *Historical Journal*, vol. 27, no. 1 (1984), pp. 199–223, at p. 216.
8. See Elaine McFarland, '"How the Irish Paid Their Debt": Irish Catholics in Scotland and Voluntary Enlistment, August 1914–July 1915', *Scottish Historical Review*, vol. LXXXII, 2, no. 214 (2003), pp. 261–84.
9. Jack Alexander, *McCrae's Battalion: The Story of the 16th Royal Scots* (Edinburgh: Mainstream, 2003).
10. This is a central argument of Derek Rutherford Young, 'Voluntary recruitment in Scotland, 1914–1916', PhD thesis, Glasgow University, 2001, on which I have heavily relied; see also Derek Young, *Forgotten Scottish Voices from the Great War* (Stroud: The History Press, 2005).

11. Ian F. W. Beckett, *The Amateur Military Tradition 1558–1945* (Manchester: Manchester University Press, 1991), pp. 226–30.
12. Trevor Royle, *The Flowers of the Forest: Scotland and the First World War* (Edinburgh: Birlinn, 2006), pp. 91–2; Ewen A. Cameron and Iain J. M. Robertson, 'Fighting and bleeding for the land: the Scottish highlands and the Great War', in Catriona M. M. Macdonald and Elaine W. McFarland (eds), *Scotland and the Great War* (East Linton: Tuckwell, 1999), pp. 81–102, at pp. 87–8.
13. Ian Hay, *The First Hundred Thousand: Being the Unofficial Chronicle of a Unit of 'K(1)'* (Edinburgh: Wm. Blackwood, 1916), pp. 120–1, cited by Peter Buitenhuis, *The Great War of words: literature as propaganda 1914–18 and after* (London: Batsford, 1989), p. 113; see also Gordon Urquhart, 'Confrontation and readership: Loos, readership and "The First Hundred Thousand"', in Macdonald and McFarland, *Scotland and the Great War*, pp. 125–44.
14. Cyril Falls, *War books: an Annotated Bibliography of Books about the Great War* (London: Peter Davies, 1930; revised edition, London, 1939), p. 278.
15. John Ewing, *The History of the 9th (Scottish) Division 1914–1919* (London: John Murray, 1921), p. 8.
16. In Andrew Lownie and William Milne (eds), *John Buchan's Collected Poems* (Aberdeen: Scottish Cultural Press, 1996), pp. 144–7.
17. Robert Service, *Rhymes of a Red-Cross Man* (London: Fisher Unwin, 1923), pp. 118–19, 149. I am grateful to Professor Ted Cowan for introducing me to Service's war poetry.
18. R. W. Campbell, *The Mixed Division (T.)* (London: Hutchinson, 1916), p. vii.
19. R. W. Campbell, *The Kangaroo Marines* (London: Cassell, 1915), pp. 5, 9.
20. Ewing, *9th (Scottish) Division*, p. 332.
21. James McDermott, *British Military Service Tribunals 1916–1918: 'a very much abused body of men'* (Manchester: Manchester University Press, 2011); see also David Littlewood, 'The tool and instrument of the military? The operations of the Military Service Tribunals in the East Central Riding of Yorkshire and those of the Military Service Boards of New Zealand, 1916–1918', PhD thesis, Massey University, New Zealand, 2015.
22. Keith Grieves, *The Politics of Manpower, 1914–1918* (Manchester: Manchester University Press, 1988), p. 173.
23. Jay M. Winter, *The Great War and the British People* (Basingstoke: Palgrave, 1988), p. 28; see also Clive H. Lee, 'The Scottish economy', in Macdonald and McFarland, *Scotland and the Great War*, pp. 11–35, at p. 20.
24. Alexander, *McCrae's Battalion*, p. 178; final losses were four officers and 225 other ranks killed, two officers and seven other ranks captured, and six officers and 341 other ranks wounded (of whom twenty-seven died). See Alexander, p. 306.
25. Nevil Macready, *Annals of an active life* (London: Hutchinson, 1924), p. 257; Nicholas Perry, 'Nationality in the Irish infantry regiments in the First World War', *War and Society*, vol. 12, no. 1 (1994), pp. 65–95, at p. 72; see also Edward Spiers, 'The Scottish Soldier at War', in Hugh Cecil and Peter Liddle (eds), *Facing Armageddon: the First World War Experienced* (London: Leo Cooper, 1996), pp. 314–35.
26. Martin Gilbert, *Winston S. Churchill*, vol. III, 1914–1916 (London: William Heinemann, 1971), p. 630.
27. Deneys Reitz, *Trekking On* (London: Faber & Faber, 1933), p. 139.
28. Young, 'Voluntary recruiting'.
29. W. N. Nicholson, *Behind the Lines: An Account of Administrative Staffwork in the British Army 1914–1918* (London: Jonathan Cape, 1939; 2nd edition, Stevenage: Strong Oak Press, 1990), pp. 37–8, 42–3, 51; Nicholson was on the staff of the division.

30. A. G. Macdonell, *My Scotland* (London: Jarrolds, 1937), pp. 80, 87.
31. This point reflects the arguments of Jay M. Winter, *Sites of Memory, Sites of Mourning: the Great War in European cultural history* (Cambridge: Cambridge University Press, 1995).
32. Patricia R. Andrew, *A Chasm in Time: Scottish War Artists in the Twentieth Century* (Edinburgh: Birlinn, 2014), especially pp. 20–2, 40–2, 68–72; Alice Strang, Elizabeth Cumming and Sheila McGregor, *J. D. Fergusson* (Edinburgh: National Galleries of Scotland, 2013), p. 21.
33. Ian Hay, *Their Name Liveth: the Scottish National War Memorial* (London: John Lane, 1931), p. 6.
34. Ann Petrie, 'Scottish culture and the First World War, 1914–1939', PhD thesis, University of Dundee, 2006, vol. 1, p. 217; for other discussions of the Scottish National War Memorial, see Juliette MacDonald, '"Let us now praise the name of famous men": myth and meaning in the stained glass of the Scottish National War Memorial', *Journal of Design History*, vol. 14, no. 2 (2001), pp. 117–28; Jenny Macleod, '"By Scottish hands, with Scottish money, on Scottish soil": the Scottish National War Memorial and national identity', *Journal of British Studies*, vol. 49, no. 1 (2010), pp. 73–96; Ian Gow, 'The Scottish National War Memorial', in Fiona Pearson (ed.), *Virtue and vision: sculpture and Scotland 1540–1990* (Edinburgh: National Galleries of Scotland, 1991), pp. 104–9; Duncan Macmillan, *Scotland's Shrine: the Scottish National War Memorial* (Farnham: Lund Humphries, 2014).
35. Quoted in Elaine W. McFarland, 'A Coronach in Stone', in Macdonald and McFarland, *Scotland and the Great War*, pp. 1–10, at p. 1.
36. National Library of Scotland (NLS), MS 26031, Grieve to GO, 28 April 1918, quoted in Petrie, 'Scottish culture', p. 72; see also Royle, *The Flowers of the Forest*, pp. 140, 296–7, 300.
37. Eric Linklater, *The Man on My Back: An Autobiography* (London: Macmillan, 1941), p. 41.
38. David Torrance, 'Today the hand of history lies on Cameron's shoulder', *Herald*, 24 February 2014, p. 13.
39. Winter, *The Great War and the British people*, p. 68.
40. McFarland, 'A coronach in stone', p. 1.
41. Colin Campbell, Letter to the editor, *Herald*, 27 February 2013.
42. Royle, *Flowers of the Forest*, p. 284; Trevor Royle, 'The First World War', in Edward M. Spiers, Jeremy A. Crang and Matthew J. Strickland, *A Military History of Scotland* (Edinburgh: Edinburgh University Press, 2012), pp. 506–35, at p. 529; see also Spiers, 'The Scottish soldier at war', in Cecil and Liddle (eds), *Facing Armageddon*, p. 314, which gives a total of 147,000 dead but relates this total to the army only, thus excluding the navy.
43. Thomas M. Devine, *The Scottish Nation 1700–2000* (London: Penguin, 1999), p. 309.
44. Winter, *The Great War and the British People*, p. 72.
45. Royle, *Flowers of the Forest*, p. 284.
46. Niall Ferguson, *The Pity of War* (London: Penguin, 1998), pp. 298–9. Ferguson cites Winter, *The Great War and the British People*, p. 75, which carries no such statistic for Scotland.
47. I am most grateful to Professor Michael Anderson for sharing with me Chapter 10 of his forthcoming book, provisionally entitled *Scotland's population histories: contrasts and comparisons from the mid-nineteenth to the early twenty-first centuries*.

Part 2

4

Performing Scottishness in England: Forming and Dressing the London Scottish Volunteer Rifles

Stuart Allan

> There is no want of the native raw material in London, which is said to be overrun by Scotchmen. All that is wanted is that it should be well worked up.

Thus spoke Scottish aristocrat, Member of Parliament, sportsman, and leading light of the rifle volunteer movement Francis Wemyss-Charteris-Douglas, Lord Elcho, later earl of Wemyss and March, as he presided over a public meeting of Scottish residents in London held at the Freemasons' Tavern in the West End, on 4 July 1859.[1] The meeting had been convened conjunctly by the Highland Society of London and the Caledonian Society of London in order to consider the formation of a Scottish volunteer corps in London. Two months earlier, the British government had accepted and authorised proposals to form a part-time military reserve of volunteer units throughout the country, answering public concerns over the perceived instability of continental politics and the potential for a French threat to the immediate security of the British Isles, with the British regular army heavily committed to imperial garrisons overseas. The countrywide response to the volunteering call, in organising activity, subscriptions raised and men enrolled had been strong. In the view of Lord Elcho,

> Such then being the popular feeling, it would be strange indeed if the sons of Scotland, who have ever been noted for their loyalty, their patriotism, and their valour attested on many a bloody field and in many a clime, had been backward in this movement.[2]

As it proved, there was no backwardness about volunteering in Scotland, nor among those Scots domiciled south of the border. In England, as part of the countrywide surge in amateur military organisation set off in 1859, recruiting for Scottish volunteer companies began in London, Liverpool and Newcastle. The Scottish volunteers achieved an enduring presence in the capital, one that has lasted into the twenty-first century. In the northern English cities the idea and recruiting effort underwent periodic revival, first as a result of the South African War and then as part of the great national recruiting effort of the first year of the First World War. By 1918 the British army's Order of Battle included the following Anglo-Scottish units, consisting in the main of pre-war part-timers and war service volunteers: 'the London Scottish' comprising of two Territorial Force battalions of the London Regiment, recruited from among Scots in London and directly descended from the volunteer corps brought into being at the Freemasons' Tavern meeting nearly sixty years earlier; 'the Liverpool Scottish', one Territorial Force battalion of another English infantry regiment, the King's (Liverpool Regiment), whose Scottish roots may also be traced to the nascent rifle volunteer movement of the early 1860s; 'the Tyneside Scottish' comprising four New Army volunteer battalions of the Northumberland Fusiliers, who could also point to short-lived antecedents in the initial rush of mid-Victorian rifle volunteering; and the 'Manchester Scottish', a New Army contingent raised in 1914 which formed half of the initial strength of the 15th (Service) (1st City of Edinburgh) Battalion of Scottish regular infantry regiment, the Royal Scots (Lothian Regiment). It would be remiss therefore to set about assessing expressions of Scottish military identity among the Scottish diaspora in the late nineteenth and early twentieth centuries without taking some account of this phenomenon in England, that most readily reachable of destinations for migrant Scots. Part-time Scottish or Highland volunteer rifle companies appeared in three English cities, including London, in 1859, around the same time in which the earliest of such peace-time Scottish civil-military organisations emerged in overseas contexts.[3] The antecedents of the Scottish volunteers in London however reached back into the late eighteenth century. In considering the interaction of expatriate Scottish associational culture with the volunteer military ethos, this may be a good place to start.

The Highland Society of London and the Napoleonic volunteer movement

The London Scottish Volunteer Rifles established in 1859 as the result of the Freemasons' Tavern meeting had two ancestors among the volunteer forces of Georgian Britain. In 1798, in response to fear of French invasion and of French-inspired revolutionary insurrection at home, voluntary local armed associations and volunteer corps were formed in parishes, wards and other districts across London and were accepted for service by the government. Recruits signed up, largely at their own expense, to drill and prepare for active duty if and as required, operating under various definitions of local responsibility for helping to keep the peace and defend property from any home-grown threat, and with some offering to serve anywhere in the country in the case of enemy invasion. This was its practical purpose, but voluntary military organisation of this kind was also, intrinsically, an assertion by the urban property-owning classes of their stake in the defence of the realm and, by extension, their right to participate in national affairs. Among the volunteer corps that sprung up across London from Westminster to Deptford was one drawing its recruits from across the metropolis, the Highland Armed Association, a unit composed, according to its Standing Orders, of 'Highlanders, and persons born in Scotland, as well as the sons of

Scotchmen and Highlanders and members of the Highland Society'.[4] This last category of membership eligibility points to a feature which was common to the Highland Armed Association of 1798 and to many of the part-time Scottish military units which would subsequently follow their example throughout the British Empire, this being the patronage of a Scottish or Highland society whose social, cultural and philanthropic purposes and interests were not exclusively, nor indeed primarily, concerned with military affairs.[5] The Highland Society of London was formed in 1778 by Highland noblemen and gentlemen whose social, commercial and professional lives found them resident, or spending a significant amount of their time, in London. From the outset, the Society's membership was strong in Highland landowners and Scottish magnates connected with the Pitt government of the day, in Highland regimental officers and other military men.[6] As well as its notable achievement in 1782 of successfully lobbying for repeal of the Dress Act of 1746, which had banned Highland dress after Culloden, its stated objectives included the preservation of the music of the Highlands, the cultivation of the Gaelic language and literature, the establishment of charitable institutions for the relief of Highlanders in economic distress, the economic improvement of the Highlands, and, further, 'keeping up the martial spirit, and rewarding the gallant achievements of the Highland Corps'.[7] This last goal it pursued actively from 1801 by striking medals and commissioning trophies for award, individually and collectively, to the officers and men of the regular Highland regiments of the British army. In 1815 the Society combined its militaristic and philanthropic purposes through its patronage of the Caledonian Asylum, a school in London for the children of Scottish soldiers, sailors and marines.

It was in keeping therefore with the membership profile and multiple aspirations of the nobles, lairds and military officers of the Highland Society of London that, when patriotic armed associations and volunteer corps were forming in the city in 1798, it should propose, at the June monthly meeting held at the Shakespeare Tavern, Covent Garden, to form a 'corps of volunteers in the Highland Uniform from the Highlanders and other Natives of Scotland resident in London under the patronage and direction of this Society'.[8] That the 'Highland Uniform' should have been at the forefront of this proposal was entirely in tune with the Society's mission since, more than pursuing publication of works of Ossian with which it had busied itself to this point, the promulgation of Highland dress was a highly visible and increasingly attainable marker of differentiation for Highland and, by extension, Scottish interests in London society. Highland dress already meant something in relation to the status of Scotland in the calculations and conduct of wartime government and, as would transpire in the ensuing decade, in the interest and regard of royal patrons. Even before the French Revolutionary War, Scottish soldiers were a recognisable group often to be seen in and around the city, and indeed were the most visibly distinctive of all among the many trades and professions followed by Scotsmen in London. As such they were a common, colourful feature incorporated by London print-sellers into their street scenes.[9] Once established, the Highland Armed Association must certainly have stood out among the fashionable, light infantry styles of dress worn by its London volunteering counterparts. Purchased at considerable expense out of subscriptions to the corps and by the volunteers themselves, the uniform chosen by the Highland Society and its new corps conformed to the dress patterns and accoutrements of the regular army Highland regiments, with red jacket, yellow-faced, feather bonnet, belted plaid (the full *breacan an fheilidh*) in the 'government', or 'Black Watch', tartan as worn by the 42nd Royal Highland Regiment of Foot, hair sporran, and diced hose.[10] Provision was also made for what was becoming another staple of Scottish military culture: three pipers were to be provided for.

The first hopes of the Highland Society were for a battalion 800-strong, but such ambitions were never to be realised and at its strongest the Highland Armed Association, or as it came also to be known the 'Royal Highland Volunteers', did not exceed around 100 officers and men during its brief existence.[11] The threats which it and its numerous counterparts were raised to combat did not materialise either, not at least to the point that required the Highland Armed Association to be called out for active duty. Its activities therefore amounted to drills and reviews, until the Treaty of Amiens of April 1802 brought an end to matters with the disbandment of volunteer units across the country. Amiens proved to be only a thirteen-month respite in long wars between Great Britain and France, however, and on the resumption of hostilities in May 1803 the corps was reactivated back at the Shakespeare Tavern, this time as the Loyal North Britons and once again under the patronage of the Highland Society of London. The change of name reflected a desire on the part of the volunteers to widen the appeal of service in the corps among Scottish gentlemen, businessmen, tradesmen and artisans in London.[12] This version of the corps endured until the peace of 1814, though mostly below its target recruiting establishment of 300, numbering on average around 200 officers and men. The Loyal North Britons had the excitement of being called out for service on two occasions in 1812 for public order duties, first amid the riots provoked by the arrest of radical MP Sir Francis Burdett, and second in the days of crisis following the assassination of Prime Minister Spencer Perceval.

Highland dress as an outward signifier of national identity remained at the centre of the concerns of the revamped regiment. In 1803, thanks to the earlier recruitment of multiple regiments of regular 'line' regiments in the Scottish Highlands for the wartime British army, and with the celebration in word, and especially in picture, of the success of Highland regiments in the British victory over the French in Egypt in 1801, Highland military appearance was well on its way to becoming synonymous with military Scotland in the eyes of the metropolis. For the volunteers, however, there was the more prosaic consideration that the cost of the Highland uniform had been identified as a disincentive to those who might otherwise have come forward to join the first incarnation of the regiment, since volunteers had to fund or part-fund the purchase of their own uniforms and Highland dress represented an additional expense.

The Loyal North Britons decided therefore to dispense with the expensive belted plaid, eschewed the *feileadh beag* or 'little kilt' that was being adopted in the regular Highland regiments, and opted instead for more economical grey breeches and boots, retaining, for the Highland effect, the feather bonnet and a tartan cloak or shoulder plaid.[13] In this, however, they ultimately failed, and that failure speaks to the cultural potency of the Highland dress and its attractions among those for whom the money was not an issue. From 1805 the commanding officer of the Loyal North Britons was Prince Augustus Frederick, duke of Sussex and earl of Inverness, sixth son of King George III. Between 1806 and 1809 Sussex was, concurrently with this military office, President of the Highland Society of London, an appointment which reflected the increasingly aristocratic profile of the Society and, furthermore, the emergence of 'Highlandism' as a cultural phenomenon reaching into the very highest ranks of the British political and social establishment.[14] The duke's fondness for the Highland dress meant that the officers of the Loyal North Britons, and possibly the rank and file also (for whom the evidence is unclear), were ultimately obliged to invest in kilts for wear on special occasions, bringing the cost of dressing and equipping the corps to an estimated £20 per head, well over the 10 guineas that had been agreed as an acceptable expense at the outset. To be properly Scottish in London, or at least to be properly a military Scotsman in London, one had to look the part.

Much has been written about the motivations, social make-up and complex political profiles of the Napoleonic-era volunteer corps. By serving in the cause of national defence, and adopting military uniform so to do, the civilian volunteers were not merely offering themselves as an adjunct to the regular army, they were presenting themselves as free and independently minded participants in the affairs of the nation. As they went about their business of parade and drill, they asserted a range of group identities related to locality, class, occupation and, in the case of the Scots in London, nationality.[15] Fellowship was an inherent part of the experience, and social relations between officers and non-commissioned ranks were more subtle than in the rigid social and authoritative hierarchies that existed in the regular army. Derived from the Highland Society of London, an early vehicle of Scottish associational culture, the Highland Armed Association and the Loyal North Britons were cultural associations in themselves. On disbandment in 1814, their temporary political and military utility at an end, the officers of the Loyal North Britons kept the flame of fellowship alive by forming a Masonic lodge which initially met at the Shakespeare Tavern.

As in the volunteer corps more generally, it should be acknowledged that the officers and men of the Scottish volunteer corps in London also expressed and asserted their masculinity. Through the wearing of military dress, and the bearing of arms, volunteers associated themselves with the culture of war, with patriotic vigour, chivalry and danger, performing this element of themselves in contrast to the domestic realities of their metropolitan lives. For the Scots drawn towards the Scottish volunteer corps, Highland dress was not only distinctive and exotic;

it was also recognised in association with the romantic idea of an ancient warrior culture, an idea which was gaining in literary and cultural traction at the same time. Not every Scottish volunteer in London served in one of these two regiments; many doubtless fitted happily enough into other corps where their local and occupational identities outweighed any wish to demonstrate their cultural origins. But for a Scotsman in London at the turn of the century, there was no more emphatic statement of national and individual virility than the military Highland dress, whatever it might have cost.

The Caledonian Society of London and the London Scottish Volunteer Rifles

Raised forty-five years after the disbandment of the Loyal North Britons, the London Scottish Volunteer Rifles championed by Lord Elcho in 1859 had no direct institutional descent from the former, but the interests and motivations which brought Elcho's unit into existence were similar to those which had influenced the earlier versions. As stated above, the London Scottish were only one manifestation of a nationwide volunteering phenomenon, and were one of many new volunteer corps in London itself. As before, it was the will and organising activity of existing private associations of Scotsmen in London that helped to foster their foundation. The Highland Society of London was involved once more, and on this occasion further impetus came from a relatively new arrival on the associational culture scene, the Caledonian Society of London formed in 1837. The membership of the latter was more broadly based than that of the rather exclusive Highland Society of London. The Caledonian Society was fashioned to appeal to the ever-greater number of middle-class Scots making their way professionally and commercially in London, in their own eyes 'the average Caledonian in London', many of whom were of Lowland origins and connections.[16] Speaking in 1854, the Secretary of the Caledonian Society spoke of its original purpose, to bring together 'the class called "middle", to have membership open to all men from all parts of Scotland; to make it in short a really Scottish institution.'[17]

It is unclear whether the move to create, or revive, a Scottish volunteer regiment in London in 1859 originated either from within the Caledonian Society or the Highland Society. Sources differ in crediting the idea on the Caledonian side to Robert Hepburn, a Scottish dental surgeon resident in Grosvenor Square and founder member of the Society, or on the Highland side to Dr Alexander Halley, a Dunkeld-born Harley Street physician and Gaelic scholar.[18] What is certain is that both men and other representatives from the two societies were present in the committee that convened the public meeting at the Freemasons' Tavern and together they had formally invited Lord Elcho to take the chair.[19] It was, however, a reflection of the differing social and age profiles of the membership of the two societies that, while both associations would go on actively supporting the London Scottish through the first decades of its history as a volunteer corps, the Caledonian Society of London was the one which was to supply the

London Scottish with numbers of its enrolled volunteers, both as officers and in the ranks.[20]

It appears, nevertheless, that it was Dr Halley of the Highland Society who made the first move towards engaging the participation of Lord Elcho in the summer of 1859.[21] The Scottish aristocrat and self-styled 'Liberal-Conservative' independent MP was an obvious choice as figurehead for the cause, since his name had already become prominent in public and press discussion of the desirability, constitution, organisation, equipment and dress of the new national volunteer force. Then in his early forties, Elcho was not a soldier, nor was he a Highlander; the family estates were in East Lothian and Gloucestershire. But from his patrician conservative perspective he was confidently vocal in matters concerning the defence of the realm and the part that volunteers might play in it. His competence to comment on the training and equipping of the volunteer force was derived from personal experience that was sporting rather than military. In common with many men of his class, Lord Elcho's attachment to Scotland was manifested most actively each year in the months of July to October, the season for stag-hunting on the sporting estates of the Scottish Highlands. In the late 1850s the craze for Highland deer-stalking was well underway, and it was from the perspective of the recreational hunter that Elcho viewed the potential value of the rifle volunteer movement, and of the Scottish contribution to it.[22]

'Rifle' was an operative word in this respect. Alluding to the recent and widely reported successes of Giuseppe Garibaldi's Italian volunteers in the 1859 campaign against the Austrians, Elcho and others contended that a volunteer force formed of private citizens trained to shoot rifles accurately at long range would offer a sound basis for strengthening British national defence.[23] He knew something about this. Progress in the technical development of reliable, accurate, high-velocity hunting rifles was one contributory factor in the burgeoning popularity of Highland deer-stalking among the sporting gentry, professional and commercial middle classes.[24] Speaking to the assembled London Scotsmen at the Freemasons' Tavern meeting, Elcho got down to specific recommendations for a weapon of choice for the volunteers, the Wesley Richards breech-loading rifle or, his own personal preference, the Lancaster smooth oval-bored rifle: 'I have myself used the oval smooth-bored rifle for the last nine years in deer-stalking, and can therefore speak practically as to its efficiency.'[25] Military efficiency demanded uniformity of calibre among the arms carried by volunteer riflemen, however, and ultimately the Enfield military rifle was made available by the government, supplanting any initiative to adopt non-regulation models.

Deer-stalking was also very much in Lord Elcho's mind when he considered the question of how a corps of volunteers ought to be dressed, observing, 'The only difference between a deer-stalker and a soldier is that one pursues deer the other men, and what experience has proved to be best suited to the one should, I humbly think, be adopted by the other.'[26] Entering into an emerging debate on the efficacy of drab or 'khaki' dress, already in use among some British units in India, in the first place he rejected the red coats worn by regular infantry, and the dark green worn by regular army rifle regiments deemed 'more visible than any other on the heath', as inappropriate for modern war.[27] The growing accuracy and firepower of infantry small arms was demonstrating camouflage to be an imperative requirement. Elcho believed the least visible and hard-wearing of cloths, the grey tweed, to be the answer. He was also convinced that trousers were unsuitable military dress, since they were a constant drag on the knee when walking, and liable to soaking when moving over wet ground. Acknowledging the relative advantages of the kilt over trousers in this regard, Elcho however chose to advocate loose tunics and loose-kneed breeches, or 'knickerbockers', worn with knee stockings, leggings and ankle boots, 'which are now in almost universal use among the sportsmen and deer-stalkers of the Highlands of Scotland, who have to undergo great fatigue, and to whom the utmost freedom of limb is essential'.[28]

In setting all this out for the assembled throng at the Freemasons' Tavern, Lord Elcho was among friends. With him on the inaugural committee of the London Scottish Volunteer Rifles were others of his class and sporting interests, including the marquis of Stafford, Liberal MP, heir to the vast Sutherland estates and an enthusiastic sportsman, and Lord Grosvenor, later first duke of Westminster, Liberal-Whig MP and another avid deer-stalker, with whom Elcho had spent many happy stalking days in the Reay forest. Elcho was evidently also confident that there were those among the wider meeting who were suitably familiar with the sport, commenting on the difficulties of judging distance in rifle-shooting, by which reason '– as many who hear me will know – that deer so often escape the sportsman's bullet'. Although a sporting holiday in the Scottish Highlands might at this stage have been beyond the means of the 'average Caledonian in London', the meeting was sufficiently impressed with Elcho's arguments to endorse the adoption of the grey tweed jacket and knickerbockers as the uniform for the London Scottish. Many other rifle volunteer units across the country followed this lead, although others chose more colourful uniforms. Elcho himself sought out the requisite cloth for what became known as 'Elcho grey', searching the tailor shops of London before finding a suitably tough Leicester-made grey tweed at Isaacs in Jermyn Street.[29] Thus the London Scottish acquired the first version of its distinctive grey uniform, derived as an idea from an elite, metropolitan view of the Scottish Highlands, and by extension of Scotland, as a place for a noble, manly recreation, skill in which was held to have application in modern warfare.

Dr Halley's sketch

In urging the knickerbockers, stockings and boots approach, Elcho had been obliged to give due consideration to the option of the kilt. Realising some might prefer it on patriotic grounds, he rejected it on practical grounds: 'Some I know are in favour of the kilt as a national dress; but though it is the best dress in the world for walking on open ground, I question its merits as a costume for skirmishing amongst the hedgerows of Kent or Surrey.'[30]

However, in drawing this conclusion Elcho reckoned without the power of the kilt as a marker for the Scottish military tradition and all that went with it, not least for Scotsmen far from home. As we have seen, promotion of Highland dress was one of the multiple formal objectives of the Highland Society of London. The Caledonian Society of London had likewise set out the aim, alongside its philanthropic and social purposes, 'to preserve the picturesque garb of old Gaul'.[31] Lord Elcho was first apprised of the move to start a London Scottish volunteer regiment when he received a visit from Dr Halley of the Highland Society. Halley was already familiar with Elcho's published letter about the most suitable uniform for rifle volunteers, and he brought with him a rough, coloured sketch drawn by a Mr Smart depicting a figure wearing what Halley imagined a 'Highland or Scottish London volunteer regiment' might look like.[32] The figure wore grey, certainly, but not the knickerbockers favoured by Lord Elcho. In this first vision of the uniform of the London Scottish, the figure wore a kilt, and a grey kilt at that.[33]

Enrolment for the corps began on 3 September 1859 at a meeting held at the headquarters of the Scottish Corporation, the principal Scottish charity in London, and Lord Elcho was appointed commanding officer. By early 1860, following a trawl for recruits of banks, insurance companies and businesses in and around London, a six-company corps was formed, with an establishment of around 500 active members. The first rules of the London Scottish Volunteer Rifles were drawn up in 1859, setting out the qualification criteria for enrolment in the corps. Effective and Honorary members were each to pay entrance and annual subscription fees and were to be 'connected with Scotland by birth, marriage, or property'.[34] Birth and marriage, which were evidently taken to encompass descent, covered the young men of the commercial, clerical and professional classes, students and apprentices, who paid for their own volunteer uniforms on top of their fees. Skilled workers, men of the respectable working class, or 'artisans' as they were still described, were also admitted on the grounds of their Scottish nationality, and for them the entrance fee could be waived (it was abolished altogether in 1862) and uniforms provided out of regimental funds. Class relationships in the corps were not defined by rank, since, beyond its first establishment, the practice developed that commissioned officers were usually expected first to have seen service in the ranks. The 'property' qualification meanwhile admitted those of eminent social standing whose Scottish connections and affections were in some cases a little more removed, and so brought within this convivial military-social network those landed and sporting interests whom Lord Elcho had been addressing with his thoughts on uniform. The area of Scotland devoted to deer forest for recreational hunting was yet to reach its peak, but by the late 1850s the private and syndicate-letting ownership of swathes of the Highlands was well established among London social and political elites.[35] The corps also absorbed two other nascent volunteer companies in London, the Scottish Artisans and the Highland Rifle Volunteers, which had formed with the backing of another cultural and dining association of Scotsmen in London, the Club of the True Highlanders, which was specifically concerned with the promulgation of Gaelic culture and providing fellowship and philanthropic support for young Highlanders in the capital. The membership of the True Highlanders was defined more by Highland origin than by class and, perhaps lacking the aristocratic influence of their counterparts, the Club had failed to gain official recognition for its volunteer corps. In consequence these early rivals to the London Scottish saw their recruits lured away by Elcho and his officers, who could offer uniforms and rifles straight away.[36]

For a time Elcho's deer-stalking version of volunteer uniform held sway in the corps. Originally there were five 'Trouser' companies clad to his specification. Significantly, however, there was one 'Highland' company, No. 1 Company of course, which instead of the grey knickerbockers worn by the others were clad in kilts fashioned of the same grey material, and glengarry Highland bonnets, as envisaged in Dr Halley's sketch. As the corps grew in the years immediately following, kilted companies proliferated. Dressed alike, they distinguished between themselves with an extra flourish of Gaelic lore, the *suaicheantes* floral bonnet badges associated with Highland clans, which were worn in the London Scottish companies to reflect the lineage of their individual company commanders. When, in 1866, the battalion's illustrious Honorary Colonel, celebrity Scottish soldier Lieutenant General Sir Hope Grant, complemented the Highland companies of the London Scottish on their 'becoming and manly dress', the writing was on the wall for Elcho's practical knickerbockers.[37] The 'Trouser' companies could not compete with the appeal of the Highland dress among potential recruits. By 1872 they had given up trying and the whole corps was wearing the peculiar kilts of Elcho grey.

As 'A' (London Scottish) Company of the London Regiment, an infantry regiment of the Army Reserve, the corps still wears its grey Highland dress uniform today, as does the Toronto Scottish, a reserve unit of the Canadian Army affiliated to the London Scottish since 1921. The emergence of this unique hybrid of Highland military uniform has come to be understood within the regiment in simpler terms. The colour first known as 'Elcho grey' has altered in shade over time in the regiment's uniform, bringing in a red tint, and is commonly described as 'hodden grey', this being a reference to home-spun course, un-dyed cloth associated figuratively with the rustic dress of the Scottish peasantry of former times.[38] It has further been suggested that the grey kilt was originally chosen to avoid issues of 'interclan feeling on the subject of tartan'.[39] Neither explanation necessarily contradicts the influence of Elcho's ideas about grey uniform, but both might conceivably have been re-imagined to conform to more popular notions of Scottish historical tradition. Inter-clan feeling did not prevent the wearing of *suaicheantes* in the first Highland companies of the corps, as we have seen. Scottish volunteer companies which were recruiting in Newcastle-upon-Tyne at the same period managed to come to an accommodation about kilts, choosing to wear the 'government' or 'Black Watch' tartan during their short-lived existence.[40] In similar circumstances in Liverpool, the choice of tartan for uniform kilts was a cause of disagreements among the volunteers and a proposed compromise in the guise of a plain grey kilt adapted from that of the London

PERFORMING SCOTTISHNESS IN ENGLAND | 83

Figure 4.1 Original sketch proposing a kilted grey uniform for the London Scottish, 1859. Trustees of the London Scottish Regiment.

Scottish did not satisfy all parties. A more amenable solution was found in 1900 when members of a Liverpool Scottish battalion raised for the South African War acquiesced in adopting 'Forbes' tartan kilts, possibly on the basis that the first commanding officer was one Major Forbes Bell, or possibly merely because 'Forbes' tartan happened to be available at a good price.[41]

Performing Scottishness

The concern with dress among these first volunteer corps of expatriate Scotsmen in London was central to the motivations and attractions of those who participated. For the Highland Armed Association and the Loyal North Britons of the Napoleonic volunteering era, and therefore for the Scottish associations that sponsored them, versions of the picturesque Highland dress which was being worn by the Highland infantry regiments of the regular army were a signifier of difference, one that was ready-made in the figurative sense. Highland military uniform was increasingly a subject of fashionable appreciation, one which those who wore and promoted it knew would be recognised in London as 'Scottish', and would draw attention to themselves and to the country they looked back to with generally positive connotations in the eyes of the beholders. For the Victorian-era volunteers of the London Scottish, the deer-stalking dress advocated by Lord Elcho was not sufficiently distinctive, fascinating or flamboyant as to be favoured for long by the officers and men who wished to join. The wearing of the kilt, with its associations of warrior ancestry and martial prowess, was an essential part of what they were joining a Scottish volunteer corps in order to do. It is not necessary to dig too deeply into the psychology of group behaviour to acknowledge that Highland dress, especially in association with the Scottish military tradition, might make the volunteers wearing it feel not only Scottish, but masculine and attractively Scottish.[42] While active members of the corps were not exclusively bachelors, few of their number can have been immune to enjoying the attention-attracting powers of kilt-wearing in an era when fashionable association between the Highlands and masculine sporting activity had only added to the mystique of the virile Highland image.[43]

Whatever the individual may have gained by it, the grey, kilted uniform of the London Scottish had considerable public impact collectively. Newspaper reports of the first great Royal Review of Volunteers in Hyde Park in June 1860 pronounced favourably on the appearance of the corps, with the Highland Company and the pipers to the fore and receiving the bulk of the press comment. A summary of the views of the London press on this occasion appeared a day or two later in Edinburgh in *The Scotsman*, to which an observation about the grey Highland dress was appended, to the effect that Lord Elcho's Scottish corps were 'considered to have solved the problem of indistinctness most satisfactorily'.[44] The London Scottish, with their Scottish music and dress, continued thereafter to stand out among the volunteers of London, as attested in 1892 by a highly impressed, and necessarily sympathetic, correspondent of the *Volunteer Service Gazette*:

The London Scottish Rifle Volunteers enjoy the distinction of being the only corps on this side of the Tweed clothed in the kilt, and perhaps more interest is taken in their welfare on this account. To the metropolitan mind the skirl of the pipes, the swing of the kilt, and the light jaunty step which appears to be begotten of the pipes, on all occasions and in all climes, have many attractions. Other corps may come and go, and the British tradesman observes them not, but let the 7th Middlesex (London Scottish) march down Piccadilly and he is at his door in a trice. Everybody seems to take more interest in them than in either of the thirty odd soberly clad battalions to be found within a very few miles of Bow Bells.[45]

This is worth bearing in mind when we also recognise that, in practical military terms, the Scottish volunteers, whether of Georgian or Victorian Britain, did nothing that was any different from the volunteer units of any other description. This, indeed, was more broadly true of Scottish military units in the regular army. Not since the very early days of raising companies of Highland soldiers to police the Highlands, using their local knowledge, had Scottish soldiers been defined by any meaningful practical attributes in terms of what they did, rather than where they came from or how they were dressed. Since then only the Lovat Scouts, a volunteer regiment raised in 1900 from among the professional deer-stalkers, ghillies and keepers of Highland sporting estates for service in the South African War, could claim to bring with them specialised military or quasi-military skills – in this case their scouting know-how and marksmanship. Otherwise, the differences between Scottish soldiers and other British soldiers, or between Scottish volunteers and other British volunteers, were entirely cultural. The London Scottish were Scottish in that they looked Scottish, and they held Burns Suppers and St Andrew's Night dinners as well as the various social and sporting activities followed by volunteer corps in general. In addition, their regimental chaplains were Scottish Presbyterian ministers, a link which developed during the 1880s into a formal relationship with St Columba's Church of Scotland in Knightsbridge. Naturally, in this respect, as a Scottish organisation and a Scottish military regiment, the corps applied itself from the beginning to nurture a strong tradition of piping. In this it was aided in 1861 when Lady Elcho presented the regiment with its first six sets of bagpipes supplied from a subscription raised by Scottish ladies resident in London.[46]

In 1898, as a supplement to the more conventional volunteer habits of drilling, annual camps and shooting matches, the London Scottish began a corps tradition of route marches in Scotland. These peregrinations offered practical training in the discipline and logistics of moving and living in the field, but they were also intended to show the corps off to the people of Scotland. While the volunteers would arrive by rail in Edinburgh, Glasgow or Perth, with dinners to attend and parades to mount, the business of marching was done through the Highlands, and favour was given to those picturesque parts of the country frequented by Lord Elcho and his ilk for their sporting pursuits. On completing the first of these, through Highland Perthshire, the corps reported itself fully conscious of its cultural responsibilities in its home base, representing Scotland in the eyes of London. At a culminating civic reception in Edinburgh, the Historiographer Royal in Scotland, Professor David Masson, addressed the corps he had joined in his youth in 1859, impressing upon his successors that 'Scotland looks to you to uphold her ancient military honour in London.' He concluded by playfully chiding them that, as 'the Scotsmen in possession and in guardianship of London' by dint of the presence of the Stone of Scone and the prophecy that 'Whaur that Stone is, Scotsmen sall maisters be', they had better get back there swiftly to do their duty.[47] Gentle teasing aside, the welcoming reception afforded to the London Scottish on their northern peregrinations indicated that the corps encountered no hesitation among the residents in being accepted formally as authentic Scotsmen, and as a credit to their country.

Back at home in London, for men of the middling sort, and older men especially by way of their Honorary membership, the London Scottish was one of a number of bodies through which they could choose to cultivate and promote Scottish cultural identity for their own enjoyment, pursuing their own interests in the company of like-minded countrymen, and opening and exploiting possibilities for advancement, patronage and philanthropy. For example, London physician Alexander Halley, in his plural Scottish social and cultural pursuits, was active in the Highland Society of London, the Gaelic Society of London, the Edinburgh University Club of London, the Gaelic Society of Inverness and the London Scottish Volunteer Rifles; while London dentist Robert Hepburn, Halley's fellow founding and Honorary member of the London Scottish, was likewise prominent in the Caledonian Society of London, and chaired the Scottish Corporation, the charitable foundation established by, and for, Scots in London in the early seventeenth century. For younger men enrolled into the corps, there was the prospect of enjoying the satisfaction, comradeship and *esprit de corps* of volunteer military service. By association with the corps and its influential Scottish-minded supporters in the Caledonian Society and its counterparts, they might also gain confirmation and augmentation of their middle-class social standing. Indeed, for the 'artisans', whose social status was more ambiguous, membership might offer a tangible social gain and an introduction, even if at a modest level, into networks of Scotsmen doing well in London.

It is not to denigrate the military efficiency or motivation of the members of the London Scottish, past and present, to say that the original corps, and the regiment it grew into, may as readily be recognised as a vehicle of associational culture among expatriate Scots in London as be recognised in its military historical context as a distinguished reserve unit of the British army. Through many changes in scale and organisational status the regiment served its purposes to general approbation in both contexts, with an unbroken tradition of service and fellowship dating back to 1859. In so doing, it maintained, to a considerable degree, its upper middle-class pedigree. Regimental headquarters were at a series of smart addresses in Westminster. The officer, or potential officer type, by

Figure 4.2 Robert Hepburn, founder member of the Caledonian Society of London, in London Scottish uniform. © National Museums Scotland.

background, education and occupation were to be found throughout the corps. Writing in 1925, the regimental historian noted that the ranks were still filled largely by a core of 'public school and university men', not necessarily aspiring to commissions, and fleshed out by a throughput of apprentices en route to professional and technical positions abroad.[48]

A social network it may have been, but its 'drill and practice' were conducted with entirely serious intent. The corps provided a service company of volunteers for active service during the South African War but, as for other volunteer regiments, it was the First World War which signified a coming of age for the London Scottish. In its early deployment as a Territorial Force battalion on active service on the western front in 1914, and especially in the celebrated Halloween action at Messines, where the battalion was instrumental in preventing a German breakthrough around Ypres, the highly creditable performance of the London Scottish was a vindication of the Territorial Force and of the reputation of the auxiliary soldier.[49] War service at this scale put the London Scottish, and its newer Anglo-Scottish cousins on Merseyside and Tyneside, on the same pedestal as the famous regular Scottish regiments which the founders of the corps had admired and sought to emulate at the outset of the rifle volunteer movement. Conspicuous success and sacrifice on the battlefield was, after all, one of the constitutive norms of the Scottish military tradition, and an element of performing 'Scottishness' in itself. In 1916 the London Scottish became formally affiliated to one of these distinguished regular regiments that had hitherto carried the torch of Scottish military identity, the Gordon Highlanders. This relationship had earlier developed during the South African War, when a company of volunteers from the London Scottish for overseas service had served with the Gordons. Informal and formal affiliation with a 'parent' Scottish regiment was a practice that was a common characteristic among the expatriate Scottish regiments of the wider diaspora in Canada, South Africa, Australia, New Zealand and other parts of the British Empire, similarly keen to establish their military credentials through endorsement by the illustrious regulars, and through practical measures such as the secondment of officers in both directions. In its formal relationship with the Toronto Scottish established after the war, the London Scottish took on, in turn, the status of 'parent' regiment to its Canadian counterpart.

When, at the outset of the regiment's history in 1859, Lord Elcho addressed the assembly of Scottish residents in London drummed up by the Highland Society and the Caledonian Society, it was a matter of recent public memory that the regular Highland regiments of the British army had emerged from the Crimean War and Indian Mutiny with their reputations enhanced, and this amid public anxiety over the political and military management of these campaigns. Lord Elcho had imagined the London Scottish forming part of a 'Scottish Brigade' of rifle volunteers, 'which shall be not less distinguished amongst the volunteers than are the Highland regiments in the line'.[50] Elcho died in June 1914 and did not live to see his London Scottish volunteers fulfil that vision, but we may presume he would have been satisfied with the effective marksmanship of his grey-kilted volunteers at Messines, demonstrated amid the khaki-clad regular infantry battalions of the British Expeditionary Force.[51] He must surely also have approved of the wide proliferation of expatriate Scottish volunteer corps across the globe in his lifetime, a Scottish military and cultural phenomenon with shared characteristics, many of which were to be found among the military-minded Scottish residents of Georgian and mid-Victorian London.

Acknowledgements

I am grateful to Andrew Parsons, Curator and Archivist of the London Scottish Regiment, for his advice about written and material sources; to Anthony Partington, Toronto Scottish Regimental Association, for his comments on a draft of this chapter; and to the Earl of Wemyss and March for his permission to quote from the Wemyss Manuscripts.

Notes

1. Wemyss-Charteris-Douglas, Francis, Lord Elcho, *London Scottish Volunteer Rifles. Speech of Lord Elcho, MP at Freemasons' Tavern, July, 4* (London: J. Ridgeway, 1859), p. 10.
2. Ibid.
3. The Highland Company of Montreal and the Toronto Company of Highland Rifles, both being formed in 1856, might lay claim to being the first of these.
4. The National Archives (TNA), HO50/43. Standing Orders, Highland Armed Association, 30 July 1798, quoted in J. O. Robson, *London Scots of the Napoleonic Era. The Highland Armed Association or Royal Highland Volunteers and The Loyal North Britons*, privately published collection of articles from the *London Scottish Regimental Gazette* (1969), p. 1. Much of the following detail about the Highland Armed Association and its successor corps the Loyal North Britons derives from Robson's booklet.
5. See Tanja Bueltmann, Andrew Hinson and Graeme Morton, 'Introduction: diaspora, associations and Scottish identity', in Tanja Bueltmann, Andrew Hinson and Graeme Morton (eds), *Ties of Bluid, Kin and Country: Scottish Associational Culture in the Diaspora* (Guelph, ON: Centre for Scottish Studies, University of Guelph, 2009), pp. 1–18.
6. John E. Cookson, 'The Napoleonic wars, military Scotland and Tory Highlandism in the early nineteenth century', *Scottish Historical Review*, vol. LXXVIII, 1, no. 205 (1999), pp. 60–75. Henry Dundas, secretary of state for war, served as Society President in 1799.
7. Sir John Sinclair of Ulbster, Bt, *An Account of the Highland Society of London, from its establishment in May 1778, to the commencement of the year 1813* (London: B. McMillen, 1813), pp. 4–5.
8. National Library of Scotland (NLS), Dep. 268/23. Records of the Highland Society of London. 'Minute book, 21 January 1793–18 May 1805'.
9. Stana Nenadic (ed.), *Scots in London in the Eighteenth Century* (Lewisburg, PA: Bucknell University Press, 2010), 'Introduction', pp. 14–45.
10. *Loyal Volunteers of London & Environs, Infantry & Cavalry, in their respective uniforms. Representing the whole of the Manual, Platoon, & Funeral Exercise, in 87 Plates, Designed and etched by T. Rowlandson* (London: Ackerman, 1799), p. 70.

11. Robson, *London Scots of the Napoleonic Era*, pp. 4–5.
12. North Briton was an accepted, uncontroversial name for a Scotsman in London at this period. The 'Loyal' prefix was shared with other volunteer corps of the day, such as the Loyal British Artificers and the Loyal Britons. *Gentleman's Magazine and Historical Chronicle for the Year MDCIII*, vol. 73, no. 94, p. 978.
13. For a time the corps boasted a rifle company, clothed in 'government' tartan jacket and plaid, thereby adapting Highland dress to the fashion for green uniforms that distinguished British riflemen in the regular army at this period.
14. The Prince of Wales and the Duke of Kent, brothers to Sussex, were also promoters, and wearers, of Highland dress. Sussex, with his radical political sympathies, gives the lie to any automatic assumption of equivalence between 'Highlandism' and Tory or Pittite political loyalties. The Highland Society of London's membership at this period included at least one other celebrity London liberal, the Scottish naval officer and radical MP for Westminster Lord Cochrane.
15. For an examination of the organisation and motivations of the volunteers in Georgian Britain, see Austin Gee, *The British Volunteer Movement, 1794–1814* (Oxford: Oxford University Press, 2003).
16. David Hepburn and John Douglas, *Chronicles of the Caledonian Society of London, Part 1, 1837–1890 by David Hepburn* (London: Caledonian Society, 1923), p. 33.
17. Quoted in Justine Taylor, *A Cup of Kindness. The History of the Royal Scottish Corporation, a London Charity, 1603–2003* (East Linton: Tuckwell, 2003), p. 148.
18. Ibid. p. 120. Hepburn is acknowledged as a founder of the regiment in displays at the London Scottish Regimental Museum, Horseferry Road. Dr Halley is given the credit for the idea in Duncan Tovey, 'The History of the London Scottish', *London Scottish Regimental Gazette*, vol. XXVI, no. 302 (February 1921), pp. 22–3.
19. Wemyss-Charteris-Douglas, *London Scottish Volunteer Rifles*.
20. Hepburn, *Chronicles of the Caledonian Society*, p. 33.
21. Wemyss-Charteris-Douglas, Francis, earl of Wemyss and March, *Memories, 1818–1912* (Edinburgh: David Douglas, 1912), vol. 1, p. 289. A proof copy of this two-volume memoir from the Wemyss MSS is available on microfilm at the National Records of Scotland (NRS), RH4/40/19.
22. For an essay on the appeal and cultural context of Highland deer-stalking in the nineteenth century, see Maureen N. Martin, *The Mighty Scot. Nation, Gender, and the Nineteenth-Century Mystique of Scottish Masculinity* (Albany, NY: State University of New York Press, 2009), pp. 38–79.
23. The Italian victories of 1859 might in fact have owed less to the impact of Garibaldi's citizen volunteers than contemporary reporting and rhetoric suggested. See Lucy Riall, *Garibaldi. Invention of a Hero* (New Haven, CT and London: Yale University Press, 2007), pp. 171–5.
24. Duff Hart-Davis, *Monarchs of the Glen. A History of Deer-stalking in the Scottish Highlands* (London: Jonathan Cape, 1978), pp. 175–6.
25. Wemyss-Charteris-Douglas, *London Scottish Volunteer Rifles*, p. 23.
26. Ibid. p. 31. An appendix to the printed speech reprinted Lord Elcho's letter to *The Times* on this subject of 23 May 1859.
27. Wemyss-Charteris-Douglas, *London Scottish Volunteer Rifles*, p. 22.
28. Ibid. p. 30. Elcho laid claim to invention of the deer-stalking knickerbocker, encouraged by conversation during a day's sport with the painter Edwin Landseer. Wemyss-Charteris-Douglas, *Memories*, vol. 1, p. 106.
29. Wemyss-Charteris-Douglas, *Memories*, vol. 1, p. 295, quoted in J. O. Robson, *The*

Uniform of the London Scottish 1859–1959 (London: London Scottish Regiment Ogilby Trust, 1960), p. 7.
30. Wemyss-Charteris-Douglas, *London Scottish Volunteer Rifles*, p. 22.
31. Hepburn, *Chronicles of the Caledonian Society of London*, p. 33.
32. The sketch by Smart, annotated by Dr Halley, is preserved in the London Scottish Regimental Museum.
33. A second sketch was drawn by Mr Andrew Maclure for a private meeting held at Robert Hepburn's house to discuss raising the corps in May 1859. This version combined Elcho's grey knickerbocker idea with a Highland shoulder plaid in grey. *London Scottish Regimental Gazette*, vol. XIX, no. 224 (August 1914), p. 140.
34. Printed as an appendix to Wemyss-Charteris-Douglas, *London Scottish Volunteer Rifles*, pp. 26–9.
35. See Willie Orr, *Deer Forests, Landlords and Crofters. The Western Highlands in Victorian and Edwardian Times* (Edinburgh: John Donald, 1982).
36. Charles Niven McIntyre North, *Leabhar Comunn nam fior Ghael, Book of the Club of True Highlanders; a record of the dress, arms, customs, arts and science of the Highlanders* (London: Richard Smythson, 1881), p. 13.
37. Lieutenant Colonel J. H. Lindsay, *The London Scottish in the Great War* (London: London Scottish Regimental Headquarters, 1925), p. 5.
38. William Grant and David Murison, *The Scottish National Dictionary*, vol. V (Edinburgh: Scottish National Dictionary Association, 1960), p. 169.
39. *The History of the London Scottish* (London: Headquarters The London Scottish, 2007), p. 1.
40. Graham Stewart and John Sheen, *Tyneside Scottish. 20th, 21st, 22nd & 23rd (Service) Battalions of the Northumberland Fusiliers. A History of the Tyneside Scottish Brigade Raised in the North East in World War One* (Barnsley: Pen & Sword, 1999), p. 10.
41. Hal Giblin, with David Evans and Dennis Reeves, *Bravest of Hearts. The Biography of a Battalion. The Liverpool Scottish in the Great War* (Liverpool: Winordie Publications, 2000), p. 4.
42. For some elementary ideas on the relationship between military culture and gender, see Martin Van Creveld, *The Culture of War* (Stroud: Spellmount, 2009), pp. 395–409.
43. Maureen N. Martin, *The Mighty Scot*, pp. 49–53.
44. Press cuttings regarding the Review were preserved by Lord Elcho. NRS, RH4/40/1, 4/15, Wemyss MSS, 'Speeches and printed letters, 1860'.
45. *Volunteer Service Review*, May 1892, quoted in Edwin Hodder, *John MacGregor. Rob Roy* (London: Hodder Brothers, 1894), p. 232. From their formation until 1908 the London Scottish companies came under the administrative umbrella of the Middlesex Rifle Volunteer Corps, which recruited in Middlesex and London.
46. National Museums Scotland (NMS), National War Museum Library, Major I. H. Mackay Scobie collection. 'Presentation of bagpipes to the London Scottish Rifle Volunteers in Westminster Hall, Wednesday, 19th June 1861', pamphlet appended to Major General J. M. Grierson, *Records of the Scottish Volunteer Force 1859–1908* (Edinburgh and London: William Blackwood & Sons, 1909).
47. 'The march through Scotland', *London Scottish Regimental Gazette*, vol. III, no. 9, September 1898, pp. 130–43.
48. Lindsay, *The London Scottish in the Great War*, p. 13.
49. Rather more prosaically, one officer reported that the action at Messines delayed until 5 November an improvised feast upon a consignment of haggis sent out by supporters at home in London for Halloween. 'A Subaltern's Diary', *London Scottish Regimental Gazette*, vol. XIX, no. 228 (December 1914), p. 222.

50. Wemyss-Charteris-Douglas, *London Scottish Volunteer Rifles*, p. 10.
51. In 1900 Lord Elcho had added his name to efforts to raise the Liverpool Scottish, which, as a Territorial Force battalion, would later go on also to see distinguished service through the First World War.

5

Canada, Military Scottishness and the First World War

Jeff Noakes

On the eleventh hour of the eleventh day of the eleventh month, Canadians gather to observe Remembrance Day. Central to the ceremony is the two minutes' silence, often followed by a piper's lament.[1] Among those taking part at the national ceremony in Ottawa are the Pipes and Drums of the Cameron Highlanders of Ottawa and of the Royal Canadian Air Force Band. Their presence, and the playing of the lament, testifies to the continuing expression of a Scottish diasporic military identity by Canadians. A century ago, at the outbreak of the First World War, military Scottishness occupied a prominent position in Canada. Tied to and sustained by the Scottish diaspora[2] and its influential position in the country, and by links to the British Empire, it was part of a broader pattern reflected in other dominions and colonies. Increasingly adopted and appropriated by broader sectors of Canadian society, Scottishness and military Scottishness was also sustained by characteristics often connected with nationalism and imperialism in Canada, including conservative, militarist and anti-modern sentiments.[3] This chapter will examine the creation and uses of Scottish military identity in Canada leading up to, during and after the First World War, using images as a way of understanding the pervasive influence of visual culture in war-time.[4] Furthermore, many of the wartime manifestations of military Scottishness in Canada – or at least those manifestations which have survived to the present day – are visual expressions of military Scottishness.

Scottish units first arrived in North America during the Seven Years War, where they formed a substantial portion of British forces.[5] Some Scottish veterans remained afterwards, settling in the former New France and elsewhere, and their numbers were gradually augmented by the arrival of other Scottish immigrants. With the outbreak of the American Revolution, Britain recruited these veterans and settlers for units including the Royal Highland Emigrants, the first Highland regiment recruited in North America. After the Revolution, these regiments were disbanded, with many veterans either returning to their Canadian homes or settling in various locations in what are now the Atlantic provinces, Quebec and eastern Ontario. Continuing Scottish immigration, including the arrival of

Loyalists leaving the new American republic, added to their numbers and would help shape the creation of military units during the War of 1812 and from the mid-nineteenth century onwards.[6]

From the 1820s to the First World War, more than two million people emigrated from Scotland. Up to the early 1840s, British North America, which later became Canada, was their most popular destination. There, Michael Vance and others have argued, 'they exercised an influence all out of proportion to their numbers'.[7] Many sought to preserve their identity and assert their place in their new homes through means including business activities, settlement plans and various Scottish societies. While some of these societies were exclusive, others, especially in smaller communities, were less so.[8] Canada was a settler society and these activities played out within an imperial matrix: Vance notes that 'the earliest Scottish social organizations . . . were linked to class and ethnic relationships conditioned by Canada's British imperial connection'.[9]

In addition to Canada's position within the British Empire, this matrix included Canada's often turbulent relationship with the United States. American forces had invaded Canadian territory during the American Revolution and the War of 1812. During the Rebellions of 1837–8, some Canadian rebels had sought refuge in the United States and had also used it as a base for operations, sometimes with assistance from American supporters such as the Hunters' Lodges, who advocated the liberation of the Canadian provinces from British control.[10] Subsequent tensions between the United States and Great Britain included the Oregon boundary dispute in western North America, and were aggravated by the American Civil War. They had significant implications for Canada, especially after Confederate agents used Canadian territory as a base for operations, including an armed raid on St Albans, Vermont in 1864. Consequences included fears of attack by the United States, which abrogated a treaty of trade reciprocity in 1866, and several raids on Canada by the American-based Fenian Brotherhood, which sought to force Britain to leave Ireland by seizing Canada as a bargaining chip.[11] Canada also had to contend with Britain's increasing reluctance to continue significant defence commitments for its partially or wholly self-governing colonies. These circumstances, often identified as among the causes of Confederation in 1867, also helped give rise to military measures that included the establishment of a small standing army supported by volunteer militia units.[12] This new Canadian force, patterned on British models, included a strong regimental system. In addition to providing a functional model for organisation, equipment and training, the British army also provided an aspirational model for both the Permanent Force and for the Militia. James Wood notes that the peace-time militia 'felt obligated to ape the ceremonial functions of the British Army of the 1860s owing to the wider public's belief that "real soldiers" wore red and modeled themselves after imperial regulars'.[13] This belief, a product of Canada's place within the British Empire, contributed to the shaping of a Canadian army that often emulated its British counterpart.

Military Scottishness

Given the prominence and influence of some members of the Scottish diaspora in many communities, it was not surprising that a number of militia units assumed a Scottish military identity; as indicated in the other chapters within this volume, this was part of a broader imperial pattern. Among the better-known Canadian examples are Montreal and Toronto, large cities with prominent and well-represented Scottish diasporic communities. In Montreal, the regiment that would ultimately become the Black Watch (Royal Highland Regiment) of Canada originated in 1862 as a volunteer militia unit, which over time reflected an increasingly pronounced Scottish identity: Carman Miller has noted that the regiment's members 'were predominately [sic] Scots and Presbyterian'.[14] In Toronto, the 48th Highlanders were established in 1891 following lobbying by Scottish societies in the city, and built on prior experience with a Company of Highland Rifles.[15] Other units also adopted Scottish identities, among them Hamilton's 91st Highlanders, formed in 1903. Its officers and many of its initial rank and file were drawn from Hamilton's Scottish community, and there were strong links between the regiment and local Scottish societies, which had helped press for its creation.[16]

This pattern continued elsewhere. In 1910, for instance, Vancouver saw the creation of the 72nd Highlanders (later the Seaforth Highlanders of Canada), while the 79th Highlanders (subsequently the Queen's Own Cameron Highlanders of Canada) were established in Winnipeg.[17] The distinctly 'national' identities of some militia regiments attracted attention and comment from some Canadians. Miller notes that

> some contemporary critics regarded 'the introduction of distinctively Scottish, Irish, English or French-Canadian regiments in the Canadian Militia as a national mistake', but others argued that it merely recognized a social reality, aided recruitment and esprit de corps, encouraged the pursuit of goals, and a commitment to loyalties which transcended ethno-religious difference.[18]

As indicated by Tanja Bueltmann's chapter on Scottish ethnic associationalism in this volume, these units served social purposes in addition to their military functions; a factor reinforced by the involvement of Scottish societies in their creation.[19] Miller's study of the Montreal militia argues that 'in a society captivated by "nationalistic" imperialism, by Christian soldiers extending the borders of commerce, religion, and government, militia units were often at the centre of a network of patriotic, professional, fraternal, athletic, and business associations'.[20] This reflected a broader pattern within the British Empire, where Scottish militia units were initially linked to elite members of the Scottish diaspora. The expression of a Scottish military identity allowed them to remain attached to their ethnicity in an imperial context, and also to assert their importance in their colonial societies. Over time, however, this pattern changed, and by the twentieth century some of those joining these units used their service to publicly assert their own sense of Scottishness. In addition to members of the Scottish diaspora, this also involved non-Scots appropriating Scottish symbols and traditions; again, they were part of a broader pattern. Regardless of the reasons for their adoption by units across the empire, however, Scottish military identities were created within the context of their host societies.[21]

In the Canadian context, military units, including those with a Scottish military identity, were created and acted within the closely intertwined strands of Canadian, and in particular English Canadian, nationalism and imperialism. Both were often closely linked to and seen as being compatible with British identity and the British Empire.[22] Anthony Michel notes that 'recent scholarship on imperialism has underscored the extent to which late nineteenth-century European Canadians considered themselves part of a British world with "a sense of belonging to a shared British culture"'.[23] Paul Maroney, in examining how Canadians attempted to understand the Northwest Resistance of 1885, when the Canadian army suppressed Métis and Cree resistance to Canadian expansion, argues that it was given meaning through local and national identity, 'but also through a sense of Britishness'.[24] The same themes were called upon at the outbreak of the South African War and the dispatch of Canadians to participate in the fighting.[25] Vance notes that Scottishness and Scottish societies were linked with patriotism and the British Empire, including through the celebration and promotion of a Scottish military identity. 'In addition to linking themselves to the potent symbol of British imperial power that the Highland regiment had become by the end of the nineteenth century,' he writes, 'Scottish society members who formed the majority of the rank and file in the regiment [Toronto's 48th Highlanders] were also provided with the opportunity to demonstrate prowess and loyalty in a broader imperial context.'[26] In doing so, Canadians were often laying claims to multiple identities. J. M. Bumsted argues that the years leading up to the First World War were 'the era of imperial federation, and while it was true that one could be an imperialist and a Canadian simultaneously, it was equally true that one could be an imperialist, a Canadian, and a Scot as well'.[27] This assertion of plural identities that included Scottishness was not limited to Canada. Elizabeth Buettner makes a similar argument that among the Scottish diaspora in British India 'a well-developed Scottish national consciousness could easily coexist with other loyalties'.[28] In the years leading up to the First World War, many Canadian militia units demonstrated and reinforced such imperial connections as they sought closer links to their British counterparts. In the case of Canadian Highland or Scottish regiments, they often modelled themselves after specific Highland units, and also often became allied to them; again, this was part of a broader pattern in the British colonial world.[29]

The Scottish identity expressed through these military units was overwhelmingly Highland rather than Lowland. In the late eighteenth century and through the nineteenth, Highlandism, drawing on romanticised notions of the Highlands and newly created 'Highland traditions', became the symbolic basis for a new Scottish identity.[30] As Edward Spiers notes, by the end of the nineteenth century,

'Highland imagery had become emblematic of a Scottish cultural and national identity, intertwined with a British identity and wedded to an imperial cause'.[31] This held true at the colonial peripheries as well. Buettner describes how in British India 'in countless toasts at St Andrew's festivities, Scotland appeared as an undifferentiated country – the Highlands writ large – despite the fact that the vast majority of those present came from other parts of the country'.[32] The image of the Highland soldier was an integral part of this identity. Paul Dickson argues that 'as Highland regiments began to represent Scotland, Scottish martial spirit became a cornerstone of identity and part of the cornerstone of imperialism and the Scottish role in it'.[33] Military Scottishness was thus fundamentally linked to and part of a broader British imperial identity.

Scottishness and military Scottishness were also acceptable identities within Canadian nationalism and imperialism, since Canadians constructed and negotiated identities within both national and imperial frameworks. These Scottish identities could, however, exclude, marginalise and obscure other identities in Canada.[34] While military Scottishness became well established, some military identities indigenous to Canada did not. Highlanders shared the characteristics of the 'martial races' identified by the British in India; Spiers has observed that 'the Highland soldier now embodied all the virtues of the "noble savage", a product of a wild, rugged and unspoiled landscape, unaffected by urban vices and leveling sentiments'.[35] This was an identity acceptable to, and used by, Scots and non-Scots in a way that the identities of other 'martial races' or 'noble savages' were generally not. While some Canadian militia regiments assumed a Scottish military identity, members of the Haudenosaunee, Aboriginal Peoples who had been allies of the British since the seventeenth century, served in the Militia at the same time but without their identity being formally recognised by, adopted by and celebrated in the military.[36] In late nineteenth-century Canadian society, some identities were more acceptable than others, particularly since some English Canadian identities were based on maintaining a distinction between 'Canadians' and the 'Indian' 'other'.[37]

The proliferation of Scottish identifiers like Highland militia regiments did not necessarily reflect a corresponding growth in the diaspora that they apparently represented. While the Scottish diaspora in Canada grew from 1870 to 1914, the number of the Scottish-born remained relatively constant at about 200,000. By 1914 most Canadians of Scottish descent had been born in North America, and they formed a diminishing percentage of the country's population.[38] While some have argued that this period witnessed the decline of a distinctly Scottish identity, others have countered that Canadians could lay claim to multiple identities, including a strong Scottish identity – a perspective more congruent with the creation and negotiation of identities in Canada and the British Empire as discussed above.[39] This assumption of multiple identities included a wider appropriation of military Scottishness. J. M. Bumsted, for example, claims that by the outbreak of the First World War, 'the Highland military tradition had been fully merged into the Canadian one.'[40] Despite the appropriation of Scottish military identity by the broader society, a diasporic connection often persisted, at least until the start of the First World War. Miller, for instance, suggests that Montreal militia units 'served as an important link in chain migration to the city', and notes that the officer commanding the 5th Royal Scots corresponded with a number of prospective Scottish immigrants. Other 'Scottish' regiments could likewise claim diasporic links, with numerous members born in Scotland or of Scottish descent. Such links were strengthened by the deliberate embracing of a Scottish military identity, including the adoption of Highland uniforms, pipes and drums, and activities such as Highland dancing and games.[41]

Anti-modernism

Scottish military identity, linked with imperialism and militarism, also had connections with anti-modern sentiment that began to emerge in the latter part of the Victorian era. Donald Wright has argued that, in addition to a school of nationalism, English Canadian imperialism could also be an expression of anti-modernism.[42] At a time when romanticised notions of the Highlands were widely disseminated by authors such as Sir Walter Scott and given prominence through the adoption of Highland traditions by Britain's Royal Family and others, the Highland soldier and Highland regiments became symbols of romanticised and profoundly anti-modern visions of clanship and the lost Jacobite cause.[43] Indeed, Wright notes that David McCord, a prominent Montreal lawyer and philanthropist at the end of the nineteenth and start of the twentieth centuries, and one of the imperialist subjects of his study, was 'steeped in the stories of Sir Walter Scott'.[44] His friend William Lighthall similarly sought refuge in an idealised French Canadian past which had never existed. In both instances, these constructed pasts helped their users negotiate the realities of contemporary society.[45]

One of these realities was the emergence of challenges to existing gender relations. Organised Scottishness, and especially military Scottishness, enhanced and reinforced male power. Vance argues that an 'emphasis on martial games not only linked organized Scottishness to the pursuit of Empire, but also reflected the patriarchal nature of Scottishness itself'.[46] War and soldiering were already gendered as male, but the Highland soldier's status as a symbol of masculinity was also reinforced by his position as a member of one of the 'martial races', who were held to be naturally better soldiers than others. Indeed, according to Heather Streets, these soldiers 'came to be "gendered" as ideally masculine'.[47] These gendered characteristics were shared with militarism and imperialism. Wright notes that describing militarism as an important part of English Canadian imperialism 'is hardly a profound observation', but argues that it was in part a 'response to changing gender relations' and challenges to the distribution of power that began to emerge in the late nineteenth century. Miller similarly observes that 'during an era increasingly interested in gender differentiation, expressed by the rise of the women's movement and the cult of manliness, the militia had an important social function as an exclusively male bastion'.[48] It shared the fundamentally masculine nature of many Scottish associations, where women were often assigned a secondary and marginalised role. Unlike such associations and related organisations like athletic clubs, many of which could present financial or social barriers to prospective members, militia service offered access to a masculine environment, social respectability and recreational opportunities to those who might be excluded from other such bodies. Those seeking these benefits could include clerks, some of whom might have felt their social position endangered by declining pay and social status, and the increasing numbers of women entering their field of work, or working-class men, who had the opportunity to participate more fully in civic life than they might otherwise have had. The Militia offered still other social benefits, of course, to those who could afford to maintain an officer's position, including the expenses of uniforms, mess bills and other social obligations, and could help place them in the sorts of social and professional networks mentioned above. Militia service also offered the opportunity for men to publicly demonstrate their masculinity, and in the case of 'Scottish' and other 'national' regiments, to lay claim to a diasporic identity, once again serving a social as well as a military function.[49]

The impact of the First World War

The outbreak of the First World War brought cataclysmic change to Canadians, their country, and its military. Mobilisation for and involvement in the war had profound consequences, including the provision of troops for the Canadian Expeditionary Force (CEF), social, economic and political change and unrest, and a crisis provoked by conscription that threatened to tear the country apart.[50] Canada participated within an imperial context, going to war as part of the British Empire, and Canadians drew upon pre-war ideas and identities to help define, direct and explain the country's war effort. As in the years before 1914, military Scottishness would form part of these ideas and identities. At the outbreak of the war, Sam (later Sir Sam) Hughes, the colourful and controversial minister of militia and defence, was eager to lead a rapid build-up of Canadian forces for overseas service. He replaced existing mobilisation plans with a direct call to arms, which he later described as 'like the fiery cross passing through the Highlands of Scotland or the mountains of Ireland in former days' – a strongly anti-modern and pro-Celtic vision.[51] Among the results were a rush to enlist, and the creation of numbered battalions which supplanted existing Canadian militia units for overseas service, in part because most of the latter were too small to individually become overseas battalions. Although militia regiments did not go overseas as fighting units, they played a significant role in mobilisation and recruiting.[52] In some instances, pre-war regimental identities appeared in newly formed battalions, including Highland examples such as the 13th Battalion (Royal Highlanders of Canada, from Montreal) and the 15th Battalion (48th Highlanders, from Toronto). In others they were amalgamated, such as the 16th Battalion (The Canadian Scottish), which brought together contingents from four different Highland regiments from three provinces.[53] Ultimately, some twenty-six CEF battalions would be Highland or Scottish, while others would adopt elements of a Scottish military identity.[54] With recruiters seeking to encourage Canadians to enlist, such Scottish battalions emerged alongside units drawing on other ethnic identities like Irishness, or cultural identities like sports or temperance.[55] Scottish and Highland imagery was also used for recruiting on a grander scale; for example, a Nova Scotia Overseas Highland Brigade was raised and trained, and sent overseas in 1916, although only one of its battalions was sent into the front lines.[56]

There was a strong diasporic link for many of the Scottish units in the first contingent of the CEF. The initial nominal roll of the 15th Battalion, for instance, which drew heavily on Toronto's 48th Highlanders, shows that 22 per cent were Scottish-born. In 1911 only 5 per cent of Toronto's population, male and female, could state the same, and in Ontario overall, only 3.5 per cent of the male population was Scottish-born. Those born in England made up some 36 per cent of the unit, in comparison with 19 per cent of the city and 13.4 per cent of the male population of the province in 1911. By way of comparison, the nominal rolls of the 3rd Battalion, also drawn heavily from Toronto, record that only 6.8 per cent of its members were Scottish-born, while its proportion of English-born recruits stood at 38.5 per cent. Given that second and third generations of the diaspora would list countries of birth other than Scotland, diasporic representation in the 15th Battalion would actually have been greater than is represented by these figures. It was definitely disproportionate to the diaspora's presence in Toronto and Ontario. Furthermore, some of the English-born recruits in the 15th might also have been members of Scotland's near diaspora, born in England. Even though the English outweighed the Scots in both cases, the substantial differences in Scottish representation between two battalions drawing on much the same population points to a continued foregrounding of the Highland identity in at least some such Scottish units.[57] While Canada's localised recruiting system was initially productive, it became less effective as pools of volunteers dried up.[58] The continued formation of new battalions – facilitated by the 1915 decision to allow any patriotic individual, organisation or community to form and recruit one – also complicated the provision of reinforcements for existing units. By 1916 the CEF needed replacements for losses, and not new, untrained battalions. In the face of declining enlistment, recruiting efforts became more extensive, intensive and intrusive. Recruiting propaganda drew heavily on pre-war cultural and ideological elements of Canadian society, as well as war-time events and ideas.[59] Basic recruiting tools included rallies and personal approaches by recruiters, while print advertisements were also extensively used, in newspapers as well as in flyers and posters.[60] Many of the latter have survived, and enable discussions of recruiting efforts and the themes associated with them, including prevailing ideas of military Scottishness. In some instances, they also present the most readily available record, given the transitory nature of speeches, the private nature of personal approaches made to individuals, and the intensely ephemeral nature of flyers and handouts. Posters can also be problematic and challenging to evaluate, however, especially when removed from their century-old context.[61] In Canada at least, they also appear to have been adopted later than in the United Kingdom. As a result, they arguably better reflect the stages of war-time recruiting that followed the initial peak of voluntarism at the war's outbreak.[62] While the introduction of conscription in 1917 acknowledged the ultimate inability of voluntary enlistment to meet the military commitments made by the Canadian government, it is not the intention here to evaluate the posters' effectiveness as recruiting tools but rather to see how they can help explore and interrogate visual aspects of military Scottishness in Canada.[63]

Interrogating the visual

Much like the recruiting process, the design and production of Canadian posters was often decentralised, although some were created by the federal government for national campaigns.[64] The content of the recruiting message was consequently diverse, often reflecting pre-war culture and ideology as well as local factors that included language – most notably French – and the presence of various ethnic communities. An imperial identity was one of the earliest themes to emerge in recruiting propaganda: Maroney argues that 'in using imperial sentiments and symbols, recruiters were drawing on a deep reservoir of ideas familiar to most potential recruits'.[65] Related to imperial identity was a Canadian nationalism that was often entwined with it, as it had been during the years leading up to the war.[66] Another theme was anti-modernism, often linked to imperial identity. Maroney identifies it as a 'common thread running through much of this propaganda . . . the basic premise being that the dull, unhealthy nature of modern life could be remedied only by a twentieth-century revival of chivalric ideals'.[67] In these respects, war-time propaganda, and especially recruiting efforts, demonstrated a continuity with pre-war anti-modern impulses, as well as with the English Canadian nationalism and imperialism to which they were linked.

Not surprisingly, a number of posters used Scottish military imagery. These portrayals of a Scottish military identity were created within a broader matrix of recruiting efforts, military service, and appeals to support the war. In some cases this reflected the Scottish identity of battalions seeking recruits, be they units affiliated with existing 'Scottish' militia regiments, or those independently created. Such imagery may well have reflected a preference for recruits with a Scottish connection, but these preferences, if they existed, were not always explicitly stated. In other cases, Scottish imagery was deployed for broader patriotic purposes, including fundraising. Regardless of their specific intent, the posters were linked to the nationalism, imperialism and frequent anti-modernism of war-time propaganda and recruiting efforts.[68] The Highland soldier in particular was a 'powerful antimodern image', and consequently occupied a prominent position.[69] Images 5.1 and 5.2 show recruiting posters for units that formed and provided reinforcements for Montreal's Black Watch. Both point to the battalions' connection with the Canadian regiment, and one is also explicit about the regiment's alliance with the Black Watch in Scotland, a continuation of one of the pre-war links established between Canadian and British regiments.[70]

Figure 5.1 'The Happy Man Today is the Man at the Front'. Canadian War Museum 19900348-020.

Figure 5.2 '5th Royal Highlanders of Canada – Black Watch – 2nd Reinforcing Company'. Canadian War Museum 19900348-019.

Both posters also make use of Scottish and especially Highland military imagery. While both have Highland soldiers as their central focus, the poster for the 2nd Reinforcing Company also includes a piper and the Royal Standard of Scotland, all upon a background of Black Watch tartan, a forceful combination of symbols. Such explicit use of Highland imagery is not entirely surprising, however, given that the posters were recruiting for Highland units. Yet, while these posters used Highland imagery, their texts did not specifically and explicitly address Scottish Canadians. Other examples of recruiting posters, however, did. A poster for the 236th Battalion, CEF (Figure 5.3), calls for those who 'possess the fighting spirit of your forefathers' – an explicit invocation of the diasporic connection – in addition to once again emphasising the image of the Highland soldier. Similar targeted appeals were made to other identifiable groups, including Irish Canadians, with a number of Irish battalions being recruited for the CEF.[71] The choice of language also defined intended audiences, even if they were not explicitly identified; the use of English or French on a poster, for example, could inherently limit its appeal, even to bilingual viewers.

Scottish and Highland imagery was also used for other war-time purposes, including fundraising and encouraging enlistment in general. Given this widely understood military and masculine symbolism, as well as the colourful potential of his uniform, the Highland soldier was a particularly useful visual symbol. In one instance (Figure 5.4), a kilted, masculine and happy Highlander who has 'done his bit' through four years of military service, emphasised by the two wound stripes on his left sleeve, exhorts the public to do 'their bit' by buying Victory Bonds. Even though conscription had been introduced by the time this poster was published, the imagery of the recruiting poster still held sway.[72] A Scottish military identity did not always have to be expressed visually; another poster (Figure 5.5) shows a textual manifestation of Scottishness, using a verse from Scottish poet John Dunlop's often anthologised early nineteenth-century poem 'Here's to The Year That's Awa". While the words may be Scottish, the soldier depicted on the poster wears a generic Canadian army uniform, and the visual symbolism is Canadian and British, featuring maple leaves on either side of the Union Jack. Despite this mixture of symbols that to a modern audience would likely appear to be strongly British, some contemporary viewers saw the poster as 'distinctively Canadian', which suggests that some aspects of Scottishness had become absorbed into contemporary understandings of being Canadian. It is also a reminder of the challenges of interpreting such material at a century's remove.[73]

In Canada, as in other belligerent countries, soldiering was gendered as male, even though recruiting messages were also aimed at women in the hope that they would influence men to enlist.[74] Meg Albrinck's examination of expressions of manliness within British recruitment posters, for instance, notes how the press and propaganda of nations involved in the war 'argued that military service exemplified not only one's [sic] patriotism but one's [sic] masculinity as well', while Maroney makes a similar observation that in Canadian posters 'all soldiers are strong, contented, and healthy; civilian males are weak, uncertain, and effeminate'.[75] The

CANADA, MILITARY SCOTTISHNESS AND THE FIRST WORLD WAR | 105

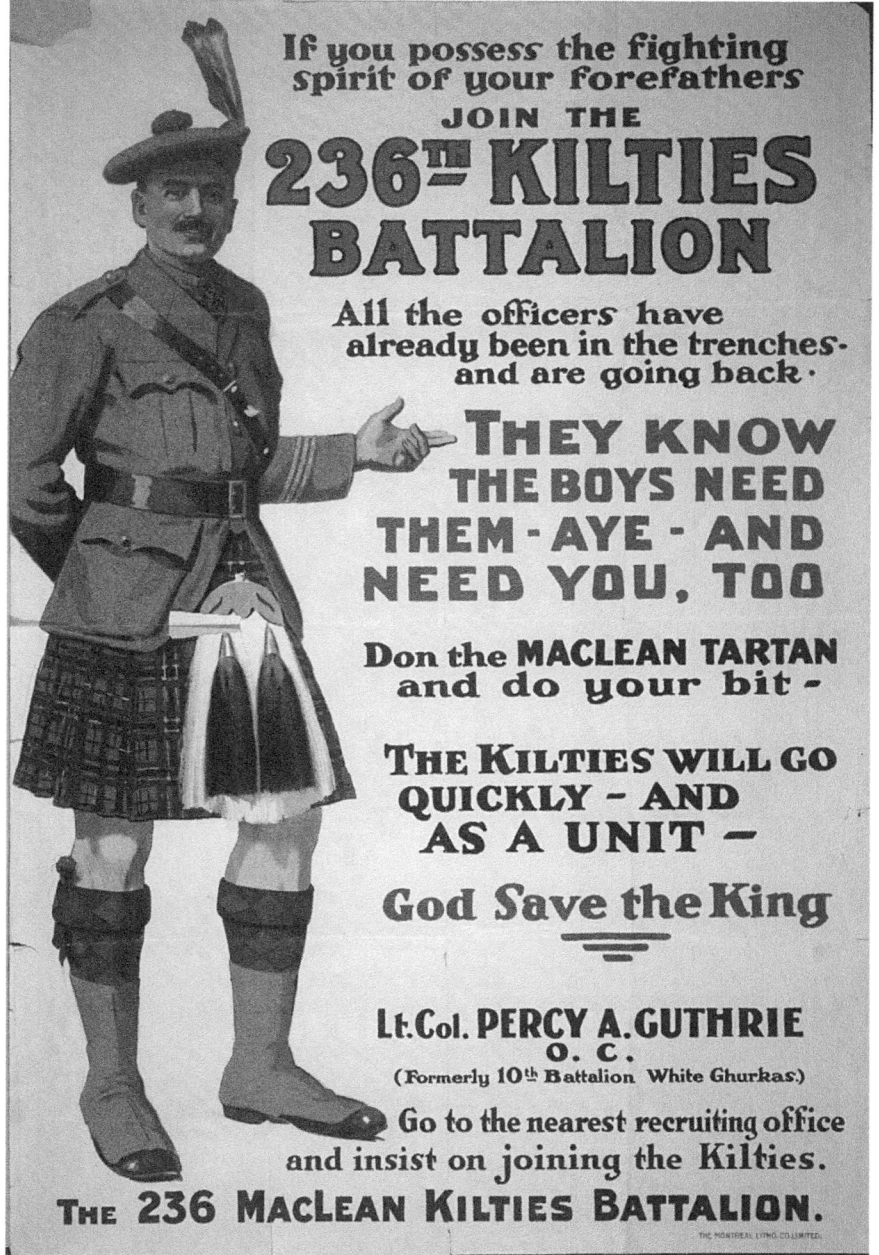

Figure 5.3 'Join the 236th Kilties Battalion'. Courtesy of Toronto Public Library.

Figure 5.4 Frank Lucien Nicolet, 'Doing My Bit', 1918. Canadian War Museum 19750046-008.

Figure 5.5 'Heroes of St Julien and Festubert', 1916. Canadian War Museum 19750046-010.

prominence given to images of the Highland soldier is a reminder that the Scottish military identity in Canada remained strongly masculine. Maroney notes that 'at all times recruiting propaganda portrayed the Highlander as the embodiment of a vigorous and healthy masculinity', and that 'the chance to become a Highlander was a type of magic elixir that promised a heightened masculinity'.[76] Such an appeal could transcend diasporic boundaries, offering to eligible Canadian men the possibility of assuming such characteristics. All they had to do was enlist.

The use of Scottish military identity in recruiting efforts extended beyond posters. New Brunswick's 236th Battalion, in addition to using Scottish military imagery in its recruiting posters, as discussed above, also made extensive use of Scottish traditions, including pipers, the lighting of hill-top bonfires, and the carrying of a fiery cross to recruiting meetings across the province.[77] Other units, like Lethbridge, Alberta's 113th Battalion, also used activities that expressed and asserted a Scottish identity, including Highland games, as part of their war-time recruiting efforts.[78] The assumption of a Scottish identity did not always result in a full Highland appearance, however, especially given the expense of Highland dress and concerns about its suitability for trench warfare. The 113th, although raised as the Lethbridge Highlanders, did not adopt full Highland dress for these reasons.[79]

As noted above, despite the employment of Scottish imagery and symbols for recruiting, many of the posters using it did not explicitly target Scottish Canadians. Fundamentally, this may have been an acknowledgement that given the increasing competition for recruits, recruiting efforts explicit in their ethnic exclusiveness could be counterproductive. While it might have been generally understood that recruitment efforts for battalions with specific ethnic and national identities were addressed to the groups they supposedly represented, even if this was not explicitly stated, the diverse composition of some Scottish battalions suggests that it did not always produce such results.[80] Like many others, they contained soldiers with a range of ethnicities and nationalities; Stanley notes that the 16th Battalion (Canadian Scottish) included 'Scots, of course, but also English, Irish, French, Americans, Italians, Dutch, Danes, Mexicans and others'. Other Scottish battalions were similar; although their nominal rolls list an appreciable majority of members as being born in the British Isles or Canada, other places of birth, most notably the United States, appear on the pages, along with references to a range of other countries.[81] There were, however, widespread barriers to members of visible minorities attempting to enlist, particularly during the first half of the war. Among the obstacles was the 48th Highlanders' early 1916 refusal to accept potential African Canadian recruits on the grounds that 'we have, being a kilted regiment, always drawn the line at taking coloured men'. The 173rd Battalion, also a Highland unit, similarly objected that '. . . we cannot see our way to accept [Negroes] as these men would not look good in Kilts'.[82] Both refusals explicitly invoked the units' Highland identities. It remains unclear, however, whether these identities were the actual reason for the objections, or whether military Scottishness was being used as an excuse to justify or conceal decisions rooted in a more fundamental racism.

The pool of Scottish diasporic recruits was also relatively limited: in the 1911 census, Canadians of French, English and Irish origin all outnumbered those of Scottish origin. Despite this, Scottish and Highland battalions were seen as being easier to raise than other units, a vital consideration as recruiting became increasingly difficult, and evidence of the wider appeal of military Scottishness to non-Scots.[83] It also reflected the general appropriation and assimilation of Scottish symbols and identifiers by Canadian society. If these were no longer seen as an exclusively Scottish purview, they would understandably have been effective for recruiting outside the Scottish diaspora.[84] Streets' work on 'martial races' suggests another significant possibility: that the Highland soldier represented the potential of what British men could become, even if they were not from the Highlands or even from Scotland – 'an emotive device designed to demonstrate that Britons had "the right stuff" to take on their rivals and enemies'. As such, the Highlander was an aspirational identity presented to potential Canadian recruits, and assumed by many of them.[85] Some Canadian commentators had acknowledged this even before the war; author and lawyer Charles Egerton MacDonald had argued in 1896 that although 'others than native Highlanders' were enlisting in these regiments, 'the Highland garb[,] the symbol of bravery associated with so many heroic deeds[,] cannot fail to have its influence on all who wear it'.[86]

As it had been before the war, Scottish military identity in Canada was also expressed within an imperial context. The British-Canadian Recruiting Mission (BCRM), established to recruit Britons and Canadians resident in the United States for the British and Canadian militaries, provides an interesting example of Canadians asserting a Scottish military identity as part of a very public performance with a broader imperial significance. The BCRM made extensive use of Canadian Scottish units and Highland imagery as part of its recruiting efforts following America's entry into the war. Bands and contingents from the Royal Highlanders of Canada, the 48th Highlanders, and the 236th Battalion toured Boston, New York and Chicago in order to generate public interest and enthusiasm for recruiting and fundraising activities.[87] The British Recruiting Week (16–20 July 1917) used pipe bands as 'the centerpiece and primary tool for recruitment'.[88] Carol Shansky argues that 'the kiltie bands were the highlight of the events and served a dual purpose by providing both parade music and nostalgia'.[89] The use of Highland imagery extended beyond parades and rallies. In one poster for the week (Figure 5.6), representations of Uncle Sam, a man in eighteenth-century clothing and a piper march together, accompanied by the prominent title 'Hoot Mon, the Kilties are Here!', while Canada's Red Ensign flies boldly from one of the piper's drones.[90] Here, a fusing of American and Scottish symbols is accompanied by a distinctively Canadian identifier, all to promote British recruiting. Highland imagery was used for British and Canadian objectives in related areas, including the promotion of the 'Hero Land' fundraising fair and spectacle in New York City.[91] Through their participation in the BCRM, Canadians were using military Scottishness to recruit for the British forces and the CEF, and to support the British and Canadian war efforts.

Figure 5.6 'Hoot Mon, The Kilties are Here! British recruiting week July 16–21', 1917. Library of Congress, Prints & Photographs Division, WWI Posters, LC-USZC4-8119.

Expressions of Canada's Scottish military identity, established in the years before 1914 and reinforced through war-time recruiting and propaganda, extended overseas with the CEF. The large number of Scottish battalions permits only a general discussion, as does the absence of a broader study of Scottish diasporic identity and the CEF. As they did in Canada, pre-war patterns and ideas persisted. Even if those serving in Scottish units were not members of the diaspora, for instance, their service and heroism was often seen at the time and subsequently as a reflection and embodiment of Scottish military traditions.[92] This was particularly the case when their actions involved identifiable expressions of military Scottishness. The story of Victoria Cross recipient Piper James Richardson, a Scottish-born member of the 16th Battalion whose playing under fire was credited with inspiring a successful attack, has been presented as an exemplar of the Scottish military tradition in Canada.[93] Canadian Highland soldiers, and Highland soldiers more generally, also gained a reputation as shock troops, further building on beliefs about the traditional martial valour of the Highlander.[94] The Scottish military identity and its associated accoutrements were also seen as boosting morale. This was an important effect in war-time, and one that was perhaps linked to the broader significance of the identity, including its associations with masculinity, imperial identity, and ideas about martial races.[95]

In addition to being portrayed as part of a Scottish military tradition, Canadian 'Scottish' battalions also actively placed themselves within the broader spectrum of Scottish diasporic units within the imperial forces. Their war-time activities reinforced and built upon links and affiliations established before the war, sometimes on a grand scale. In July 1918, for instance, the 13th and 15th Battalions, the original overseas embodiments of Montreal's Royal Highlanders of Canada and Toronto's 48th Highlanders, sponsored a Highland Gathering at Tincques in France. It included representatives from all of the Canadian Corps' Highland battalions, as well as from most of the battalions of the 15th (Scottish), 51st (Highland) and 52nd (Lowland) Divisions. A day of Highland Games was followed by the playing of 'Retreat' by the massed pipe bands of the units involved.[96] The widespread adoption of a Scottish military identity by CEF battalions also influenced some depictions of Canadians by others. Figure 5.7 is a British poster from the latter part of the war. Showing the 'Commonwealth in Arms', it depicts the various member countries of the Commonwealth as soldiers, with both the Canadian and the South African wearing kilts, a reflection of the strong and visible presence of a Scottish military identity in both countries' expeditionary forces, and also arguably of their connections with other Scottish diasporic units.[97]

The inter-war period

The First World War brought Canada increased international prominence, but also left it exhausted and divided. It was not necessarily seen as an unmitigated tragedy, however, but rather – in large parts of English-speaking Canada, at

Figure 5.7 'The British Commonwealth in Arms'. Canadian War Museum 19900348-004.

least – as a victory brought about through service and sacrifice.[98] Although the war changed Canada's relationship with Great Britain, it did not mark the end of imperialism in Canada, nor did it bring an end to a sense of connection to the British Empire. The active expression and use of a Scottish military identity likewise continued and in some respects expanded in inter-war Canada, paralleling experiences elsewhere in the Commonwealth.[99] During this time, a number of Canadian militia units turned to the prestige and public recognition of this identity, which now included the recent war record of Highland and Scottish CEF units, as a means of attracting and retaining personnel. Among the units that became Scottish were the Cameron Highlanders of Ottawa, the Stormont, Dundas and Glengarry Highlanders, and the Calgary Highlanders. These newly 'Scottish' units almost uniformly adopted a Highland identity. Only one of these regiments – the Lorne Scots – wore trews; the rest were kilted.[100]

As a recruiting and retention measure, these steps were understandable. Canadians had relatively little interest in the militia in the immediate post-war years. In 1919 and 1920, summer training was cancelled due to a lack of interest attributed to war-weariness; when it started again in the summer of 1921, it was on a much smaller scale than it had been before the war.[101] Public interest may also have been diminished because the post-war militia found its training and parades overshadowed by recollections of the war and the observance of Armistice Day (later Remembrance Day), and by a public memory of victory through war-time service by citizen soldiers. Peace-time training was not congruent with such popular perceptions. The lack of interest likely also reflected the disruption of local regiments caused by the mobilisation of the CEF, and by the sundering of links between these regiments, the defence of Canada and overseas service, especially in the general public's perception.[102] This inter-war 'Highland turn' might thus be seen as a peace-time implementation of the war-time belief that Highland units were easier to recruit, and an acknowledgement of the continued effectiveness of the Highlander as an aspirational image and identity.

Other aspects of Scottish military identity, including the use of pipes and drums, also persisted and flourished in at least some parts of inter-war Canada. Not only were pipe bands useful for recruiting and for establishing and reinforcing regiments' standings within their communities – an echo of the pre-war social function of the Militia – but they also helped form the basis for regimental customs and traditions, which often continued to be modelled on British precedents. In other instances, the pipes and drums may have been intended to evoke war-time manifestations of military Scottishness associated with the CEF, and to lay claim to that legacy. In the face of limited military funding in the 1920s and 1930s, these bands were often sustained by officers' private donations. Even with these strictures, the largest pipe bands in early 1930s Ontario were affiliated with militia regiments, as opposed to civilian organisations.[103]

In addition to the attention they brought to Canada's Scottish diasporic military units, First World War experiences also contributed to the spread of tartanism and the continued foregrounding of Scottish identity in parts of Canadian civilian life. Some manifestations of inter-war tartanism in Nova Scotia, for instance, were directly linked to war-time experiences. The first 'Gathering of the Clans' in Sydney, Nova Scotia was held in 1919 to welcome returning service personnel. Angus L. Macdonald, the premier who actively promoted a Scottish identity for the province, had served in two CEF battalions (the 25th and 185th) with Scottish identities, and his intense fascination with Scotland and Scottishness may well have begun during the war.[104] Broader societal factors helped reinforce this trend. McKay points to research arguing that the inter-war emergence of a 'Scottish simulacrum' in Nova Scotia was affected by post-war uncertainty about British imperialism and the world economy, as well as by the anti-modernist sentiments that accompanied them.[105] In the uncertainty of the inter-war years, it was also useful for conservative political ends and to reinforce existing authority.[106] In this respect, it was a continuation of pre-war and wartime associations with imperialist nationalism and anti-modern sentiments, as well as a reaction to the consequences of the First World War and the uncertainties of the inter-war years.

The outbreak of the Second World War was greeted in Canada with less celebration and more apprehension than the events of 1914. Mobilisation did not replicate the improvised haste of 1914; among the consequences was the dispatch overseas of many existing regiments, rather than the creation of numbered battalions.[107] As a result, existing military units, including those with Highland and Scottish identities, were seen as taking an active part in overseas activities, a contrast with the First World War's perception of a separation between the militia at home and active service abroad. Scottish military identity persisted in the Canadian military during the Second World War, despite measures that hindered some of its more obvious expressions, like the general prohibition on the wearing of the kilt due to fear of the consequences of gas attack.[108] When possible, distinctive 'Highland' or 'Scottish' touches were retained. No bands accompanied the first two Canadian divisions sent overseas, for instance, but each Highland regiment was permitted to take six pipers.[109] A Scottish diasporic identity was certainly seen as significant enough to the Canadian military that the pipes and drums of the Argyll and Sutherland Highlanders of Canada accompanied the Canadian Berlin Battalion during the July 1945 Victory parade in Berlin.[110]

The war also witnessed new adoptions and manifestations of a Scottish military identity by Canadians. In 1942 the Royal Canadian Air Force (RCAF), which already drew upon some expressions of military Scottishness, acquired its own tartan.[111] The war also witnessed the creation of women's branches of Canada's air force, army and navy, and one of these branches, the Canadian Women's Army Corps (CWAC), established a pipe band and a brass band.[112] The CWAC pipe band presents an interesting example of women adopting elements of a Scottish military identity which was typically gendered as male. They were, however, also drawing upon existing civilian uses of Scottish diasporic identity, since Pipe Major Lillian Grant had been playing the bagpipes since the age of twelve, and had earlier led the women's pipe band 'The Highland Lassies'.[113] Both the pipe and brass bands played to wide attention and acclaim in North America and Europe, but the pipe band's adoption of a traditionally masculine identity encountered limits. Much to its members' dismay, a proposed kilted uniform was not granted official approval on the grounds of tradition and modesty, which held that kilts were incorrect Highland dress for women.[114] Some elements of a Scottish military identity were to remain an exclusively masculine purview.

Measures such as the creation of tartans and the adoption of pipe bands were arguably taken for morale, publicity and recruiting purposes, echoing earlier uses of a Scottish military identity in Canada. As with the First World War and the inter-war years, they suggest a continuing belief in and use of a Scottish military identity to attract and retain recruits, and to sustain morale. They also suggest that elements of a Scottish military identity were seen as noteworthy parts of a military image, and as part of the trappings of a successful service. This was perhaps especially so for more recently established entities like the CWAC – a war-time creation – or the RCAF, established in 1924. Once again, a Scottish military identity was serving as an aspirational model, as well as a demonstration of the continued influence of the Scottish diaspora and the appropriation of elements of its identity by other Canadians.[115]

Unlike the inter-war years, in the aftermath of the Second World War few regiments adopted Scottish identities. One of them was the Lake Superior Regiment, which became the Lake Superior Scottish Regiment in 1949. As it had in the 1920s and 1930s, this new identity was assumed as a recruiting measure.[116] Although fewer in number, these adoptions of a Scottish military identity testified to its continuing appeal and significance in a country where ties to Britain were still strongly felt by many.[117] The 1950s and early 1960s witnessed unprecedented peace-time levels of military expenditures as a reaction to the Cold War, and Highland and Scottish regiments formed part of the regular army as well as the reserves. Scottish military identity persisted even through the disruptive and homogenising experience of Canadian military integration and unification in the 1960s. The creation of a unified Canadian Forces, in which functional 'elements' replaced the Royal Canadian Navy, Canadian Army and Royal Canadian Air Force, swept away fundamental traditional distinctions between the services, as well as many of the uniforms and traditions that they had adopted, although Highland units were permitted to retain distinctive elements of their dress. At much the same time, defence cutbacks relegated the same units to the reserves.[118] Despite these changes, however, Scottish military traditions and expressions of military Scottishness continue to the present day.[119] The order of service for Remembrance Day services in Canada, as mentioned at the beginning of this chapter, usually includes a lament by a piper following the two minutes' silence. Elements of Scottish military identity have also been adopted as part of uniquely Canadian ceremonies, such as those relating to the anniversary of the taking of Vimy Ridge in 1917 – one of the touchstones of the First World War in Canadian popular memory.[120]

The persistence of a Scottish diasporic military identity in Canada a century after the First World War testifies to an enduring appeal, influence and significance. The identity has changed over time, however, as have some of the reasons for its adoption and some of the ways in which it has been expressed. First becoming widespread as an assertion of the Scottish diaspora's identity and influence, it became increasingly appropriated by broader Canadian society from the late nineteenth century onwards. The Highland soldier, cornerstone of Scottish military identity, also served as an imperial symbol, an exemplar of a martial race and an aspirational image of British masculinity, compatible with and reinforcing contemporary Canadian nationalism and imperialism. The First World War, with its use of Scottish military identity, and especially the image of the Highland soldier, as a tool for recruiting and morale and to muster public support for the war effort, both expanded the uses of the identity and accelerated the process of its appropriation.[121] Its survival until the present day, albeit in changed form, has left a legacy for Canadians, the Canadian military and Canadian history, and offers ample opportunity for further research and discussion.[122]

Notes

1. Veterans Affairs Canada, 'A Guide to Commemorative Services', http://www.veterans.gc.ca/eng/remembrance/get-involved/veterans-week/guide-to-commemorative-services (last accessed 11 August 2014).
2. On the use of 'diaspora' in this context, see Tanja Bueltmann, Andrew Hinson and Graeme Morton, *The Scottish Diaspora* (Edinburgh: Edinburgh University Press, 2013), pp. 16–33.
3. J. M. Bumsted, 'Scottishness and Britishness in Canada, 1790–1914', in Marjory Harper and Michael Vance (eds), *Myth, Migration and the Making of Memory* (Halifax, NS: Fernwood, 1999), pp. 89–104, at pp. 98–100; Wendy Ugolini, 'Scottish Commonwealth Regiments', in Edward M. Spiers, Jeremy A. Crang and Matthew J. Strickland (eds), *A Military History of Scotland* (Edinburgh: Edinburgh University Press, 2012), pp. 485–505, at p. 485; Michael Vance, 'A Brief History of Organized Scottishness in Canada', in Celeste Ray (ed.), *Transatlantic Scots* (Tuscaloosa, AL: University of Alabama Press, 2005), pp. 96–119; Donald Wright, 'W. D. Lighthall and David Ross McCord: anti-modernism and English-Canadian imperialism, 1880s–1918', *Journal of Canadian Studies*, vol. 32, no. 2 (1997–8), pp. 134–53; Ian McKay, 'Tartanism Triumphant: The Construction of Scottishness in Nova Scotia, 1933–1954', *Acadiensis*, vol. XXI, no. 2 (1992), pp. 5–47.
4. In his discussion of First World War posters, for instance, Jay Winter argues that 'in wartime, images overwhelm words'. Winter, 'Imaginings of War: Posters and the Shadow of the Lost Generation', in Pearl James (ed.), *Picture This: World War I Posters and Visual Culture* (Lincoln, NE: University of Nebraska Press, 2009), pp. 37–60, at p. 37.
5. Hew Strachan, 'Scotland's Military Identity', *Scottish Historical Review*, vol. 85, no. 2 (2006), pp. 315–32, at p. 321; George F. G. Stanley, 'The Scottish Military Tradition', in W. Stanford Reid (ed.), *The Scottish Tradition in Canada* (Toronto: McClelland & Stewart, 1976), pp. 137–60, at pp. 141–5.

6. H. P. Klepak, 'A Man's a Man because of That: The Scots in the Canadian Military Experience', in Peter E. Rider and Heather McNabb (eds), *A Kingdom of the Mind: How the Scots Helped Make Canada* (Montreal and Kingston: McGill-Queen's University Press, 2006), pp. 40–59, at pp. 41–5; Stanley, 'Scottish Military Tradition', pp. 145–50; Bueltmann et al., *Scottish Diaspora*, pp. 193–5.
7. Thomas M. Devine, *The Scottish Nation: A History, 1700–2000* (New York: Viking, 1999), pp. 470–5; Gillian I. Leitch, 'Scottish Identity and British Loyalty in Early-Nineteenth-Century Montreal', in Rider and McNabb, *A Kingdom of the Mind*, pp. 211–26, at pp. 212–13; Vance, 'A Brief History', p. 105.
8. Edward J. Cowan, 'The Myth of Scotch Canada', in Harper and Vance, *Myth, Migration and the Making of Memory*, pp. 49–72, at pp. 66, 61–2; Vance, 'A Brief History', p. 97; Michael Vance, 'Powerful Pathos: The Triumph of Scottishness in Nova Scotia', in Ray, *Transatlantic Scots*, pp. 156–79, at p. 174. Larger towns and cities could also sustain a number of Scottish organisations, often with different populations of members drawn from the local Scottish Canadian community. Shannon O'Connor, 'The Scottish-Canadian Community in Toronto: Class, Gender & Identity, 1871–1914', paper presented at the 2008 History on the Grand Symposium, Cambridge, Ontario, pp. 6–10; Bueltmann, Hinson and Morton, *Scottish Diaspora*, p. 117.
9. Vance, 'A Brief History', p. 96.
10. For these events, see, among others, George F. G. Stanley, *Canada Invaded, 1775–1776* (Toronto: Samuel Stevens Hakkert, 1977); Jon Latimer, *1812: War with America* (Cambridge, MA: Belknap Press of Harvard University Press, 2007); D. Peter Macleod, *Four Wars of 1812* (Vancouver: Douglas & McIntyre, 2012); Elinor Kyte Senior, *Redcoats and Patriotes: The Rebellions in Lower Canada, 1837–38* (Stittsville, ON: Canada's Wings in collaboration with the Canadian War Museum, 1985).
11. Barry Gough, *Fortune's a River: The Collision of Empires in Northwest America* (Madeira Park, BC: Harbour Pub., 2007); Robin W. Winks, *The Civil War Years: Canada and the United States* (Montreal: McGill-Queen's University Press, 1998); Peter Vronsky, *Ridgeway: The American Fenian Invasion and the 1866 Battle that made Canada* (Toronto: Allen Lane, 2011).
12. Ugolini, 'Scottish Commonwealth Regiments', p. 487; Jeffrey Grey, 'War and the British World in the Twentieth Century', in Phillip Buckner and R. Douglas Francis (eds), *Rediscovering the British World* (Vancouver: UBC Press, 2005), pp. 233–50, at pp. 236–7; Klepak, 'The Scots in the Canadian Military', pp. 45–8. The standard formulation of this interpretation can be found in Charles Perry Stacey, *Canada and the British Army, 1846–1871: A Study in the Practice of Responsible Government* (revised edition, Toronto: University of Toronto Press, 1963).
13. James Wood, *Militia Myths: Ideas of the Canadian Citizen Soldier, 1896–1921* (Vancouver: UBC Press, 2010), p. 22.
14. Ugolini, 'Scottish Commonwealth Regiments', pp. 485–8; Klepak, 'The Scots in the Canadian Military', pp. 47–50; Carman Miller, 'The Montreal Militia as a Social Institution before World War I', *Urban History Review*, vol. 19, no. 1 (1990), pp. 57–64, at p. 58.
15. Vance, 'A Brief History', p. 102; Kim Beattie, *48th Highlanders of Canada, 1891–1928* (Toronto: 48th Highlanders of Canada, 1932), pp. 1–5. In the 1850s and 1860s, Toronto had had a Company of Highland Rifles, which was at one time attached to the Queen's Own Rifles. Following its disbandment, some of its members helped form the Caledonian Society of Toronto, which later helped lobby for the creation

of a Highland regiment. Alexander Fraser, *The 48th Highlanders of Toronto, Canadian Militia* (Toronto: E. L. Ruddy, 1900), pp. 24–6. On the lineage of the Montreal and Toronto regiments, see 'The Black Watch (Royal Highland Regiment) of Canada' and '48th Highlanders of Canada', in Canada, Department of National Defence, Directorate of History and Heritage, *Official Lineages: Volume 3, Part 2: Infantry Regiments*, http://www.cmp-cpm.forces.gc.ca/dhh-dhp/his/ol-lo/vol-tom-3/par2/index-eng.asp (last accessed 1 June 2014).

16. Klepak, 'The Scots in the Canadian Military', p. 50; Michael Mitchell, *Ducimus: The Regiments of the Canadian Infantry* (Canada: s.n., 1992), p. 172; Argyll and Sutherland Highlanders of Canada (Princess Louise's) Historical Committee, *Historical Records of the Argyll and Sutherland Highlanders of Canada (Princess Louise's), 1903–1928* (Hamilton, ON: Robert Duncan, 1928), pp. 6–12.

17. Bernard McEvoy and A. H. Finlay, *History of the 72nd Canadian Infantry Battalion, Seaforth Highlanders of Canada* (Vancouver, BC: Cowan & Brookhouse, 1920), pp. 1–7; Murray Burt, *Winnipeg's Ladies from Hell: how the Queen's Own Cameron Highlanders of Canada fought, remembered and grew in the regiment's first century of war and peace* (Winnipeg: The Queen's Own Cameron Highlanders of Canada Centenary, 2010), pp. 2–3; Stanley, 'The Scottish Military Tradition', p. 150.

18. Miller, 'The Montreal Militia', p. 59.

19. See, for instance, Wood, *Militia Myths*, p. 3; Miller, 'The Montreal Militia', p. 57; Paul Maroney, '"The Great Adventure": The Context and Ideology of Recruiting in Ontario, 1914–17', *Canadian Historical Review*, vol. 77, no. 1 (1996), pp. 62–98, at p. 63.

20. Miller, 'The Montreal Militia', p. 57. Miller notes that 'of the 84 members of Montreal's 5th Royal Scots officers' mess in 1912, little more than a quarter were active militia officers. The rest were retired officers, prominent public men, and honorary members including Lord Strathcona, Lord Mount Stephen, Sir Hugh Montague Allen, Sir Hugh Graham, and Hugh Paton'. Ibid.

21. Ugolini, 'Scottish Commonwealth Regiments', p. 500; Elizabeth Buettner, 'Haggis in the Raj: Private and Public Celebrations of Scottishness in Late Imperial India', *Scottish Historical Review*, vol. LXXXI, 2, no. 212 (2002), pp. 212–39, at p. 225; Bumsted, 'Scottishness and Britishness in Canada', pp. 98–100; Jonathan Hyslop, 'Cape Town Highlanders, Transvaal Scottish: Military "Scottishness" and Social Power in Nineteenth and Twentieth Century South Africa', *South African Historical Journal*, vol. 47, no. 1 (2002), pp. 96–114, at p. 98.

22. In this particular context, 'English' refers to the language and its associated cultural patterns and expressions, rather than specifically to people from or with ancestral links to England, although at the time under discussion many English Canadians fell into this category. In *The Sense of Power*, his reappraisal of Canadian supporters of imperial federation prior to 1914, Carl Berger argues that 'Canadian imperialism was one variety of Canadian nationalism'. Berger, *The Sense of Power: Studies in the Ideas of Canadian Imperialism* (second edition, Toronto: University of Toronto Press, 2011), p. 9. This work, originally published in 1970, has had an enduring effect on Canadian historiography. For more recent criticism of Berger's thesis, see Phillip Buckner, 'The Long Goodbye: English Canadians and the British World', in Buckner and Francis, *Rediscovering the British World*, pp. 181–207, at pp. 182–90. For a criticism of Buckner's discussion, see Kurt Korneski, 'Britishness, Canadianness, Class, and Race: Winnipeg and the British World, 1880s–1910s,' *Journal of Canadian Studies*, vol. 41, no. 2 (2007), pp. 161–84.

23. Anthony P. Michel, 'To Represent the Country in Egypt: Aboriginality, Britishness,

Anglophone Canadian Identities, and the Nile Voyageur Contingent, 1884–1885', *Social History/Histoire Sociale*, vol. 39, no. 77 (2006), pp. 45–77, at p. 47.
24. Paul Maroney, 'Lest We Forget: War and Meaning in English Canada, 1885–1914', *Journal of Canadian Studies*, vol. 32, no. 4 (1997/8), pp. 108–24, at p. 111.
25. Ibid. pp. 112–13; Buckner, 'The Long Goodbye', pp. 189–90. See also Mary G. Chaktsiris, '"Our Boys With the Maple Leaf on Their Shoulders and Straps": Masculinity, the Toronto Press, and the Outbreak of the South African War, 1899', *War and Society*, vol. 32, no. 1 (2013), pp. 3–25.
26. Vance, 'A Brief History', pp. 102–3.
27. Bumsted, 'Scottishness and Britishness in Canada', p. 101.
28. Buettner, 'Haggis in the Raj', p. 214. See also ibid. pp. 215–16, 231, and Grey, 'War and the British World', p. 234.
29. Klepak, 'The Scots in the Canadian Military', p. 50; Beattie, *48th Highlanders of Canada*, pp. 12–13; Historical Committee, *Historical Records of the Argyll and Sutherland Highlanders of Canada*, pp. 13–16; Ugolini, 'Scottish Commonwealth Regiments', pp. 485–90.
30. Devine, *The Scottish Nation*, pp. 231–45; Charles Withers, 'The Historical Creation of the Scottish Highlands', in Ian Donnachie and Christopher Whatley (eds), *The Manufacture of Scottish History* (Edinburgh: Polygon, 1992), pp. 143–56; Ugolini, 'Scottish Commonwealth Regiments', p. 486.
31. Edward Spiers, 'The Highland Soldier: Imperial Impact and Image', *Northern Scotland*, vol. 1, no. 1 (2010), pp. 76–87, at p. 84.
32. Buettner, 'Haggis in the Raj', p. 227.
33. Ugolini, 'Scottish Commonwealth Regiments', p. 486; Paul D. Dickson, Some Thoughts on the Nature of Scottish Regiments', *International Review of Scottish Studies*, vol. 26 (2001), pp. 3–18, at p. 14.
34. See, for instance, Vance, 'Powerful Pathos'; McKay, 'Tartanism Triumphant'.
35. Strachan, 'Scotland's Military Identity', p. 316; Mike O'Brien, 'Manhood and the Militia Myth: Masculinity, Class and Militarism in Ontario, 1902–1914', *Labour/Le Travail*, vol. 42e (1998), pp. 115–41, at pp. 119–20; Heather Streets, *Martial Races: The Military, Race and Masculinity in British Imperial Culture, 1857–1914* (Manchester: Manchester University Press, 2004), pp. 52–62; Spiers, 'Highland Soldier', p. 79.
36. At the 1908 training camp in Niagara, for instance, more than half of the members of the 37th Halidmand Rifles were from the Six Nations Reserve. O'Brien, 'Manhood and the Militia Myth', pp. 123–4.
37. Tony Michel's study of the Canadian contingent of Nile Voyageurs, sent at British request to take part in the Nile Expedition intended to relieve General Gordon at Khartoum, provides useful insights into the construction of cultural identities in Victorian Canada as they were enacted in a military context. As he notes, 'To many anglophones, the call for voyageurs provided an opportunity to demonstrate Canadian loyalty and usefulness to the Empire. The role of Aboriginal boatmen in the expedition, however, complicated such questions of national representation.' Anglophone Canadians drew a distinction between 'Canadian' and 'Indian', but to their irritation, the British military and the British press did not often do so. Michel, 'To Represent the Country in Egypt', pp. 47–8, 56.
38. Bumsted, 'Scottishness and Britishness in Canada', p. 101; J. M. Bumsted, *The Scots in Canada* (Ottawa: Canadian Historical Association, 1982), p. 10.
39. Cowan, 'The Myth of Scotch Canada', p. 64; Bumsted, 'Scottishness and Britishness in Canada', pp. 98–100; Ramsay Cook, 'Identities Are Not Like Hats', *Canadian*

Historical Review, vol. 81, no. 2 (2000), pp. 260–5, at pp. 264–5; Buckner, 'The Long Goodbye', pp. 183–6.
40. Bumsted, 'Scottishness and Britishness in Canada', p. 101.
41. Miller, 'The Montreal Militia', pp. 61–2; H. M. Urquhart, *The History of the 16th Battalion (The Canadian Scottish), Canadian Expeditionary Force in the Great War, 1914–1919* (Toronto: Macmillan of Canada, 1932), pp. 15–16. On the pre-war diasporic links of 'Scottish' militia regiments, see, among others, Ibid. pp. 356–63; Fraser, *History of the 48th Highlanders*; Historical Committee, *Historical Records of the Argyll and Sutherland Highlanders of Canada*, pp. 6–12, 29–31.
42. Wright, 'Lighthall and McCord', pp. 134–5.
43. Ugolini, 'Scottish Commonwealth Regiments', p. 486; Spiers, 'Highland Soldier', p. 79; Strachan, 'Scotland's Military Identity', pp. 325–7; Withers, 'The Historical Creation of the Scottish Highlands', pp. 152–4; Streets, *Martial Races*, pp. 55–9.
44. Wright, 'Lighthall and McCord', p. 137.
45. Both McCord and Lighthall were actively involved in the Montreal militia, although not in Scottish or Highland regiments. Lighthall had wanted to volunteer for service during the Northwest Resistance in 1885, but his law partner objected. Too old to serve overseas during the First World War, Lighthall nonetheless was in the Victoria Rifles Reserve for much of the conflict, and helped found the Great War Veterans' Association. Ibid., pp. 142–3; Alan Gordon, *Making Public Pasts: The Contested Terrain of Montreal's Public Memories, 1891–1930* (Montreal and Kingston: McGill-Queen's University Press, 2001), pp. 51–2.
46. Vance, 'A Brief History', p. 107. See also Marjory Harper and Michael E. Vance, 'Introduction', in *Myth, Migration and the Making of Memory*, pp. 14–48, at p. 37; O'Connor, 'The Scottish-Canadian Community in Toronto', pp. 15–17.
47. Chaktsiris, '"Our Boys With the Maple Leaf"', pp. 5–6; Winter, 'Imaginings of War', pp. 39–40; O'Brien, 'Manhood and the Militia Myth', pp. 119–20; Streets, *Martial Races*, p. 10.
48. Wright, 'Lighthall and McCord', p. 143; Miller, 'The Montreal Militia', p. 60. See also O'Brien, 'Manhood and the Militia Myth'.
49. Bueltmann, Hinton and Morton, *Scottish Diaspora*, p. 116; O'Connor, 'The Scottish-Canadian Community in Toronto', pp. 6–11; Miller, 'The Montreal Militia', pp. 59–60; O'Brien, 'Manhood and the Militia Myth', pp. 118–31.
50. G. W. L. Nicholson, *Canadian Expeditionary Force, 1914–1919* (Ottawa: Queen's Printer, 1962); Tim Cook, *At the Sharp End: Canadians Fighting the Great War, 1914–1916*, vol. 1 (Toronto: Viking Canada, 2007); Tim Cook, *Shock Troops: Canadians Fighting the Great War, 1917–1918*, vol. 2 (Toronto: Viking Canada, 2008).
51. Quoted in Nicholson, *Canadian Expeditionary Force*, p. 18.
52. Andrew Iarocci, *Shoestring Soldiers: The 1st Canadian Division at War, 1914–1915* (Toronto: University of Toronto Press, 2008), p. 25. Maroney, 'The Great Adventure', pp. 63, 71; Stephen J. Harris, *Canadian Brass: The Making of a Professional Army, 1860–1939* (Toronto: University of Toronto Press, 1988), pp. 92–100; Tim Cook, *The Madman and the Butcher: The Sensational Wars of Sam Hughes and General Arthur Currie* (Toronto: Allen Lane Canada, 2010), pp. 67–8.
53. Iarocci, *Shoestring Soldiers*, p. 26; Wood, *Militia Myths*, p. 219. The four regiments contributing to the 16th Battalion, CEF were the 91st Canadian Highlanders (from Hamilton, Ontario), the 79th Queen's Own Cameron Highlanders (from Winnipeg, Manitoba), the 72nd Seaforth Highlanders of Canada (from Vancouver, British Columbia) and the 50th Regiment (Gordon Highlanders) from Victoria, British Columbia. Urquhart, *The History of the 16th Battalion*, pp. 5–17.

54. Paul Maroney, 'Recruiting the Canadian Expeditionary Force in Ontario, 1914–1917', MA thesis, Queen's University, Kingston, Ontario, 1991, p. 104. The 25th Battalion was one unit with a Scottish identity that was never officially 'Highland' or 'Scottish'. F. B. MacDonald and John J. Gardiner, *The Twenty-Fifth Battalion, Canadian Expeditionary Force: Nova Scotia's Famous Regiment in World War One* (Sydney, NS: City Printers, 1983), pp. 22–3, 205–6.
55. Robert Rutherdale, *Hometown Horizons: Local Responses to Canada's Great War* (Vancouver: UBC Press, 2004), p. 82; Maroney, 'Recruiting the CEF in Ontario', pp. 104–11.
56. W. James MacDonald, *Honour Roll of the Nova Scotia Overseas Highland Brigade, 85th, 185th, 193rd, 219th Battalions* (Sydney, NS: Cape Breton University Press, 2007), p. 21.
57. The figures for the 15th Battalion are derived from Canadian Expeditionary Force, Fifteenth Battalion, *Nominal Roll of Officers, Non-Commissioned Officers and Men* (Ottawa: Department of Militia and Defence, 1915). For the 3rd Battalion, they are derived from Canadian Expeditionary Force, Third Battalion, *Nominal Roll of Officers, Non-Commissioned Officers and Men* (Ottawa: Department of Militia and Defence, 1915). The figures for the characteristics of Toronto's population are from O'Connor, 'The Scottish-Canadian Community in Toronto', table 1.4, p. 22. For the male population in Ontario, it is derived from *Fifth Census of Canada, 1911* (Ottawa: King's Printer, 1913), vol. 2, table XVII, p. 442. There are some constraints on the utility of these figures. The 15th Battalion included drafts from other militia regiments outside the Toronto area, and because of the boundaries of census districts in the Toronto area, the figure for the city's population is based upon an estimate. Most importantly, the figure for Toronto includes both men and women living in Toronto, and the figures for both Toronto and Ontario include men outside of military age. It has long been noted that the majority of the CEF's first contingent had been born in the British Isles, in comparison with the Canadian population as a whole. Robert Craig Brown and Donald Loveridge, 'Unrequited Faith: Recruiting the CEF, 1914–1918', *Revue Internationale d'Histoire Militaire*, vol. 54 (1982), pp. 53–79, at p. 57. On the drafts added to the 15th, see Beattie, *48th Highlanders of Canada*, p. 21.
58. The foundational work in the historiography of Canadian recruitment during the First World War remains Brown and Loveridge's 'Unrequited Faith'. For a discussion of existing works and of an ongoing project to re-evaluate enlistment patterns based on a new review of CEF service records, see Jonathan F. Vance, 'Provincial Patterns of Enlistment in the Canadian Expeditionary Force', *Canadian Military History*, vol. 17, no. 2 (2008), pp. 75–8.
59. Brown and Loveridge, 'Unrequited Faith', pp. 59–61; Nicholson, *Canadian Expeditionary Force*, pp. 212–18, 222–5; Harris, *Canadian Brass*, pp. 105–13; Rutherdale, *Hometown Horizons*, pp. 79–85. Maroney, 'The Great Adventure', p. 74.
60. Maroney, 'The Great Adventure', pp. 75–9. Maroney identifies the spoken word as the principal method of recruiting in Ontario.
61. On First World War posters, see, among others, Jim Aulich and John Hewitt, *Seduction or Instruction? First World War Posters in Britain and Europe* (Manchester: Manchester University Press, 2007); Pearl James (ed.), *Picture This: World War I Posters and Visual Culture* (Lincoln, NE: University of Nebraska Press, 2009); David Bownes and Robert Fleming, *Posters of the First World War* (Oxford: Shire Books, 2014).

62. *The Globe*, a major Toronto newspaper, noted the relative absence of posters from recruiting campaigns even in mid-1915, and called for their more extensive use as part of recruiting efforts. See, for instance, 'Plan to put "Pepp" in Call to Arms', *The Globe*, 6 July 1915, p. 6; 'Ottawa Must Wake Up' (editorial), *The Globe*, 16 July 1915, p. 4. Given the decentralised nature of Canadian recruiting efforts, however, it is possible that other locations in Canada were making more extensive use of recruiting posters at this time.
63. Historians differ about how authentically and accurately recruiting posters reflected public sentiment and attitudes. See, for instance, Winter, 'Imaginings of War', and Meg Albrinck, 'Humanitarians and He-Men: Recruitment Posters and the Masculine Ideal', in James, *Picture This*, pp. 312–39.
64. For non-Canadians, it is worth noting Canada's substantial francophone population, located largely but by no means entirely in Quebec. Some of the centrally produced posters were made in French and English versions, with similar graphics, but many of the locally produced posters were created only in English or French. In addition to the obvious fact of language, French-language propaganda also sometimes used different cultural and social references; some were specific to Canadian francophones, but others were linked to France. Marc H. Choko, *Canadian War Posters: 1914–1918, 1939–1945* (Laval, QC: Éditions du Méridien, 1994), pp. 69–74.
65. Maroney, 'The Great Adventure', p. 80. This pattern was repeated elsewhere in the empire. Bownes and Fleming, *Posters of the First World War*, p. 6.
66. Maroney, 'The Great Adventure', pp. 82–3.
67. Ibid. pp. 81, 79.
68. Maroney, 'Recruiting the CEF in Ontario', pp. 104–11; McKay, 'Tartanism Triumphant', p. 15.
69. Maroney, 'The Great Adventure', p. 83, n. 102; Maroney, 'Recruiting the CEF in Ontario', pp. 107–10.
70. Ugolini, 'Scottish Commonwealth Regiments', p. 493.
71. See, for instance, Canadian War Museum 19780473-030, 'Irish Canadians: Enlist in an Irish and Canadian Battalion', n.d.; Maroney, 'Recruiting the CEF in Ontario', p. 111. Interestingly, Mark McGowan notes that, in Toronto at least, Irish Canadian units 'were not necessarily an irresistible attraction to English-speaking Catholics'. Mark G. McGowan, *The Waning of the Green: Catholics, the Irish, and Identity in Toronto, 1887–1922* (Montreal and Kingston: McGill-Queen's University Press, 1999), p. 258.
72. Fundraising posters often drew upon recruiting campaign tropes, even after the introduction of conscription. Bownes and Fleming, *Posters of the First World War*, p. 6.
73. 'Kilties now Ready for Mobilization', *The Globe*, 28 August 1915, p. 19. The French version of this poster (Canadian War Museum 19880207-002, 'Les Héros de St Julien et de Festubert', 1916) uses a verse from Paul Déroulède's poem 'Sur Corneille', written in the aftermath of the Franco-Prussian War.
74. Albrinck, 'Humanitarians and He-Men', pp. 331–4; Maroney, 'The Great Adventure', pp. 93–6.
75. Albrinck, 'Humanitarians and He-Men', p. 313; Maroney, 'Recruiting the CEF in Ontario', p. 131.
76. Maroney, 'Recruiting the CEF in Ontario', pp. 110–11. See also Rutherdale, *Hometown Horizons*, pp. 192–223.
77. Maroney, 'Recruiting the CEF in Ontario', pp. 105–6. The similarity to Hughes' 1916 description of his vision of the call to arms is worth noting.

78. Rutherdale, *Hometown Horizons*, pp. 83–5. The 113th was another battalion that had adopted a Highland identity because it was believed it would make recruiting easier. Maroney, 'Recruiting the CEF in Ontario', p. 105.
79. Rutherdale, *Hometown Horizons*, p. 83. Full Highland accoutrements were expensive; in 1913 their cost for the newly formed 50th Regiment was some $35,000, more than $734,000 in 2014 Canadian dollars. Cook, *The Madman and the Butcher*, pp. 54–5.
80. Stanley, 'The Scottish Military Tradition', p. 151. Such associations between ethnic and religious communities and militia units existed before the war. Miller, 'The Montreal Militia', pp. 58–9.
81. Stanley, 'The Scottish Military Tradition', p. 151. The nominal roll for the 185th Battalion, recruited as a Highland unit in Cape Breton, Nova Scotia, reveals that the overwhelming majority of officers, non-commissioned officers and soldiers were born in Canada or the British Isles, but some, primarily privates, were born in locations including the United States, Newfoundland, St Pierre et Miquelon (a French possession), the Russian Empire and Italy; at least two were listed as having been born in Syria. The nominal roll for Hamilton, Ontario's 173rd Battalion (Canadian Highlanders) reflects a similar pattern, including a small number of soldiers from Macedonia, Romania, Italy, Serbia, Sweden, Denmark, Russia and Poland. Both of these battalions were raised in and around significant industrial cities (Sydney, Nova Scotia and Hamilton, Ontario respectively), and Cape Breton was at the time also home to large-scale coal-mining. These economic factors would have been a draw for pre-war immigration that could help explain some of the battalions' (relatively limited) diversity. Canadian Expeditionary Force, 185th Battalion, *Nominal Roll of Officers, Non-Commissioned Officers, and Men* (Ottawa: Department of Militia and Defence, 1917); Canadian Expeditionary Force, 173rd Battalion, *Nominal Roll of Officers, Non-Commissioned Officers, and Men* (Ottawa: Department of Militia and Defence, 1917). Many of the CEF nominal rolls are now available online to researchers thanks to the work of the Canadian Expeditionary Force Study Group.
82. James W. St.G. Walker, 'Race and Recruitment in World War I: Enlistment of Visible Minorities in the Canadian Expeditionary Force', *Canadian Historical Review*, vol. LXX, no. 1 (1989), pp. 1–26. The first quotation is from Ibid. p. 10. The second quotation is in Sarah-Jane Mathieu, *North of the Color Line: Migration and Black Resistance in Canada, 1870–1955* (Chapel Hill: University of North Carolina Press, 2010), p. 106.
83. *Fifth Census of Canada, 1911*, vol. 2, table 7, p. 162. Bumsted, 'Scottishness and Britishness in Canada', p. 101; Maroney, 'Recruiting the CEF in Ontario', pp. 104–5.
84. Bumsted, 'Scottishness and Britishness in Canada', pp. 98–101; Ugolini, 'Scottish Commonwealth Regiments', p. 487.
85. Streets, *Martial Races*, pp. 9–10.
86. Charles Egerton MacDonald, 'The Highland Regiments and their Origin', *The Canadian Magazine*, vol. VII, no. 3 (July 1896), p. 263.
87. Richard Holt, 'British Blood Calls British Blood: The British-Canadian Recruiting Mission of 1917–1918', *Canadian Military History*, vol. 22, no. 1 (2013), pp. 26–37, at pp. 27–9; Carol L. Shansky, 'Patriotism and the Skirl of the Pipes: The Scottish Highland Pipe Band and World War I Recruiting in New York, 1916–1918', *Journal of Musicological Research*, vol. 33, nos. 1–3 (2014), pp. 241–67, at pp. 243–50.
88. Shansky, 'Patriotism and the Skirl of the Pipes', pp. 256–64, at p. 256.
89. Ibid. p. 264. When the Canadian war art programme commissioned painter and muralist Arthur Crisp to depict these recruiting efforts, almost all of his preliminary

works incorporated soldiers in Highland uniforms. The final work, *British and Canadian Recruiting on Boston Common* (Canadian War Museum 19710261-0124, Beaverbrook Collection of War Art), prominently features members of the 236th Battalion. For a discussion of this particular artistic project, see Jim Burant, 'War, Remembrance, and the Canadian War Memorials: Arthur Crisp's contribution to the Nation's Memory of the First World War', *Hamilton Arts & Letters*, vol. 5, no. 2 (2012–13), http://samizdatpress.typepad.com/fall_winter_201213_hamilt/arthur-crisp-war-remembrance-and-the-canadian-war-memorials-1.html (last accessed 6 February 2015).

90. This poster is also reproduced on p. 257 of Shansky's article.
91. Shansky, 'Patriotism and the Skirl of the Pipes', pp. 256, 264–7; Holt, 'British Blood Calls British Blood', p. 29. For an overview of 'Hero Land', see Beverly Gordon, *Bazaars and Fair Ladies: The History of the American Fundraising Fair* (Knoxville: University of Tennessee Press, 1998), pp. 157–9.
92. Ugolini, 'Scottish Commonwealth Regiments', pp. 494–5; Stanley, 'The Scottish Military Tradition', p. 151.
93. Ugolini, 'Scottish Commonwealth Regiments', p. 495. Richardson's actions were mentioned in the CEF's official history. Nicholson, *Canadian Expeditionary Force*, pp. 184–5.
94. Klepak, 'The Scots in the Canadian Military', p. 52; Devine, *The Scottish Nation*, p. 309.
95. Ugolini, 'Scottish Commonwealth Regiments', pp. 493–4; Streets, *Martial Races*, pp. 52–62; Spiers, 'Highland Soldier', p. 79.
96. Nicholson, *Canadian Expeditionary Force*, p. 385.
97. The South African Brigade, which included a Scottish battalion, was deployed as part of the 9th Scottish Division in Europe. Ugolini, 'Scottish Commonwealth Regiments', p. 493; Hyslop, 'Cape Town Highlanders, Transvaal Scottish', pp. 105–6.
98. Historians disagree about the impact of the war on Canadians, and especially on how they came to remember and commemorate its losses. See, for instance, Jonathan F. Vance, *Death so Noble: Memory, Meaning, and the First World War* (Vancouver: UBC Press, 1997); Ian Hugh Maclean Miller, *Our Glory and Our Grief* (Toronto: University of Toronto Press, 2002); Buckner, 'The Long Goodbye', pp. 190–1; Cook, *Shock Troops*, pp. 621–48.
99. Buckner, 'The Long Goodbye', pp. 190–9; Ugolini, 'Scottish Commonwealth Regiments', pp. 496–7.
100. Klepak, 'The Scots in the Canadian Military', p. 32; Stanley, 'The Scottish Military Tradition', pp. 151–2; Richard E. Ruggle, *For Our Heritage: A History of the Lorne Scots (Peel, Dufferin and Halton Regiment)* (Brampton, ON: The Lorne Scots Regimental Museum, 2008), pp. 65–71. On the lineages of the various regiments, see Canada, Department of National Defence, Directorate of History and Heritage, *Official Lineages: Volume 3, Part 2: Infantry Regiments*, http://www.cmp-cpm.forces.gc.ca/dhh-dhp/his/ol-lo/vol-tom-3/par2/index-eng.asp (last accessed 1 June 2014).
101. Wood, *Militia Myths*, pp. 265–7.
102. Ibid. pp. 273–4, 219. On Armistice Day and Remembrance Day in inter-war Canada, see Vance, *Death so Noble*, pp. 211–19; Buckner, 'The Long Goodbye', p. 196.
103. Fraser Clark, 'Tunes of Maple Glory: An Examination of Ontario Militia Bagpipers in the 20th Century', *International Review of Scottish Studies*, vol. 28 (2003), pp. 88–100, at pp. 92–5; J. R. Madden, 'The History of Bands in the Canadian Army', AHQ Report No. 47, 6 February 1952, http://www.cmp-cpm.forces.gc.ca/dhh-dhp/his/

rep-rap/ahqrd-drqga-eng.asp?txtType=3&RfId=236 (last accessed 1 June 2014), pp. 9–10. Clark argues that the inter-war period was the 'golden age' of the regimental band, and particularly the regimental pipe band, and that in inter-war Canada, piping was centred on the Militia. Clark, 'Tunes of Maple Glory', p. 90.

104. McKay, 'Tartanism Triumphant', pp. 15, 17–19. The 185th was a Highland battalion. Although the 25th was never officially 'Highland' or 'Scottish', it asserted a strong Scottish identity, and steps were underway towards the war's end to make it a Highland unit. Among the manifestations of its Scottish military identity were a goat mascot named Robert the Bruce and a kilted pipe band. MacDonald and Gardiner, *The Twenty-Fifth Battalion*, pp. 22–3, 205–6. Macdonald's interest in manifestations of a Scottish military identity in Canada also appeared in a 1936 suggestion to the minister of national defence that a 'Macdonald Regiment' be created if the Canadian Militia was re-organised. McKay, 'Tartanism Triumphant', p. 29.

105. McKay describes it as 'a local version of a general middle-class search for something *outside* and better than the crisis-ridden modern world it inhabited'. Ibid., pp. 8–9, 15–19. See also Vance, 'The Triumph of Scottishness in Nova Scotia', pp. 164–5. These factors might also have helped shape militia units' decisions to adopt a Scottish military identity; further research in this area could prove interesting.

106. McKay, 'Tartanism Triumphant', pp. 40–3. See also Vance's observation about the earlier uses of Scottishness and Scottish societies for conservative ends and to reinforce elite authority. Vance, 'Organized Scottishness in Canada', pp. 100–2. Similarly, in non-military Canadian contexts, a focus on the Highlands obscured other Scots identities. Ian McKay notes how the inter-war construction of a 'Highland' identity for some rural areas of Cape Breton supplanted and excluded the identities associated with other, more urban and industrial areas, where the majority of the population lived, along with the identities and ways of life associated with them. McKay, 'Tartanism Triumphant', pp. 23–4. See also Vance, 'The Triumph of Scottishness in Nova Scotia', pp. 159–60.

107. Ugolini, 'Scottish Commonwealth Regiments', p. 497; Charles Perry Stacey, *Official History of the Canadian Army in the Second World War, Volume I: Six Years of War* (Ottawa: Queen's Printer, 1955), pp. 47–56. On Canada's initial Second World War mobilisation, see Stacey, *Official History*, pp. 38–71; Charles Perry Stacey, *Arms, Men and Governments: The War Policies of Canada, 1939–1945* (Ottawa: Queen's Printer, 1970), pp. 1–37.

108. Klepak, 'The Scots in the Canadian Military', pp. 52–3; Stanley, 'Scottish Military Tradition', pp. 152–3. Strictly speaking, the units of the Active Service Force had no direct connection with the militia units that bore the same names, but, as Stacey notes, 'whatever the law might say there was a close connection in every other respect, and this was recognized by the public, the regiments and the Army at large. The units of the Active Service Force were regarded as being what, for most practical purposes, they were: service battalions of their militia regiments.' Stacey, *Six Years of War*, p. 48.

109. Madden, 'The History of Bands in the Canadian Army', p. 13.

110. Charles Perry Stacey, *Official History of the Canadian Army in the Second World War, Volume III: The Victory Campaign* (Ottawa: Queen's Printer, 1960), pp. 620–1; H. M. Jackson (ed.), *The Argyll and Sutherland Highlanders of Canada (Princess Louise's), 1928–1953* (Hamilton, ON: The Regiment, 1953), pp. 223–35.

111. Canada, Department of National Defence, *On Windswept Heights: Historical Highlights of Canada's Air Force* (Ottawa: Department of National Defence, 2009),

pp. 61–2. Klepak notes that 'several squadrons' had pipe bands in the early years of the RCAF, although without providing further details. Klepak, 'The Scots in the Canadian Military', p. 55.

112. For an overview of Canadian women's services in the Second World War, see Barbara Dundas, *A History of Women in the Canadian Military* (Montréal: Art Global, 2000), pp. 37–90. Both a brass band and a pipe band were authorised in August 1942, and were used for recruiting in Canada before being sent overseas in 1945. J. N. Buchanan, 'The Canadian Women's Army Corps, 1941–1946', AHQ Report No. 15, 1 May 1947, http://www.cmp-cpm.forces.gc.ca/dhh-dhp/his/reprap/ahqrd-drqga-eng.asp?txtType=3&RfId=203 (last accessed 1 June 2014), p. 38; W. Hugh Conrod, *Athene, Goddess of War: The Canadian Women's Army Corps; Their Story* (Halifax, NS: William Macnab & Son, 1983), pp. 264–76; Janet Cape, '"Athene's Pipers" Made History', *Piping Today*, 38 (2009), pp. 30–4.

113. Conrod, *Athene*, p. 265; Cape, '"Athene's Pipers"', p. 30. Military bands in general have historically been gendered as male; for a discussion of the subject in a North American context, see Elizabeth Gould, 'Re-Membering Bands in North America: Gendered Paradoxes and Potentialities', in Carol A. Benyon and Kari K. Veblen (eds), *Critical Perspectives in Canadian Music Education* (Waterloo, ON: Wilfrid Laurier University Press, 2012), pp. 101–21.

114. Conrod, *Athene*, p. 272; Cape, '"Athene's Pipers"', p. 33; Gould, 'Re-Membering Bands', p. 114.

115. The RCAF tartan owed its origins to yet another instance of a Scottish diasporic identity being asserted through a quintessential event: Burns Night. A station commander in Canada, Group Captain Elmer G. Fullerton, wanted to celebrate his Scottish identity with a Burns Night mess dinner; he designed the tartan so that the band could wear full Scottish regalia. Canada, Department of National Defence, *On Windswept Heights*, p. 61. With respect to aspirational models, Wood's observation about the need for pre-First World War militia units to reflect the appearance and functions of the British military in order to assert their legitimacy in the eyes of the public is worth remembering. Wood, *Militia Myths*, p. 22.

116. Stanley, 'The Scottish Military Tradition', p. 153; George F. G. Stanley, *In the Face of Danger: The History of the Lake Superior Regiment* (Port Arthur, ON: The Lake Superior Scottish Regiment, 1960), pp. 324–5. Formally, it was the Lake Superior Regiment (Motor), which became the Lake Superior Scottish Regiment (Motor). 'Lake Superior Scottish Regiment', in Canada, Department of National Defence, Directorate of History and Heritage, *Official Lineages: Volume 3, Part 2: Infantry Regiments*, http://www.cmp-cpm.forces.gc.ca/dhh-dhp/his/ol-lo/vol-tom-3/par2/index-eng.asp (last accessed 1 June 2014).

117. Buckner has argued that many Canadians considered themselves part of a British world well into the 1950s and 1960s. Buckner, 'The Long Goodbye', pp. 199–203.

118. Marc Milner, 'More Royal than Canadian? The Royal Canadian Navy's Search for Identity, 1910–1968', in Phillip Buckner (ed.), *Canada and the End of Empire* (Vancouver: UBC Press, 2005), pp. 272–84, at p. 282; Klepak, 'The Scots in the Canadian Military', p. 54. For an overview of integration and unification, see J. L. Granatstein, *Canada's Army: Waging War and Keeping the Peace*, second edition (Toronto: University of Toronto Press, 2011).

119. Klepak, 'The Scots in the Canadian Military', pp. 55–6.

120. The ninetieth anniversary observance of Vimy Ridge Day in Ottawa, for instance, included a piper dressed in a First World War uniform. On Canada and Vimy Ridge, see, among others, Geoffrey Hayes, Andrew Iarocci and Mike Bechthold (eds),

Vimy Ridge: A Canadian Reassessment (Waterloo, ON: Wilfrid Laurier University Press, 2007).
121. Klepak, 'The Scots in the Canadian Military', p. 32; Stanley, 'Scottish Military Tradition', pp. 151–2.
122. This chapter began as a paper presented at the 'Wha bears a blade for Scotland?' research workshop held at the University of Edinburgh on 23–4 March 2012. I am indebted to Dr Wendy Ugolini and David Forsyth for the opportunity to share these ideas, and to the other participants for their comments and observations. I would also like to thank my colleagues at the Canadian War Museum, including Dr Andrew Burtch, Dr Nic Clarke, Dr Peter Macleod, Dr Tim Cook and Dr Mélanie Morin-Pelletier, for their advice and assistance. Finally, I would also like to thank the editors for their very helpful comments and suggestions. The views presented in this paper are those of the author, and do not necessarily reflect those of the Canadian War Museum or the Canadian Museum of History.

6

'A military fervour akin to religious fanaticism': Scottish Military Identity in the Australian Imperial Force

Craig Tibbitts

Since European settlement in 1788, in total, about 600,000 Scots have made their homes in Australia.[1] While earlier in the twentieth century as many as 12 per cent of Australians claimed to be of Scottish descent, the most recent census shows a figure of 7.6 per cent.[2] Today, the main legacy of the early Scots settlers is a small but strong Scottish cultural identity and heritage within Australia's now much larger and more diverse population. The influence of Scottish military traditions and identity in Australia dates back to the arrival of a battalion of the 73rd Highland Regiment in New South Wales in 1810. From the 1860s several home-grown 'Scottish' volunteer militia units were then established in the Australian colonies. This chapter discusses the influence of Scottish military heritage and traditions in Australia from the mid-nineteenth century onwards, focusing particularly on a perceived dominant Scottish influence within a small number of Australian infantry battalions during the First World War. This includes the 56th Australian Infantry Battalion, one of a limited number of units where a larger proportion of officers and men were of Scottish descent, or had pre-war service in militia units with Scottish heritage and identity. A junior Australian officer serving with the 56th observed of Scotsmen in his unit that they displayed 'A military fervour akin to religious fanaticism',[3] underlining how, within these units, the links to Scottish heritage were seen as a positive factor and a strength. Yet against this was set a general view across the Australian forces and among senior command during the First World War that units should identify exclusively as Australian.

Throughout the second half of the nineteenth century up to the First World War, around two million Scots emigrated overseas, primarily to the USA and the British Dominions: a remarkable rate of migration given the total population of Scotland by the middle of the nineteenth century was still under three million. The initial waves of migration resulting from the Highland Clearances saw most Scots emigrants go to North America, but about 10,000 made the longer journey to Australia between 1837 and 1857.[4] During the second half of the nineteenth century even more headed south, and by the beginning of the twentieth century

Scottish migrants had outstripped the numbers of Irish migrating to Australia. It is estimated that during this peak period, from 1850 to 1914, some 265,000 Scots settled in Australia.[5] The majority coming to Australia were Lowlanders, except for those who settled on the north coast of New South Wales (NSW). Particularly in the Clarence River District, almost all were Highlanders, mainly from the Isle of Skye. One of the main centres in this region, Maclean, is still known as 'the most Scottish town in Australia'. Many towns, rivers and regions in Australia bear Scottish names and the early immigrants seemed keen to establish these quickly, though not all were ultimately successful. For example, the regions of New Scotland and Caledonia Australis were later renamed New England and Gippsland. The Scots clearly had a struggle on their hands to assert their dominance within these areas, competing particularly with English and Irish settlers and officialdom in general.[6] The flow of Scottish migration to Australia was also fairly consistent before and after the peak period. The Scots made a strong impression on Australia; many were successful in the fields of politics and banking, and as merchants, doctors and, certainly, soldiers. Indeed, in all these arenas, Scots rose to prominence and were proportionately over-represented.[7] In general terms, as Malcolm Prentis argues, their perceived hard work ethic, adaptability to harsh conditions and better education, coupled with egalitarian, democratic political ideals, made them appear a good match for the young nation of Australia.[8]

Establishing Scottish military traditions in Australia

The presence of Scottish military units in the Australian colonies dates back to soon after white settlement in 1788 when the First Fleet from Great Britain arrived in Sydney Cove. There the first colony was established – a mix of soldiers, sailors, free settlers and convicts. The New South Wales Corps, the first military force in the colony, is estimated to have had about 10 per cent Scotsmen in its ranks. This formation was replaced in 1810 when the new governor, Lachlan Macquarie, brought out his own 1st Battalion, 73rd Regiment of Foot, formerly known as the 73rd Highland Regiment. Other Scottish regiments came for garrison duties in later years, namely the Royal North British Fusiliers (21st Regiment) and the King's Own Scottish Borderers (25th Regiment). There were also several prominent figures of Scottish descent serving with the Royal Navy or Royal Marines in the colonies from the earliest days.[9] British military forces were gradually withdrawn from Australia in the second half of the nineteenth century due to financial constraints and commitments elsewhere around the empire, so that by 1870, the last British troops to garrison the Australian colonies departed.

A series of crises around this time underlined the need to provide for Australia to provide its own defence and led to the creation of new volunteer military units. The Crimean War and the threat of Russian attack was a factor, followed by an assassination attempt on the Duke of Edinburgh, Prince Alfred, in Sydney in January 1868, which led to more unrest and fear. Fighting in various parts of Africa and the ongoing threat of war between Britain and Russia fuelled a perceived need to strengthen the colonial military forces in Australia.[10] As part of this pursuit, Scottish identity and military heritage began to emerge.

The promotion of Scottish military traditions in the Australian colonies seems to have emerged from a variety of individuals and organisations. Mostly they came from Scotsmen who had formerly served in imperial regiments, especially Scottish Highland ones, often those influential Scots settlers who were prominent in politics, the church or business.[11] The influence and support of Scottish-Australian institutions such as schools like the Scotch College in Melbourne, Victoria and various Scottish societies, such as the Caledonian Society and the Scotch Thistle Club, played a significant role. Scotch College, a Presbyterian school for boys established in Melbourne in 1851 by the Reverend James Forbes, had created its own Cadet Unit by 1884. Beginning with drill, the cadets later progressed to military manoeuvres, weapons training, and by the outbreak of the First World War were involved in deeper studies of warfare.[12]

During the latter half of the nineteenth century and into the beginning of the twentieth, there were also other competing diasporic military identities in Australia, namely the English and Irish. Both of these, however, seemed weaker and less consistent than the Scottish. In New South Wales, for example, there was an attempt to raise a 'Union Regiment' at the end of the nineteenth century, including English, Irish and Scottish elements. This existed only briefly, while the Scottish Rifles, raised in 1885, continued as a viable volunteer military unit. Thus, while the Scots arguably struggled to compete in a wider cultural context with the numerically significant English and Irish presence, they enjoyed more success in establishing and maintaining volunteer units, styled with their own military heritage. This was clearly down to support from the Scottish community in Australia, in general, as well as the patronage of some wealthy and influential Scottish-Australian individuals. English- and Irish-styled units lacked the same level of conviction and support from their expatriate communities, nor apparently did they hold quite the same level of interest or leadership in martial matters.[13]

The establishment of volunteer militia regiments with Scottish identity in the Australian colonies began in South Australia. A volunteer force first raised in 1854 became the Adelaide Regiment of Volunteers in 1860, adding a Scottish Company (of Scots migrants to South Australia) in 1866. However, the regiment was disbanded and re-raised several times over the next decade. The timings more or less matched the Crimean, American Civil, Franco-Prussian and Russo-Turkish Wars, but other factors such as lack of sufficient equipment and money were also telling. Further, while many Australians felt somewhat isolated and defenceless against potential raids or takeovers from Britain's rival Great Powers, when those perceived threats inevitably diminished, so too did Australians' interest in voluntary soldiering. Some units did not survive this constant raising and disbanding process, and if they did, emerged in a modified form. The South Australian experience is a good example. By November 1867 the Adelaide Regiment of Volunteer Rifles had been redesignated the Prince

Alfred's Rifle Volunteers following the Duke of Edinburgh's visit to Australia, with the Scottish Company styled The Duke of Edinburgh's Own. However, due to a lack of funding the regiment soon disbanded.[14]

In New South Wales the Duke of Edinburgh's Highlanders existed between 1868 and 1878, and took to wearing the Black Watch tartan. In 1885 the Queensland Scottish Volunteer Corps and the New South Wales Scottish Rifles were established, with the Victorian Scottish Regiment following in 1898. The New South Welshmen affiliated with the Black Watch, while the Victorians chose the Gordon Highlanders. There followed the Cameron Highlanders of Western Australia and the South Australian Scottish Regiment, both established in 1899, the latter being affiliated with the Seaforth Highlanders. Later came the establishment of the Byron Regiment (northern NSW and Queensland) in 1914 (affiliated with the Argyll and Sutherland Highlanders) and the last established, the Queensland Cameron Highlanders, in 1938.[15] Why these affiliations were chosen is not clear. Apart from the Clarence River District of New South Wales's connection to the Highlands and Skye, no other region had apparent links to specific areas of Scotland. It appears therefore that affiliations with certain Scottish regiments were chosen because of their martial fame. This identification with a Scottish 'parent' regiment was also perhaps driven by whichever regiment appealed to the man most influential in organising or financing the Australian volunteer unit.

With their impressive uniforms and accoutrements, the highly visible Scottish volunteer units tended to attract much media attention and were highly regarded by the public. In May 1901, for example, the Maclean Company of the New South Wales Scottish Rifles was in Melbourne for the opening of the federal parliament. *The Age* newspaper reported:

> ... the Maclean Company of Scottish Rifles, or the 'Dandy Fifth' as they are popularly designated, in the picturesque garb of old Gaul supplied an effective note of military pomp and colour to the scene. The piper of the Scottish Rifles (Piper J. B. Mackay of Maclean), elicited a cheer as he stepped into the middle of the street and treated the multitude to a few strains of martial music.[16]

The 'Scottish' militia regiments also seemed to take their training more seriously than other volunteer formations, and showed pride in their units and Scottish heritage as well as their association with famous old Scottish regiments such as the Black Watch, Gordon Highlanders and Cameron Highlanders.[17] In 1893 Major General Edward Hutton, Commander of the New South Wales Military Forces, inspected the Scottish Rifles and reported:

> The small existing Corps of Scottish Rifles is animated by an excellent military spirit and has a good standard of efficiency. An increase in its number is anticipated under the new capitation grant allotted for 1894. It is most desirable in the interests of the Colony that this small corps should be augmented in numbers and receive every encouragement.[18]

These Scottish-Australian regiments also raised pipe bands and were closely involved with their local communities. Drilling and marching, participating in the annual Easter Camp and attending the Highland Gathering often made the news and brought them into contact with the wider public. Social and recreational activities were an important adjunct to their existence and the units also held smoking concerts and dances. Interest and support for the units stemmed from the interest and appreciation of the local Scots communities. With membership restricted to those of Scottish birth or descent, it is likely that the cultural homogeneity of the Scottish units resulted in a closer kinship across the range of their activities.[19]

It is, however, worth noting that there was some opposition to the creation of Scottish military units in Australia. In Victoria, for example, as early as 1854 the overall military commander and the defence minister blocked the initiative, the latter stating he was 'not sure that it was desirable to create national distinctions in this colony where we are properly one nation'.[20] However, through the persistence of the Caledonian societies, and after gaining further political support, the Victorian Scottish Rifles were created in Melbourne in 1898.

With the outbreak of war in South Africa in 1899, many Scotsmen living in Australia enlisted and many women also joined the various nursing services. It is estimated that some 2,200 Scots-Australian men enlisted, and of the sixty nurses who served in South Africa a quarter were of Scottish descent.[21] The Scottish militia regiments in Australia wished to go to South Africa as units, but circumstances prevented this, as skilled horsemen were needed from Australia, not more infantry units. Still, many individual members of these units left to serve with Australian mounted units, while others joined units formed in South Africa, or imperial regiments. Eighty-five members of the New South Wales Scottish Rifles fought in the war, seven of whom died. Two of those lost were highly regarded officers serving with imperial regiments; Lieutenant G. J. Grieve with the Black Watch and Lieutenant K. K. MacKellar, with the 7th Dragoon Guards.[22] In addition, over 900 men from Australia and New Zealand also joined the Marquis of Tullibardine's Scottish Horse and served with distinction in South Africa. The marquis singled out his 'Australians' as his very best horsemen and soldiers, and in scouting felt perhaps they could only be equalled by a good Highland stalker. Thirty-nine Australians also gained commissions serving in South Africa with the Scottish Horse.[23]

During the South African War the Australian colonies federated into the Commonwealth of Australia in 1901. Subsequent reforms of the colonial military forces in 1911 meant the end of the volunteer units, and most of the Scottish ones were absorbed into the Commonwealth Forces, their Scottish identity largely lost or marginalised. Only some in New South Wales, Victoria and South Australia managed to preserve at least some visible threads of Scottishness. The New South Wales Scottish Rifles benefited greatly at this time from the presence of Major Ewen Sinclair-Maclagan DSO of the Border Regiment, who served as their adjutant from 1902. Born in Edinburgh, this career British officer, though only in his early thirties, had impressive military experience. He had served in India and Waziristan, and more recently in South Africa. There he had been wounded in action, mentioned in despatches and awarded the Distinguished Service Order. Posted to Australia in 1901, Sinclair-Maclagan was made deputy assistant adjutant general for New South Wales, as well as adjutant of the New South Wales Scottish where his experience was viewed as being of 'inestimable advantage to the regiment'.[24] He would go on to play an important role in the development of Australian military forces before returning to England. However, so impressed were the Australian military authorities that Sinclair-Maclagan was recruited to the staff of the new Royal Military College, Duntroon, which opened in 1911. Sinclair-Maclagan would rise to even greater prominence during the First World War.

In 1911 the Commonwealth government announced the introduction of a new compulsory military service scheme and the creation of a new Citizens Army. All volunteer militia units would be incorporated into the new scheme, which meant losing their existing distinctive heritage. With the introduction of the new scheme the following year, in New South Wales the Scottish Rifles were absorbed into two new Sydney battalions, the 25th and 26th Infantry. With the Scottish Rifles ceasing to exist in 1912, there were calls from Scottish associations to make the 25th Infantry Regiment a kilted one, and have it renamed the 1st Battalion, New South Wales Scottish Regiment. This would be affiliated with the Black Watch, with kilts being supplied by the federal government. This plan progressed positively but was thwarted by the outbreak of war in 1914. In Victoria the state's Scottish Rifles suffered a similar fate, being renamed the 52nd Infantry, although Scottish-style dress continued to be worn by volunteers and officers. Commanded from 1911 by Major David Wanliss, a Scots immigrant from Perthshire, the 52nd Infantry, along with the 51st, would become closely associated with the 5th Battalion of the Australian Imperial Force.[25]

Other factors also influenced considerations about having national or ethnic-based units. The inspector general of the military forces of Australia, Major General George Kirkpatrick, argued in favour of retaining Scottish, English and Irish regiments, and thereby not falling under the new re-organisation of the forces on the grounds that such a force, a *corps d'elite*, could fill a vital role. Since the Australian Defence Act precluded the militia from serving overseas, Kirkpatrick felt if such a force existed it could be ready for despatch overseas in the event of an emergency or the sudden outbreak of war. However, Kirkpatrick had a powerful adversary on this issue. Commonwealth defence minister George Pearce was equally *against* having other national identities in the Australian military forces. Apart from the added expense of the uniforms, and his misgivings about creating an 'elite' unit, Pearce opposed it more on nationalistic grounds. In 1913 he told the parliamentary senate:

> If our men are going to fight for this country, we want them to fight for it because it is a country which they love and are proud of. We want them to be

proud because they are Australians, not because their fathers and mothers were Scotch, Irish, English, or Welsh. I am the son of an Englishman, but I am proud to be an Australian, and I never want to be called anything else.[26]

In the recently federated nation, a sense of 'Australianism' was beginning to emerge, and to a growing extent at the expense of the national heritage of the 'Mother Country' (Great Britain) as well as colonial parochialism. Naturally, federal politicians like George Pearce were keen to promote such sentiments, but when the nation went to war as Australia the following year, it would soon become apparent that a majority of the Australian populace held similar feelings.

When war in Europe broke out in 1914, a number of Australian-born men were already serving in the British army. In August 1914 those among the first Australians to die in the Great War actually fell serving with Scottish regiments. Lieutenant Leslie Richmond of the 1st Battalion, Gordon Highlanders died at Mons, while Captain Charles Dalglish of the 1st Battalion, Black Watch was killed at Soblonnières a few weeks later. Such deaths were usually reported in the local newspapers in Australia, where often the parents still lived.[27]

In Australia, the response to the outbreak of war was swift. The Australian government offered a force of 20,000 men, but more than double that number enlisted and an expeditionary force was quickly raised. Within days of the outbreak of war, the organisation of the 1st Division of the Australian Imperial Force (AIF) commenced. With government regulations at the time prohibiting home forces serving overseas, members of the existing army (permanent or militia forces) would have to volunteer and join one of the new AIF units. The Australian Imperial Force would thus be formed with completely new units and recruited on a state-based scheme. Despite this, some existing militia units with Scottish identity lobbied for inclusion in the AIF, aided by support from Scottish societies and influential persons. Particularly in Melbourne and Sydney, it was the Scottish societies and associations that pressed the case hardest. They had battled over the years prior to the war to have their local militia units kilted and named Scottish. The 25th (Militia) Battalion in Sydney, for example, had just gained such approval, but the outbreak of war and subsequent organisation of the AIF left that idea shelved. In Melbourne strong supporters of the Victorian Scottish were the businessmen politicians Sir John MacIntyre and Sir Malcolm McEacharn.[28] But such ideas were soon quashed by figures such as Pearce and, as had been the case with the South African War, soldiers of Scottish background would have to join the Australian Imperial Force as individuals in the new national units, contributing to this new Australian force rather than signalling a different form of allegiance. Despite this, efforts were still made to 'stack the deck' in a handful of AIF battalions, relying on their high proportion of officers, NCOs and men of Scottish background with pre-war military service to exert influence. With senior officers and many men recruited from Australian-Scottish militia units, the 4th Infantry Battalion (New South Wales) and the 5th Infantry from Victoria, for example, did their best to shape their new battalions in this way. Several companies of these two units were almost entirely manned by recruits from the NSW and Victorian Scottish militia. They brought with them their Scottish military culture and accoutrements and sought to transplant this into their newly raised AIF units. This could be achieved more easily at the sub-unit level and through the raising of pipe bands. The 27th from South Australia and 52nd from Victoria were raised in 1915 and 1916 respectively, and also made similar attempts. Overall, however, these moves caused some friction among men within the units and none of these battalions ever succeeded in incorporating full Highland uniform, nor in making their units truly 'Scottish' in either name or appearance.

What worked against such desires were the higher authorities of the Australian forces and indeed the majority of officers and men in the battalions. It soon became clear that most men who served wanted to be seen as Australians, or perhaps identify with their states, such as New South Wales, Victoria or Queensland, and *not* be members of 'Scottish'-styled units. Particular evidence for this comes from the 5th Battalion (Victoria) unit history. Upon formation in 1914 there were hopes among the men of A and B Companies that the whole battalion might be a 'kilted one' but they were outnumbered by the other six companies who opposed the idea.[29] However, the 5th Battalion (Victoria) contained many men from the former Victorian Scottish Rifles, including their commanding officer, Lieutenant Colonel David Wanliss, the Perthshire man who emigrated to Australia and had commanded the 52nd Infantry in Melbourne. They continued to push hard to make the 5th a Scottish unit, if not in name, then in character. Disputes and arguments ensued, even on the troopship making its way to Egypt in late 1914, as the 5th Battalion history records:

> The pipers were active . . . and long and bitter were the arguments between the two schools of thought represented on the boat. With admirable zeal, the true Scottish-Australian defended the pipes, striving manfully to convince his opponent, and at the same time remove any doubts in his own mind as to the real musical value of the instrument. The Sassenachs [English or English descent], who greatly outnumbered their antagonists, sneered loudly at the idea of an Australian regiment tolerating such 'blanky windbags', and were not averse to groaning like stricken souls when 'On the Banks of Allan Water' droned out from the officers' deck and mess.[30]

The 4th and 5th Battalions were in fact the only ones to take pipe bands with them, although they would not last long: many of the 4th Battalion's pipers were killed or wounded at Lone Pine on Gallipoli in August 1915. Other attempts to cling to Scottish heritage, usually by officers of Scottish descent, were also evident. Photographs surviving in the Australian War Memorial collection show members of the 5th Battalion wearing their Victorian Scottish Rifles glengarries on Gallipoli, against regulations. However, it seems such attempts came from a persistent minority, likely those seeking to preserve a sense of pride in their Scottish heritage as well as pride and connection to their pre-war militia units and surviving comrades.

It should also be appreciated that across the entire first contingent of the AIF, while 27 per cent of the force was British-born, mostly being of English descent, the far greater majority at almost 73 per cent were Australian-born.[31] While there were plenty of Irishmen too, the Scottish-born presence in the AIF overall was only ever around 2.5 per cent.[32]

As had been the case in Australian society, many Scots became prominent figures in the AIF during the war. Eight of the seventy-two AIF generals were Scottish-born or raised, most notably divisional commanders such as William Bridges, Duncan Glasfurd and Ewen Sinclair-Maclagan, mentioned above. Bridges had also been the first commandant of Australia's military college, RMC Duntroon, and the original commander of the 1st Australian Division.[33] He was mortally wounded by a sniper on Gallipoli just three weeks into the campaign. Many brigade and battalion commanders were also Scottish-born, while others were Australian-born but of Scottish descent, although these identities were not widely acknowledged or foregrounded at the time.

4th and 56th Battalions, AIF

Since 2007 the author has conducted extensive research on the 56th Australian Infantry Battalion. The 4th Battalion, through its close association to the 56th, has also been studied to a lesser extent, although a detailed history of that unit was published in 2007.[34] From these studies a certain sense of Scottish military identity in these two particular New South Wales battalions was found to be clearly evident. Two years prior to the First World War the dissolving of the New South Wales Scottish Rifles saw their ranks absorbed into the new 25th and 26th militia battalions in Sydney. Upon raising the 4th Battalion, AIF there in 1914, many recruits came from these two units, bringing what remained of their Scottish military heritage. At this point this largely comprised of a sense of belonging to a Scottish unit, being surrounded by their militia comrades, and, to a lesser extent, some small token items of Scottish dress such as glengarries and bagpipes. A good many of the 4th's officers, such as Charles Macnaghten, William McDonald, William McKenzie, Allan Scott and Iven Mackay, were ex-Scottish Rifles, as was their brigade commander, Colonel Henry MacLaurin. Thus the ranks of the 4th were soon heavily stacked with officers, some older Scottish NCOs and many others with clear Caledonian connections, particularly being of Scottish descent. In fact there were so many Scotsmen, ex-Scottish Rifles members and a fair contingent of Irishmen that an early nickname for the battalion was 'the Macs and Micks'.[35]

The 4th Battalion cut its teeth in the Gallipoli campaign during 1915, including the savage battle of Lone Pine in August where it suffered heavy casualties. After the abandonment of the peninsula at the end of the year, the AIF regrouped in Egypt in early 1916 before departing to the Western Front. The 4th Battalion remained part of the 1st Brigade, 1st Australian Division for the remainder of the war, fighting principally on the Somme and in Flanders during 1916–17. During the German Spring Offensive of 1918 the division played an important role in defending Hazebrouck and the Channel ports. Then in the summer the 1st Australian Division rejoined the rest of the Australian Corps for the final 'Hundred Days' advance to victory from Amiens to the Hindenburg Line and beyond. Iven Mackay, the Australian-born son of a Presbyterian minister from Scotland, eventually commanded the 4th during some of its more intense periods of fighting during 1916.

With the re-organisation and expansion of the Australian Imperial Force in early 1916, the Australians sought to expand from two to five divisions. To effect this in a manner that spread the experience evenly, half the establishment was taken from each of the original battalions to provide a veteran nucleus for those newly raised. As the whole of the complement transferring from an old battalion went into a particular new one, the expression used at the time was that the old battalion had given birth to a 'pup' battalion. In this way was the 56th Battalion spawned. After organising in Egypt and a brief period holding the Suez Canal defences, the 56th Battalion, as part of the new 5th Australian Division, joined the rest of the AIF in France in July 1916. Their first major action was the disaster at Fromelles within just weeks of arriving at the front, but the 56th was fortunate in being kept in reserve and suffered fewer casualties. They spent the rest of 1916 on the Somme, then by May 1917 were committed against the Hindenburg Line, first at Louverval, then Bullecourt. The 56th spent the last few months of 1917 in Belgium, during the push to take Passchendaele, and fought one of their biggest battles in the taking of Polygon Wood. With the German onslaught in spring 1918, they were shifted back to the Somme and fought at Villers-Bretonneux, Amiens and Péronne. Their last action was at Estrées, on the Beaurevoir Line, in early October.

Judging from their unblemished battle record, it is clear that the 56th was a good battalion; well led, dependable and skilful on the attack and in defence. Out of the line they suffered from no major collapses of discipline or control. The leadership, of course, came from the officers and non-commissioned officers and it is here that we begin to see the influence of the Scotsmen or those who had previously served in the New South Wales Scottish Rifles take effect. Some of the battalion's more prominent officers were either Scottish-born or of Scottish descent, and most of these had been members of the New South Wales Scottish Rifles before the war. The commanding officer was Lieutenant Colonel Allan Humphrey Scott, who led the battalion from its creation in February 1916 until October 1917, and shaped it very much in his image. He was the son of English-born parents, though his father's name, Donald Allan Hyde Scott, perhaps indicates some Scottish roots. His pre-war service in the Sydney Scottish Rifles stood him in good stead and he duly took command of a company in the 4th Battalion. On Gallipoli he excelled, winning the Distinguished Service Order, and at times took command of the battalion. He was a natural choice to take over the 56th when it was created from the 4th. Continuing to perform well in France, he also often acted as brigade commander and was certainly earmarked to become a general in the near future. However, he was killed by a German sniper at Polygon Wood on 1 October 1917, just after his battalion had won their greatest victory. Even in death, this man's military Scottish connections were strangely present. The same sniper's bullet also killed Lieutenant Colonel Dudley Turnbull DSO of the Gordon Highlanders. Scott had fatefully stayed behind to acquaint Turnbull with the positions he was to take over.

The 56th Battalion's second in command was Major James Anderson DSO MC, yet another who had served pre-war with the Sydney Scottish Rifles. Late in the war the 56th was commanded by the legendary Norman Marshall who had won the Distinguished Service Order three times as well as the Military Cross. Marshall was Scottish-born, from Callander. Several Scotsmen were also in command of platoons and companies, including Captain Edward Dalkeith MC and Lieutenants Mack Macdonald, Sammy Dykes, Bobby Myles and Thomas 'Jock' Gordon MM, all of whom were very highly regarded by their fellow officers and men.[36] Indeed, the latter forms a useful case study as a junior officer in the 56th.

Thomas Fowler Gordon (Figure 6.1) was born in 1888 near the town of St Andrews in Scotland and is thought to have emigrated to Australia around 1912. A twenty-six-year-old grocer, he enlisted in the AIF on 30 October 1914 in Sydney, as a private in the 2nd Reinforcements for the 3rd Australian Infantry Battalion. He joined the 4th Battalion in December 1915 and was transferred to the 56th Battalion in Egypt in February 1916. At Fromelles in July, Gordon, now a sergeant, won the Military Medal for his bravery in getting supplies of grenades up to the fighting front through intense enemy shell fire. He was considered 'largely instrumental in assisting the men to hold back the Germans while the [14th] Brigade retired later on in the morning'.[37] Six weeks later, Gordon was commissioned as second lieutenant and spent the remainder of the year at the Second Army School of Instruction. On 24 November 1917 the 56th Battalion was holding the front line near Hollebeke in the Wytschaete sector of the front when Gordon was hit in the chest by an enemy shell fragment. He was rushed away to a casualty clearing station but died there a week later.

Gordon's correspondence with his sweetheart, Maggie Philp of Bonnyrigg, near Edinburgh, has only recently come to light. Along with letters from his best pal and fellow officer, Lieutenant Jack Watt, they offer some insights into how 'Jock' Gordon was regarded in the 56th Battalion. Following his death, Watt immediately wrote to Maggie, expressing his profound sympathies. The letter closes with the following statement:

> A braver soldier, a more honest or upright man never drew breath, & every man in the regiment would lay down his life for him. Never once, since the memorable landing in Gallipoli did he miss a Stunt. The landing, May 18th, Lone Pine, The Evacuation, Egypt, Fromelles, The Somme, Louverval, Bullecourt, Ypres, Polygon Wood, Broodseinde Ridge & Hollebeke, found him the same brave soldier. To you, Miss Philp, I offer my deepest sympathy, & I pray that God may give you strength to bear up during your sad affliction. I have been Tom's closest

pal all through, & perhaps the one in whom he confided. Might I be allowed to tell you, how you were loved by my dearest friend. How for years he had been yearning to make you his own little wife. Just as success was right on his path, his young life was taken from him. Shortly he was to get his Captaincy, & we are all agreed that his death was our battalion's greatest loss. I am so sorry that I cannot write more at present, it has been a big blow to us all.[38]

Such sentiments reflect characteristics apparently commonly attributed to the officers of Scottish background in the battalion; bravery under fire, a strong sense of duty, commitment to leadership in battle and a desire to be in the thick of military action.

Another of the 56th's officers was Lieutenant Harold Williams. Although without pre-war Scottish connections himself, his two books which were published in the mid-1930s, *The Gallant Company* and *Comrades of the Great Adventure*, provide us with some important observations of the strong Scottish influence in the 56th. In several passages he wrote of the leadership the battalion had inherited from the revered 4th Battalion, and of the 'strong Scottish flavour' in the unit, again inherited from the 4th. For example, Williams notes how several Scottish-born NCOs were prominent in the battalion, including Company Sergeant Major Robert Stewart DCM MM, Corporal John McKenzie, Lance Corporal John Dunsmuir and the mercurial Sergeant John McGhee. The latter, born in Stranraer, Wigtownshire, joined the 4th Battalion in 1914, putting his age as thirty-nine, when in fact he was over fifty. He fought on Gallipoli and left the peninsula with eight wounds to his body from the Anzac Landing and Lone Pine, plus a host of other medical problems. In France, although very unwell, he was still reportedly keen to be in the front line with his men. Whenever the Germans shelled their positions, it was said that McGhee would go prowling up and down the trenches brandishing rifle and bayonet, alerting the men in every bay to 'Get y'r bayonets ready, boys; he'll be coming over.' Williams eulogised McGhee in a way that seems to capture the Scottish martial spirit not only of the veteran fighter but also extends to embrace others in the battalion:

> This old Scot knew the traditions of the Scottish regiments as a child knows its ABC. Well over military age, he had enlisted at the outbreak of war in the 4th Battalion, which had a decidedly Scotch flavour about its personnel and was commanded by that old fire-eater Colonel Macnaghten. This battalion was one of the best in the peerless 1st Australian Division. The calibre of the officers and NCOs that came across from this battalion to take command of the 56th has already been noted. Somehow in these men (of whom McGee [sic] was a sample) there seemed to burn a military fervour akin to a religious fanaticism... At every opportunity McGee [sic] would talk to us of the greatness of the old 4th Battalion. We gathered from his remarks that this was the only unit under the British flag that could be mentioned in the same breath as the Highland Light Infantry [in which he had previously served] or the Royal Scots.[39]

In the ranks of the 56th were other prominent Scotsmen. One noteworthy example was a twenty-five-year-old private, Peter Duncan, from Glasgow. Duncan was one of the battalion's most trusted scouts, and known for his endurance and disregard for pain and danger. In one particularly moving passage, Williams recalls the night before going into battle at Louverval on 2 April 1917, with the men sitting around a campfire and Duncan leading them in song; 'that mournful Scottish dirge, "The Land of the Leal". It seems Duncan was sure he would not survive the next day and indeed, he was killed the next day leading the scouts ahead of the Battalion's successful attack.'[40]

In total, 140 Scottish-born men served in the 56th Battalion, which represents 4 per cent of the total, a figure significantly higher than the AIF average of 2.5 per cent. Of the Australian-born men – 76 per cent of the total – many more were clearly, or at least highly likely, of Scottish descent. An examination of the battalion nominal rolls highlights the presence of a number of Australian-born men whose names suggest that they were either the children or grandchildren of Scottish settlers.[41] Names such as Wallace Roy Macgregor, Bruce Boswell Grant, Robert Bruce Bain and William Wallace Stewart provide rather clear indications. Often another key indicator was their home towns; many battalion members came from areas of New South Wales heavily settled by Scots immigrants. The above-mentioned Private Stewart, for example, hailed from Inverell, a town on the MacIntyre River founded by Alexander Campbell.[42] A further strong indicator of a distinct 'Scottish flavour' to the 4th and 56th Battalions can be roughly deduced by the 'Mac count'. While there were 160 men with Mac surnames in the 56th, their parent unit had over 300. Furthermore, stated religion provides another indicator of Scots background; in the 56th, 451 men were of the Presbyterian faith. A final quotation from Williams provides further insight into how the battalion's Scottish connections were regarded, both during the First World War and in subsequent decades. He describes a time when the battalion came out of the line in late 1916. Some of the 56th were drinking with members of the Black Watch that Peter Duncan had met and invited over:

> Dissimilar in dress and facial expression, and reared in totally different environments, there is yet a strange kindred between the Scotsman and Australian. In demeanour both seem to be akin to men of a past age, an age in which men existed by their strong right arms. Apparently this characteristic in Scot and Aussie had been only thinly veiled by civilization. One has only to study this band of singing, drinking soldiers to realize how easily the gloss of peace and enlightenment can be discarded by these fellows. Now, as they roar the jocular advice to the Allemand, the song takes a more sinister meaning. Sung by these chaps, it is no longer a jingle of humorous words; rather, a bellow of defiance such as would be emitted by the warriors of a primitive fighting race before joining battle with their hereditary enemies.[43]

'A remarkable friendship'

War correspondent and later official historian of the AIF, C. E. W. Bean, referred to a 'remarkable friendship' that grew between the Australians and Scots during the war, while another historian called it 'probably the warmest the AIF had with any of their comrades in arms'.[44] Bean's statement is borne out by the published and private literature of the AIF during the war, where there is frequent reference to a genuine affection between Scottish and Australian troops. One such example comes from Lieutenant Norman McNicol of the 37th Battalion, who saw '. . . a special affinity between the "Jocks" and the men from Australia. They fraternised on every possible occasion in France, and such friendly feelings were also manifested in Scotland towards any wandering Australian.'[45] There were likely a variety of reasons for this apparently strong affinity between the troops from the two nations. However, there did seem to be certain traits that the 'Diggers' and 'Jocks' had in common. Popular cultural representations of both groups of men tended to focus on their self-deprecating sense of humour and their readiness to take down anyone getting too 'high and mighty'. In a positive military sense the Scots and Australians believed that they shared the required traits of toughness, stoicism and adaptability to harsh conditions; they were both known for their initiative and independence and seemed to hold a strong mutual admiration of each other's fighting qualities, either behind the lines, or in front of them. Away from the front line, they also shared a tendency to buck authority and both earned reputations for being heavy drinkers and for wild behaviour away from the front.[46]

With such an affinity having developed, as well as the lure of ancestral connections and its celebrated scenery, it is not surprising that many Australians made their way to Scotland when on leave in the UK. Many would have their first impressions of the country while recovering from wounds in the numerous convalescent homes in Scotland and sought to renew friendships and relationships. Others took the opportunity to visit members of their own extended families or to stay with the families of their Scottish-born comrades.[47] This did genuinely seem to be an affinity that extended to the civilian population, although the need to send more Australian military police to Edinburgh perhaps indicates the Australians may not have been universally popular while on leave in Scotland. A final indicator of the strength of this friendship comes from the knowledge that many Scottish ex-servicemen who emigrated in the immediate aftermath of the First World War chose Australia – some 36,000 (about 42 per cent of the total).[48] Such an influx of Scottish veterans to Australia may well have strengthened a sense of military Scottishness there. However, in the wake of such a traumatic war, this may have been reduced by war-weariness and a general decline in involvement in military activities, including those to volunteer movements.

The question of kilted Australian units

The question of raising Australian units with distinct Scottish heritage persisted throughout the conflict, and was raised again late in the war. By 1918 Australia, being one of the very few nations not to introduce conscription, was suffering from an acute lack of reinforcements for its hard-pressed and depleted units. In June that year the secretary of defence wrote to General Birdwood, Commander of the Australian Imperial Force, advising that Scottish organisations in Australia had offered to raise a brigade of infantry. This offer was on the condition that it be raised as a kilted formation, otherwise the men could be used to reinforce existing battalions with the object of transforming them into kilted units. Birdwood consulted with Australian Corps commander Lieutenant General John Monash and other divisional commanders on the matter and all agreed it was not advisable to support the offer, concluding:

> The fame of the AIF has been made by the Australian soldier as such and representative of all that is best in the British race which naturally makes us wish to encourage and preserve this national character of Australian soldiers. Every unit now has its own traditions which are jealously guarded and this makes any proposal for change in composition of units extremely inadvisable.[49]

Monash went on to also dismiss the establishment of a new brigade as impractical, but was careful to stress his hope that the Scottish organisations in Australia would understand his point of view. He hoped they would nevertheless go ahead and recruit as many Scots-Australians as possible, but to fill the ranks of the existing Australian units and 'fight in the uniform of their adopted land whose soldiers have proved that they possess military virtues rivalling the long established and recognised hardihood and valour of the men from their old country'.[50] Here we see a continuation of the trend whereby a growing confidence in Australian military identity was eclipsing any lingering ethic identities.

Following the Armistice came a lengthy delay in shipping the Australian force home. In the intervening months a very successful educational programme was implemented to provide soldiers with new skills and ideas to benefit them upon their eventual return to Australia. Many with a background in farming took advantage of organised agricultural tours in Scotland, visiting Sir John Findlay's Angus cattle stud at Aberlour and the Royal Herd at Abergeldie. Others took courses in up-to-date methods of agriculture and stock-breeding provided through institutions such as the North of Scotland School of Agriculture in Aberdeen, the University of Edinburgh and various other agricultural schools and colleges.[51]

With the Armistice came counting the losses and compiling rolls of honour for those who had fallen during the war. Two files of correspondence surviving in the Australian War Memorial's archive demonstrate the desire to compile nominal rolls along clan lines. In early 1919 MacKinnon of MacKinnon, chief of the clan in Scotland, wrote to the AIF Administrative Headquarters in London. Referring to a list he had received back in mid-1916 of all men and women of his clan serving with the Australian forces, MacKinnon now sought a finalised list. The request was passed to the officer in charge of records, one Lieutenant Stuart MacLeod, with the instruction to please investigate 'for your countryman'. The final list named 171 members of Clan MacKinnon serving with the Australian forces and provides a useful small-scale case study for exploring the functioning of military Scottishness in the AIF during the First World War. Of the 171, 10.5 per cent had next-of-kin in Scotland, against 85 per cent with next-of-kin in Australia. Regarding units, while several MacKinnons served in units with some sort of 'Scottish flavour' such as the 4th, 5th and 56th Infantry Battalions, the majority were spread out among a great variety of units with no Scottish connections or ideals.

In addition, Lieutenant Colonel John MacRae-Gilstrop wrote to the Australian Military Records Office in London later in 1919. On behalf of Clan MacRae, he was also looking for a finalised nominal roll, in the form of an update to one requested in 1916. Once more the officer in charge of records who responded to the request was likely to have been a Scotsman or of Scottish descent: this time a Lieutenant Norman MacPherson. The list supplied revealed similar results to MacKinnon, with a total of 159 MacRaes serving with the Australians and, again, mainly spread throughout the various types of units. It may also be assumed that Clan MacKinnon and Clan MacRae were not the only ones seeking such information from the Australian forces. Unfortunately these types of routine, seemingly dull administrative files were heavily culled from the Australian War Memorial's collections in the 1950s and 1960s. There may well have been other similar files regarding requests from many more clans.[52]

For those who paid the ultimate price, the Scottish National War Memorial atop Castle Rock in Edinburgh records on its Rolls of Honour the names of some 4,300 men who died serving with the Australian forces, and who were either Scottish-born or had a Scots parent. These rolls were compiled between the end of the war and the memorial's 1927 dedication from lists obtained from the War Office, the Imperial War Graves Commission and from Commonwealth countries such as Australia.[53]

Following the First World War, Australian military traditions were thoroughly dominated by the glory and the sacrifice of the AIF's achievements. Militia units were re-organised and most took on the numbers of former AIF units. The phenomenon of military Scottishness seemed irrelevant to many. However, although budget cutbacks in the wake of the Depression saw an end to some existing military units, in the early 1930s the militia began to expand again as the threat of another war in Europe loomed. Again it was proposed to raise a Scottish, kilted regiment in NSW. Yet once more, opposition to such plans was raised. In some respects the opposition concerned the expense of the uniforms but there was also some feeling, not only among senior military figures but also among the general public, that the proud traditions created by the AIF in the Great War were more important than sustaining a Scottish identity and superseded it in fact.[54] Eventually, however, defence minister Pearce ended his long-held opposition to Australian soldiers wearing kilts, hoping the popular uniform might attract more men to volunteer in the Citizen Military Forces. Thus, in 1935, a Scottish Regiment was re-formed in Sydney as the 30th Battalion, NSW Scottish Regiment. The *Sydney Morning Herald* reported glowingly on an early review of the regiment:

> All ranks stepped by with military precision and presented an impressive picture in the glittering sunshine. It was noticeable, however, that the strength of the 30th Battalion (NSW Scottish) overshadowed that of the other infantry battalions, which, it is said, are in need of recruits. Some authorities consider that it is the kilts and others claim that it is the proud association with the famous Black Watch Regiment; but the fact remains that this battalion is very popular.[55]

Similarly, the Queensland Cameron Highlanders were raised in 1938, fought the Japanese in Papua during the Second World War, and survived through until its conclusion before being disbanded.

Post-Second World War cutbacks in the forces, re-organisations and merging of units again led to the disbandment of some proud Australian units, such as the New South Wales Scottish Regiment in 1962. Nevertheless, today some units still cling to their lineage and Scottish heritage. For example, 2/17th Battalion's A Company is the 'Scottish Company', which still takes that heritage seriously and seeks to preserve such an identity. Affiliations with battalions of the Royal Regiment of Scotland have likewise been maintained. In Victoria, the 5th/6th Battalion, Royal Victoria Regiment (an Australian Army Reserve unit) perpetuates the lineage and heritage of the Victorian Scottish Regiment, and maintains affiliations with the 4th Battalion, The Royal Regiment of Scotland (The Highlanders).

And indeed Anzac Day, Australia's premier day of recognition and commemoration of its military past and present, has always had, and still does have, a Scottish flavour to it. This is not because of any Scottish dominance in the Australian military, past or present, as this chapter has demonstrated, but because of the ongoing appeal of Scottish pipe bands and their association with martial marching music. Therefore, interspersed with the myriad veteran and current units marching each Anzac Day in Australia you will see Scottish pipe bands (mostly civilian now) and hear that distinctive skirl of the bagpipes from afar.

Notes

1. Malcolm Prentis, *The Scots in Australia* (Sydney: University of New South Wales Press), p. 76.
2. Australian Bureau of Statistics, 2006 Australian Census data, http://abs.gov.au/websitedbs/censushome.nsf/home/historicaldata2006 (last accessed 4 August 2014).
3. Harold Roy Williams, *The Gallant Company* (Sydney: Angus & Robertson, 1933), pp. 74–5. This book was republished by Pen & Sword in 2012 under the title *An Anzac on the Western Front*.

Figure 6.1 Lieutenant Thomas Fowler Gordon MM, courtesy of George Gordon.

Figure 6.2 Melbourne, Australia, 25 April 1943. The Pipe Band of the 5th Battalion (Victorian Scottish Regiment) leading returned men of their regiment in the Anzac Day March. © Australian War Memorial.

Figure 6.3 Canberra, Australia, 25 April 1951. The Canberra Pipe Band leading in the ex-servicemen to their position on the parade ground for the official ceremony to commemorate Anzac Day at the Australian War Memorial. © Australian War Memorial.

4. Prentis, *The Scots*, p. 24.
5. Prentis, *The Scots*, p. 77.
6. Ibid. p. 247.
7. Ibid. p. 285.
8. Ibid. pp. 134–5.
9. Ibid. p. 143.
10. Martin Buckley, *Scarlet and Tartan: the story of the regiments and regimental bands of the NSW Scottish Rifles (Volunteers), the 30th Battalion (NSW Scottish Regiment), 'A' Company and Pipes and Drums, 17th Battalion, Royal New South Wales Regiment* (Sydney: Red Hackle Association, 1986), pp. 4–6.
11. For more on Scottish ethnic associationalism in this period, see Tanja Bueltmann's chapter in this volume.
12. Jim Mitchell, *A Deepening Roar: Scotch College, Melbourne, 1851–2001* (Melbourne: Allen & Unwin, 2001), p. 29.
13. Buckley, *Scarlet and Tartan*, pp. 11–12.
14. George Odgers, *Army Australia: An Illustrated History* (French's Forest, New South Wales: Child & Associates, 1988), p. 28; Robert Kearney, *Silent Voices: The Story of the 10th Battalion AIF during the Great War, 1914–1918* (French's Forrest, NSW: New Holland, 2005), p. 18; 27th Battalion, *The 27th Battalion Centenary: The Historical Record of the 27th Battalions, 1877–1977* (Adelaide: 27th Battalion, Royal South Australian Regiment, 1977), pp. 2–3.
15. Buckley, *Scarlet and Tartan*, pp. 284–90.
16. Eleanor McSwan, *Maclean and the Scottish Connection*, second edition (Maclean, NSW: Maclean District Historical Society Inc., 2009), p. 53.
17. Buckley, *Scarlet and Tartan*, p. 12.
18. Ibid. p. 11; Martin Buckley, *The Scottish Rifles in Northern New South Wales* (Goonellabah: M. J. Buckley, 1984), pp. 3–5.
19. Ibid. p. 11; Buckley, *The Scottish Rifles*, pp. 3–5.
20. F. W. Speed (ed.), *Esprit de Corps: The History of the Victorian Scottish Regiment and the 5th Infantry Battalion* (Sydney: Allen & Unwin, 1988), p. 1.
21. Prentis, *The Scots*, p. 146. The nurses' figure has been lowered from 'more than half' in Prentis to around one-quarter, using more recently available Australian War Memorial statistics and online information. Available at https://www.awm.gov.au/exhibitions/nurses/boer/ (last accessed 11 February 2015).
22. Buckley, *Scarlet and Tartan*, pp. 12–14.
23. John E. Price, *Southern Cross Scots: the Australian and New Zealand participation in the Marquis of Tullibardine's Scottish Horse during the South African War of 1899–1902* (Cheltenham: Victoria, 1992), pp. 21, 85–7, 169–70.
24. Lieutenant Colonel G. R. Campbell, *Twenty-one years' volunteering in New South Wales, 1885–1906: the story of the N.S.W. Scottish Rifles* (Sydney: Turner & Henderson, 1907), pp. 22–3; A. J. Hill, 'Sinclair-Maclagan, Ewen George (1868–1948)', *Australian Dictionary of Biography*, National Centre of Biography, Australian National University, http://adb.anu.edu.au/biography/sinclair-maclagan-ewen-george-8438/text14791 (last accessed 21 February 2015).
25. NSW Scottish Regimental Association, 'History of the NSW Scottish Regiment', www.nswscottish.org.au/history; Speed, *Esprit de Corps*, pp. 16–17 (last accessed 15 August 2014).
26. John Connor, *Anzac and Empire: George Foster Pearce and the Foundations of Australian Defence* (Melbourne: Cambridge University Press, 2011), pp. 35–6.
27. Jennifer King, 'WWI Scottish regiment soldier may have been first Australian-born

casualty', ABC News online, 19 September 2014, http://www.abc.net.au/news/2014-08-23/leslie-richmond-first-aust-born-soldier-killed/5685774 (last accessed 19 September 2014); Aaron Pegram 'First to fall', *Wartime: official magazine of the Australian War Memorial*, Issue 67 (Winter 2014), pp. 52–6.
28. Prentis, *The Scots*, p. 147; L. L. Robson, 'The origin and character of the first A.I.F., 1914–1918: Some statistical evidence', *Historical Studies*, vol. 15, no. 61 (1973), pp. 737–49; NSW Scottish Regimental Association, 'History of the NSW Scottish Regiment', http://www.nswscottish.org.au/history.html; Speed, *Esprit de Corps*, pp. 16–17, 23–6 (last accessed 15 August 2014).
29. Speed, *Esprit de Corps*, pp. 25–6.
30. Albert William Keown, *Forward with the Fifth* (Melbourne: Specialty Press, 1921), pp. 36–7. An excellent revision of this book with additional illustrations is also available. Compiled by Carl Johnson, published by History House, Blackburn, Vic. in 2002.
31. For the whole AIF across the four years of enlistment in the war, the proportion levelled out to about 80 per cent Australian-born and just under 20 per cent British-born. See Charles Edwin Woodrow Bean, *The Official History of Australia in the War of 1914–1918*, vol. 1, p. 84; Robson, 'The origin and character of the first AIF' and National Archives of Australia online resource, *Mapping Anzacs*, http://discoveringanzacs.naa.gov.au/.
32. While only 2.5 per cent of the AIF were Scottish-born, 15 per cent of the entire force recorded their religion as Presbyterian, a good indicator of the numbers of those of Scottish descent in the ranks. National Archives of Australia, *Mapping Anzacs*, now the online resource *Discovering Anzacs*, http://discoveringanzacs.naa.gov.au/ (last accessed 1 February 2015); Jean Beaumont, Australian Defence Force Sources and Statistics (2001), p. 116; Bill Gammage, *The Broken Years: Australian Soldiers in the Great War* (Canberra: Australian National University Press, 1974), p. 281.
33. RMC Duntroon opened in 1911 on the grounds of the former grazing property of Robert Campbell on the outskirts of Canberra. He named the property after his ancestral home of Duntrune in Argyllshire.
34. Ron Austin, *The Fighting Fourth: A History of Sydney's 4th Battalion 1914–1919* (McCrae, Vic.: Slouch Hat Publications, 2007).
35. Ibid. p. 6; Australian War Memorial (AWM), 1DRL/0358, Captain R. G. Horniman (4th Battalion).
36. AWM, 3DRL/2715, Diaries of Captain Norman Alexander Nicolson; Williams, *Gallant Company*, p. 95; Letters of Lieutenant J. C. Watt, privately held. Letters made available courtesy of David Hamilton of Edinburgh.
37. AWM28, Recommendation files for honours and awards, AIF, 1914–18 War, Sergeant Thomas Fowler Gordon, Military Medal.
38. Letters of Lieutenant J. C. Watt.
39. Williams, *Gallant Company*, pp. 74–5.
40. Ibid. pp. 118–19.
41. AWM9, 37/6, 56th Infantry Battalion AIF – Nominal Roll.
42. Campbell, a native of Scotland, had arrived in Australia in 1824 and established a property, 'Inverell', in the area in 1836. The name was said to derive from the Gaelic 'Inver' (meeting place) and 'Ell' (swan), the latter being in abundance in the area at this time. The town and surrounding district were later named after it. Inverell Shire Council, Inverell's History, http://www.inverell.nsw.gov.au/development/heritage/inverells-history.html (last accessed 3 March 2015); Geographical Names Board of New South Wales, http://www.gnb.nsw.gov.au (last accessed 3 March 2015).

43. Williams, *Gallant Company*, pp. 95–6.
44. Charles Edwin Woodrow Bean, *The Official History of Australia in the war of 1914–1918, Volume III, The Australian Imperial Force in France, 1916* (Sydney: Angus & Robertson, 1929), pp. 753–4; Eric Andrews, *The Anzac Illusion: Anglo-Australian Relations during World War 1* (Melbourne: Cambridge University Press, 1993), pp. 172–3, 188.
45. Norman Gordon McNicol, *The Thirty-Seventh: History of the Thirty-Seventh Battalion A.I.F.* (Melbourne: Modern Printing, 1936), p. 167.
46. Bean, *The Official History, Volume III*, p. 754; Prentis, *The Scots*, p. 14.
47. Several examples of impressions of leave in Scotland are held in the Australian War Memorial Private Records Collection: AWM, 1DRL/0176, Caldwell; AWM, 1DRL/0205, Collett; AWM, 1DRL/0266, Ellsworth; AWM, 1DRL/0345, Henderson. In addition, the letters of Hugh McEachern, held privately.
48. Prentis, *The Scots*, p. 29.
49. AWM10, 4311/4/16, 'Formation of kilted regiments in AIF'.
50. Ibid.
51. AWM25, 303/83, 'Education and non-military employment – Correspondence regarding tours of Scotland and Suffolk'; AWM19, TE 10/332, 'AIF Education Service – Placement of men on farms in Scotland'; AWM20, 6418/1/10, 'AIF Education Service – Reports – Agricultural training in Scotland'; AWM20, 6418/1/15, 'AIF Education Service – North of Scotland College of Agriculture'.
52. AWM18, 9983/22/22, 'Records of Australian clansmen who fought overseas – Asked for by Chief of the MacKinnons'; AWM18, 9983/22/48, 'Request for list of the members of Clan McRae in the AIF'.
53. Scottish National War Memorial, 'History', http://www.snwm.org/content/about-history (last accessed 4 March 2015).
54. Buckley, *Scarlet and Tartan*, pp. 55–6.
55. Ibid. p. 69.

7

South Africa and Scotland in the First World War

Jonathan Hyslop

If the South African contribution to the war effort made a material difference to the Allied cause in 1914–18, it was on the scrublands of South-West Africa and on the savannahs of Tanganyika, rather than in the fields of France and Flanders. Early during the conflict, South African forces rapidly and decisively suppressed a pro-German rebellion by dissident Afrikaners. Prime Minister Louis Botha personally led the South African invasion of the vast, though ill-defended, German colony in what is now Namibia, giving the British Empire one of its few victories of 1915. And in German East Africa (now Tanzania), Minister of Defence Jan Smuts in 1916 led an imperial army, including a large South African contingent, against the Schütztruppe and Askaris of Von Lettow Vorbeck. Though Smuts's efforts have been much disparaged by subsequent historians because of his inability to crush his antagonist, under his leadership the British did in fact gain control over the key urban and agricultural areas and communications routes.[1] Yet when the Botha government began, even before the conflict was over, to commemorate South Africa's military achievements, they concentrated on the role that the country had played on the western front. Here, South Africa had sent a mere brigade of white combat troops and a contingent of black troops to serve as labourers. Both were, of course, a tiny element in the vast Allied armies, far too small to affect the outcome of the struggle. They were there for reasons of political symbolism, to help stake South Africa's claim to a seat at the peace negotiations. Given the uncertainly evolving political relationship between the Dominions and Whitehall, it was by no means clear that the 'colonials' would be directly represented when the post-war settlement was made. A military presence in the central theatre of the war would provide Pretoria with the moral leverage to get a voice in the process when the time came.

The South African government's approach to celebrating the nation's role in the war took an oddly Scottish turn. The centrepiece of their official story of the conflict was the heroic resistance of the South African Brigade at Delville Wood, during the battle of the Somme, among them the kilted South African Scottish Regiment, more formally known as the 4th South African Infantry.[2] In five days of intense, often hand-to-hand fighting, the four battalions repulsed the attacks of four German divisions, at the cost of their own destruction. Although this 'Scottish' regiment did not survive the war, the myth of Delville Wood was carried into the future by the two Scots-identified units of the South African military, the Transvaal Scottish, based around Johannesburg, and the Cape Town Highlanders. To this day, the visitor to the Transvaal Scottish regimental museum will reverently be shown a cross made from one of the shell-scarred trees of the wood. And, as we shall see, to put their message about the war across, the South Africans turned to Scotland's then best-known author: John Buchan.

This chapter explores the South African–Scottish connection during, and in the aftermath of, the First World War. I have previously argued that a strand of what I termed 'military Scottishness' ran through twentieth-century South African society.[3] This connection flowed in both directions between the two countries. Some Scottish social and political institutions engaged with the 'Scottish' military forces in South Africa in a way which used the notion of an international Scots military brotherhood to support their own conceptions of national identity. Both Scots and white South Africans used the prestige of South African–Scottish militarism to help define their identities *vis-à-vis* England. White South Africans engaged in complex social battles among themselves over the relationship between military Scottishness and South African identity. There were also some interesting examples of the use of Scottish military symbolism by black people: even in the late twentieth century, a group of Pedi rural migrant workers could be found in Johannesburg's Alexandra township dancing in kilts.[4]

Essentially, this was a global politics of cultural appropriation. By the turn of the nineteenth century, decades of literary and popular celebration had endowed the figure of the Scottish warrior with a prestige that spread around the world. As he was invented by Scott and his successors, the Highland fighter was a figure who, in the British imperial imagination, combined the romantic history of doomed struggles against English domination with that of the bravery and loyalty to the empire of the regiments who were the foremost soldiers of Victoria's army. By seizing upon this valuable cultural resource, and creating their own Scottish militias, British emigrants could share the aura of military glamour. The rough and ready elites of colonial towns could re-invent themselves as aristocratic Scottish officers. And given the often fraught nature of the relationship between settler colonials and the metropolis, military Scottishness was also a way of politically underlining that the British diaspora was prepared to fight for the empire, but in turn deserved political respect from the imperial authorities. For Scottish emigrants, the Scottish military identity also helped to maintain a sense of self-identity and institutional links to their home country. By the same token, Scots themselves were often enthusiastic about these global extensions of the forms of cultural identity that they had created in the nineteenth century. Links with Scottish organisations abroad intensified and gratified a sense of Scotland's importance in the wider world. But they also reinforced the ability of Scots to make their own claims within Britain, as being a lynchpin of both the empire and the union, yet having a distinct identity. Even for colonial subjects, as the case of the Pedi dancers illustrates, the Highland soldier might come to stand not, as one might expect, simply for the invader, but for an image of strength and unity. Many different people in the colonial world could put the image of the kilted soldier to work for their own purposes.

This argument draws on John MacKenzie's insight that Scottishness as an identity, and empire, had shaped each other. For MacKenzie, the endeavours of the Scots in the empire 'looped back' and became a factor in the life of Scotland.[5] Paradoxically, participation in the British Empire strengthened Scots' claims to distinctiveness. Our understanding of the Scots in South Africa has been enriched by MacKenzie's survey of the history of the Scots in that part of the world, down to 1914.[6] In it he rightly makes a powerful and justified critique of the lack of a 'four nations' approach in much writing on southern Africa, where Britishness tends to be collapsed into Englishness. In this chapter, I explore the role of a specifically South African version of Scottish identity in relation to the Great War.

In colonial southern Africa, the idea of a Scottish military identity had an appeal that stretched well beyond Scottish immigrants. The nineteenth-century British popular imagination was imbued with the idea of the Scot, and especially the Highlander, as the embodiment of imperial military virtue. For a culture shaped by tales and images of Waterloo, Balaklava and the Relief of Lucknow, the Highlander was the unequalled hero.[7] And a burst of Scottish emigration to South Africa at the turn of the century had important effects. From roughly 1890 to 1906, with only a brief interruption during the early stages of the South African War, British immigrants poured into the goldfields of the Transvaal. It was only in this period that British emigration to South Africa ever seriously rivalled the numbers flowing to Canada and Australasia. And this immigration was hugely disproportionately Scots. At a time when Scots comprised about one in seven of the population of the United Kingdom they were about one in three British immigrants to South Africa.[8]

Thus the conditions were provided for a flourishing of 'Scots' military identity in the southern hemisphere. Well before the 1899–1902 South African War, the Cape Town Highlanders Regiment (CTH) had been established by Scottish immigrants as part of the Cape Colony's volunteer military. The CTH modelled themselves on the Gordon Highlanders.[9] The regiment offered social prestige to the officers and military glamour to the men. In 1902 the marquess of Tullibardine, heir to the duke of Atholl, then in the recently conquered Transvaal, initiated the formation of an ostentatiously Scottish unit, wearing a kilt in the Atholl tartan, which rapidly evolved into the Transvaal Scottish Regiment (TS). The Johannesburg Caledonian Society played a key part in setting up the formation.[10] Initially, the TS did solely comprise men of (at least partially) Scots descent, and used the Caledonian societies as a recruitment network.[11] However, it was not long before the regiment began to run out of 'real' Scots, and to recruit other British immigrants, and later European immigrants and Afrikaners. A number of other British colonial volunteer units in southern Africa, such as the First City Regiment in Grahamstown in the Cape, also adopted elements of Scottish identity. In the first decade of the twentieth century, the key role of these regiments was in colonial control of indigenous people. In 1906 the Transvaal Scottish went to Natal, where they participated in the bloody suppression of the Zulu Bambatha Rebellion.

But they were also turned against the militant labour movement of white workers in the Transvaal. In January 1914, after a white workers' general strike on the Rand, the government declared martial law, and the Transvaal Scottish were deployed as part of an operation which rounded up hundreds of labour activists. This reflected important class and political cleavages in the South African Scots 'community'. Scots artisans were to the forefront of the leadership of the remarkably strong trade union movement that emerged in South Africa after 1902. These unions combined anti-capitalist militancy with a commitment to racial protection of their jobs by excluding black labourers from skilled work.[12] The officers of the Transvaal Scottish, drawn from the managerial and professional classes, undoubtedly felt a sharp antagonism towards the strikers and their syndicalist-influenced leaders. Many of those in the ranks of the Transvaal Scottish were from working-class backgrounds; but they were for the most part able to reconcile themselves to the defence of a social order which promised them economic opportunities which had been out of reach at home.

All of this points to the complexity of Scottish national identity, great enough in Scotland itself, but made even more tangled by the colonial military context. Tullibardine, a Scottish aristocrat, could set up a regiment identified with the quasi-feudal tradition of his family in a cosmopolitan colonial mining town. This putatively Scottish regiment then recruited many non-Scots, who keenly took up a view of themselves as Highland soldiers. And the Scots of the Rand, far from constituting a unified 'community', were divided by political and class factors to an extent that the regiment was rounding up their 'fellow countrymen' at the point of a bayonet. This was truly the 'invention of tradition' and the 'imagination' of community at work.

The South African Scottish Regiment 1915–18

Following the creation of the Union of South Africa in 1910, the existing military units of the four component territories were re-organised, during 1912–13, into a single national army. Regiments which identified as 'Scottish' were a feature of the new military establishment, most prominently the Transvaal Scottish and the Cape Town Highlanders. As urban, imperial loyalist and English-speaking units, they were among the most reliable formations available to the Botha-Smuts government, which was viewed as a British puppet regime by a number of the senior Afrikaner officers in the Defence Force. At the beginning of the First World War, when Botha was confronted with the daunting tasks of quelling Afrikaner rebellion and conquering German South-West Africa, he needed all the loyal forces available. Thereafter, a South African Brigade was assembled to fight on the western front. This included a battalion constituted as the South

African Scottish, comprised from members of the TS and CTH, as well as new recruits drawn in through the Caledonian societies. The honorary colonel of the SA Scottish was mining magnate Sir William Dalrymple, whose presence points to the way in which the Scottish military identity had become part of the underpinning of the new South African social order. Stirlingshire-born Dalrymple had attained great wealth on the Rand during the mining boom of the 1890s, and had subsequently participated in the formation of the TS. A virulent opponent of the British immigrant labour unions, he had enthusiastically backed Smuts's tough handling of the employees on the mines.[13]

The complexity of South African 'Scottish' military identity was quickly becoming apparent. From the time of the post-Boer War restoration of self-government to the whites of the old republics in 1906–9, the lack of support from Afrikaner politicians for British immigration frustrated any prospect of South Africa continuing to be a major country of Scots migrants on a scale comparable to, say, New Zealand. At the outset of the war, therefore, there simply were not enough Scottish immigrants volunteering to make wholly Scots units viable. Thus, in the first intake into the SA Scottish there were far more South African-born than Scottish-born, and the combined numbers of English, Welsh, Irish and continental European-born men somewhat exceeded the numbers of actual Scots.[14] What is striking though is the way in which these non-Scots embraced the kilt-and-bagpipes paraphernalia of this regiment and the notion of being 'descended' from a line of Highland warrior tradition. An idea of the heady rhetoric in South African Scots circles is provided by the remarkable case of Charles Murray. The Aberdeenshire-born Murray was one of the founding officers of the TS, and for a long period a leading figure in the Rand Caledonian societies. By 1914 he had risen from humble beginnings to the position of Secretary of South Africa's Department of Public Works. But he was also a part-time poet, and had recently emerged as Scotland's most popular writer of vernacular, or 'Doric', verse. His poems of rural Aberdeenshire life, written in dense dialect, had developed a significant following in his home country.[15] Murray threw himself into support for the war effort, writing a call to arms which appealed to contradictory strands in Scottish history. The men he summoned to the ranks were to see themselves as simultaneously the inheritors of the Covenanters and the Jacobites:

> Wha bears a blade for Scotland? She's needin' ye sairly noo,
> What will ye dae for Scotland for a' she has done for you?
> Think o' the old time Slogans, the thread runnin' throu' your plaid,
> The cairns o' the Covenanters whaur the martyrs' banes are laid;
> Ay, the faith o' the godly fathers, is it naething to you the day?
> Wha bears a blade for Scotland? Noo is the time to say[16]

Though Murray's poem was directed primarily to the Scots at 'home', the imagery of military Scottishness was extensively used in drumming up recruits, and maintaining support for the war effort in South Africa and beyond.

SOUTH AFRICA AND SCOTLAND IN THE FIRST WORLD WAR | 155

Figure 7.1 Sporran worn by the noted poet Charles Murray, a founding officer of the Transvaal Scottish Regiment, a volunteer unit formed in Johannesburg, South Africa in 1902, with the support of the Caledonian Societies of South Africa. © National Museums Scotland.

Figure 7.2 Scottish military 'Balmoral' bonnet worn by Captain M. L. Norton of the 4th South African Infantry, 1915. The badge shows the springbok national symbol. The motto 'Union is Strength' is given in English and Afrikaans, stressing the unity of the white South African nation. © National Museums Scotland.

The Caledonian societies were extremely active in generating support for the war effort. In her wry memoir of her family, who were pillars of the Caledonians, Barbara Kinghorn writes of her mother:

> At the outbreak of the First World War Miss McKirdy was nine years old. She stood on the steps of the Johannesburg City Hall, dressed in a red velvet coat trimmed with swansdown and recited 'You're a better man than I am Gunga Din' so movingly that scores of young men dashed off to the recruiting office to join the army. In later years she would say to us, 'In my whole life that is the one thing I wish I'd never done'.[17]

The little girl's brother died in the war.

The South African Brigade trained at Potchefstroom, in the western Transvaal. In August 1915 they were sent by rail to Cape Town, where they embarked for England.[18] Initially, they were barracked at Borden, with the expectation that they would go to the western front. However, a German-backed uprising by the Sanussi in Libya was threatening the western border of Egypt, and the brigade was diverted into the British campaign to put it down. After being shipped to Egypt in January 1916, the SA Scottish spent some days at a camp near Alexandria before moving east to Mersa Matruh. The SA Scottish Regiment missed some of the early fighting in which the rest of the brigade had taken part, but they then participated in an advance to Sollum in March. The campaign's success was threatened by a lack of water supplies. But the imperial force quickly went on to take Halfaya Pass and surged towards the Tobruk road, crushing the Sanussi forces with small losses on their own side.[19] The campaign over, the brigade was shipped from Alexandria to Marseilles, and from there dispatched to the western front. Here the Scots connection was reinforced, for the SA Brigade was assigned to the otherwise wholly Scottish 9th Division. The South Africans arrived in the Steenbecque-Morbecque training area on 4 June, their Springbok mascot Nancy making a symbolic statement of identity. This was surely significant: whereas the original Cape Town Highlanders had had a pet stag to emphasise their Scottishness, this generation wanted to signal their distinctiveness within the empire. By this time the Springbok had become the symbol of the internationally successful South African rugby and cricket teams, and thus signalled national masculinity.

On 14 July the brigade was ordered to the Somme. The 9th Division was attempting to capture Delville Wood and Logueval, on a four-mile strip of front south of Pozières. On their arrival at Delville Wood on 15 July, the South Africans came under heavy fire but drove through to take the wood. The fight was bitter; elements of several German divisions were thrown against the brigade at various times. It was not until 20 July that the brigade was relieved. The killed and wounded were so numerous that, out of over 3,000 members of the brigade, only three officers and 140 other ranks were able to march out at the end.[20]

Delville Wood was almost immediately hailed as a South African epic. The ambition of the Smutsites was to make this into the same kind of heroic

Figure 7.3 Two kilted soldiers of the 4th South African Infantry share a match on a wintry Western Front, 1916. © National Library of Scotland.

formative event for the new (white) South African nation that Gallipoli had been for Australians. It certainly resonated profoundly with British-origin South Africans. But despite the presence of a substantial number of Afrikaners in the South African Brigade, too few Afrikaners at home ever identified with the war effort for the commemoration of the event ever to succeed in having this unifying effect. From 1919 onwards, Armistice Day parades were held in the major South African cities by the Union Defence Force, and always the epic of Delville Wood was invoked. Yet such attempts to highlight the South African role in the imperial war effort faced active resistance. General J. B. M. Hertzog, the undisputed leader of Afrikaner nationalism at the time of the war, had equivocated over the armed revolt by some Afrikaners in 1914. But he was consistently hostile to the war effort, and did not hesitate to exploit resentment over Smuts's treatment of the rebels. Hertzog's National Party (NP) promoted cultural initiatives and social organisations which focused on building Afrikaner identity. When the NP came to power in 1924, they moved to replace the Union Flag with a distinctive South African flag, and 'God Save the King' with the Afrikaner anthem 'Die Stem'.[21] The Union Defence Force was identified in the minds of Afrikaner nationalists with the British interests. While British loyalists honoured Armistice Day, the NP celebrated heroes of the 1914 revolt such as Jopie Fourie, an army officer who had been shot by Smuts for his role in the rebellion, General Beyers, the rebel leader who had drowned in a river while escaping Botha's forces, and the great Boer War commander Christiaan De Wet, who had been imprisoned for his role in the uprising. Delville Wood had immense resonance for immigrant British loyalists, and some for those Afrikaners who supported Smuts' pro-imperial stance. But it was meaningless to hardcore Afrikaner nationalists.

As a consequence of the devastation at Delville Wood, a new levy of volunteers was raised in South Africa to rebuild the brigade, including the SA Scottish. They were back in action during the latter stages of the Somme battles, and the SA Scottish suffered ghastly casualties. In early April 1917 the SA Brigade was again thrown into the front at Arras. General Smuts came to inspect the regiment before they marched out, but his presence did not bring them luck. Though their initial push was successful in gaining its objectives, on 12 April the SA Scottish suffered casualties of six officers and 200 men. After a respite over the summer, the brigade was in action again at Ypres in September. The SA Scottish lost fifty-six killed and 197 wounded. They were in the trenches once more over the New Year. The numbers of soldiers in the SA Brigade able to fight on shrank rapidly, and in a re-organisation at the turn of the year it was reduced from four to three battalions. In March 1918 the South Africans were positioned in the Heudicourt sector, where they were deployed against the massive German Spring offensive. In a desperate resistance, they were subject to gas attack and to an accidental bombardment by British artillery. The SA Scottish was reduced to such small numbers that they had to be integrated into the 2nd Battalion South African Infantry. After a brief attempt to re-form the Scots, the task was abandoned, bringing the distinctive Scottish formation in the contingent to an end. By the end of the war only one battalion of South African infantry was left on the western front.[22]

The Afrikaner as Scot: the case of Deneys Reitz

The complexity of the South African relationship to the Scottish military tradition, and to Scottishness more broadly, at the time of the Great War is perhaps best exemplified by the case of Deneys Reitz.[23] In the last year of the conflict, Reitz became Second in Command, and for a time Acting Commander, of 1st Battalion, Royal Scots Fusiliers, on the western front. Yet Reitz had fought for the Boers against the British in the war of 1899–1902. Moreover, he was the son of F. W. Reitz, who had been both President of the Boer republic of the Orange Free State and State Secretary of Paul Kruger's Transvaal. Deneys had participated in General Smuts's famous guerrilla raid on the Cape. Disgusted by the British victory, he went into a temporary self-imposed exile in Madagascar before returning home. In the immediate aftermath of the Boer War, he penned a memoir of the campaign. When it was eventually published in 1929, under the title *Commando*, the book rapidly established its position as a classic literary account of guerrilla warfare. Reitz's willingness to fight for the empire he had so recently encountered in the field derived chiefly from his loyalty to his Boer War commander, Smuts. After Reitz had returned, disease-ridden, from his sojourn in Madagascar, Smuts and his family had cared for Deneys, something for which he remained eternally grateful. Subsequently, Smuts had persuaded Reitz that the future required reconciliation between the British and Afrikaners, under the aegis of the British Empire. When, after the unification of South Africa in 1910, Smuts became the leading figure in the government of Botha, Reitz warmly supported both leaders. He accepted their view that white South Africans needed unity under the rubric of South Africanism, within a broader loyalty to the empire. When war broke out, Reitz had fought on the government side against the insurgent Afrikaner rebels, and then joined the military campaigns against the Germans in South-West Africa and Tanganyika. On arriving in England in 1917, Reitz initially enlisted as private in the British army, but baulking at the prospect of basic training, used a family connection – his uncle, the South African High Commissioner – to wangle himself a commission. Reitz had another very good connection – he met up with his old chief General Smuts, now a member of the Imperial War Cabinet, at the Savoy Hotel, and was introduced by him to Winston Churchill. Smuts arranged for Reitz to go on a senior officers' course, and he was soon promoted to major. After training, Reitz was posted to the 7th Irish Rifles, and with them he had his first taste of trench warfare on the western front. Before long, though, Reitz was transferred to the Royal Scots Fusiliers (RSF).

But while political ideology led Reitz to the trenches, there was also a deeper cultural underpinning to his being able to take on the role of commander of a Scottish regiment, in the form of a complex history of Afrikaner connections with Scotland. There were historic links in South Africa between the Boer elite and Scotland, rooted in a shared Calvinist religion and educational experiences.

During the nineteenth century a number of Scots Presbyterian ministers – some of whom became very influential – were imported to lead Boer Dutch Reform Church congregations, while the sons of some wealthy Afrikaner families were sent to attend university in Scotland. The Reitz family were a classic example. Both Deneys's father, F. W. Reitz, and his grandfather had studied in Scotland. His grandfather had claimed to have presented Walter Scott with a lion skin as a present from the Cape-based poet William Pringle, and to have been present at the banquet where Scott admitted his authorship of the Waverley novels. Whether these stories were true or not, there certainly was a close Reitz family cultural identification with Scotland. Deneys recounted that 'at our home scarcely a night passed without a reading from Burns or Scott'.[24] Very exceptionally for members of their rather insular community, the entire Reitz family were able to make a visit to Europe in 1894. Deneys Reitz retained strong memories of this trip, and especially of a visit to a family in Auchindrayne, the Cathcarts, with whom his father and grandfather had stayed: 'we felt we were among our own people', he recounted.[25] Though the closeness of Scots links in the Reitz family was unusual, it reflected a broader pattern, and certainly helped equip Deneys for his future transnational role. Between the British takeover of the Cape in 1806 and the Jameson Raid of 1895, upper-class Afrikaner culture in the Cape and the Orange Free State became closely modelled on that of Britain. Part of this was the specifically Scottish religious, educational and literary connection. It was only the trauma of Cecil Rhodes's attempt to overthrow the Boer Transvaal Republic in the raid that tipped these elite Afrikaners towards confrontation with the imperial power.[26] And for some Afrikaners, in the post-war period, this cultural past provided support in accepting reconciliation with the British. Thus Reitz's sense of the Scots as 'our own people'.

There was a remarkable density of social networks and connections between Scotland and southern Africa, created by the age of mass migration, fast and cheap steamship travel and mass communications. Now the war led to an intensification of these links. Reitz's experience as a British army officer in France demonstrates this close interweaving. When he was posted to the 6/7th Royal Scots Fusiliers near Arras in 1917, he found that the battalion's Commanding Officer, Colonel de Haviland, was the Sergeant at Arms of the South African parliament, and one of the lieutenants was also from Cape Town.[27] Later, returning to France after medical treatment for wounds in England, Reitz was transferred to the 1st Battalion of the RSF. That battalion was commanded by Colonel E. I. D. Gordon, who in Reitz's view was 'to all intents and purposes a South African'. Gordon was married to a South African and owned a farm in the western Cape.[28] The RSF were brigaded with 2nd Royal Scots and 7th Shropshire Light Infantry, and their brigadier was yet another South African, General William Tanner, who had commanded the South African Brigade at Delville Wood.[29] Later, the battalion acquired a South African adjutant.[30] Even Reitz's batman, MacColl, wanted to emigrate to South Africa – sadly, he died in combat.[31] All the while, Reitz's Scottish links were deepened. While recovering from his hospitalisation, he was sent for some weeks to the RSF depot at Fort Matilda on the Clyde, attended a gas course in Edinburgh, and viewed the Grand Fleet at Rosyth.[32] In his second volume of memoirs, *Trekking On*, Reitz provides a stunning account of the horrors of combat during the great German offensive of March 1918, in which the RSF made a heroic stand. His writing is deeply humane and informed by a deep scepticism of the effectiveness of the British high command. But his identification with the RSF was total: 'I was glad to have witnessed so mighty a conflict in the company of such brave men.'[33] The strength of Reitz's identification with the RSF does not only speak to the characteristic feelings of loyalty and group identity among soldiers who have been through traumatic combat experiences together. It also needs to be read in terms of his family history of Scots cultural linkages. And it was supported by a set of social networks between South Africa and Scotland, based on the mobility of migrants across the empire.

Severely wounded for a second time, Reitz was sent to a small hospital in London, situated in 'the private dwelling house of Mrs Muirhead Campbell, a patriotic Scotch [sic] lady'.[34] After three months of recovery, he was sent back to the RSF depot in Scotland, but it took a very long time for his wounds to heal sufficiently for him to be declared fit for active service. He returned to the front in September, participating in the great Allied advance, and was present when his battalion took part in breaching the Hindenburg Line. Subsequently, Reitz was transferred to command in another battalion but retained a great affection for the RSF: 'we were brigaded together so I was still in the same family circle'.[35]

Reitz's story is one of the extraordinary malleability of political identities. As a member of the Afrikaner elite, he had deep Scots cultural connections. Despite having fought the British army in the past, this background, his political alignment with Smuts, and the existence of South African–Scottish networks enabled Reitz to become an effective 'Scots' soldier in the new war.

John Buchan and the South African army

In 1916 John Buchan was asked by the South African government to write a book on the South African military contingent's role in the war in Europe. Apparently Buchan accepted, although he was not able to set to work until after the Armistice.[36] Thereafter, his writing moved along quickly, and in March 1920 *The History of the South African Forces in France* was published in London by Thomas Nelson & Sons. At the time he was asked to take on the task, Buchan was already the most popular novelist in Scotland, and possibly in the English-speaking world as a whole. He had published three enormously successful books – *Prester John* in 1910, *The Thirty-Nine Steps* in 1915 and *Greenmantle* in 1916 – all of them thrillers about the thwarting of conspiracies against the empire (respectively African, German and German/Islamic). Buchan was immensely well connected and on a political path that would lead him eventually to the governor-generalship of Canada. During 1916 he had been commissioned in the Intelligence Corps and had become a speechwriter and publicist for Field

Marshal Douglas Haig. During the next year he would be appointed Director of Information under Lord Beaverbrook.[37]

The South African decision to seek Buchan's help was in some respects a strange one, but one that casts some light on the relationship between South Africa, the empire and Scotland in the war-time years and their immediate aftermath. Botha and Smuts had been highly effective field commanders for the Boers during the South African War of 1899–1902. It was only as late as 1906, won over by the conciliatory policies of the Campbell-Bannerman government, that they had decisively thrown in their lot with the British Empire. By contrast, Buchan had been a member of the 'Milner Kindergarten', the small group of bright young Oxford graduates brought in by the resented, anti-Afrikaner regime of the imperial proconsul Lord Milner to reconstruct the Transvaal in the aftermath of the war. But there was by the time of the First World War an important parallelism between the political projects of Botha and Smuts on the one hand and Buchan on the other. The two South Africans believed that they could forge a united nation of British and Boers, which stood under the protection of the empire, but maintained a strong and distinctive South African identity. Smuts was in the process of elaborating a whole philosophy, rooted in the influences of Anglo-Hegelians during his studies at Cambridge, which underpinned this politics with cosmic notions of 'parts' resolving into greater 'wholes'.[38] Buchan, somewhat similarly, saw Scotland as a distinct nation, yet believed his nationalism to be perfectly compatible with Scotland as part of the union and as a bulwark of the empire. He had a long-standing interest in vernacular Scottish poetry. In the years after the First World War Buchan was active in attempts to promote the Scots tongue, and published an anthology of Scots verse. He was also to become part of the so-called Scottish Renaissance movement of the 1920s. This grouping reflected the sense among a wide spectrum of Scottish intellectuals that a more assertive national identity was needed. Its primary focus was on the promotion of Scots language and literature. Support for it generally went along with a critical view of what were seen as the Anglicising educational policies of the time. But though it contained some radical members, such as Hugh MacDiarmid, the movement was not an inherently politically critical one.[39] Buchan saw the empire as flexible enough to give scope to national identities of its component parts, within a greater unity. He was thus well placed to understand the Botha–Smuts version of a new South Africa, which similarly combined national and imperial loyalties. In some of Buchan's tales of derring-do, the hero, Richard Hannay, who has made his career as an engineer on the Transvaal mines, is symbolically supported by his side-kick, the Afrikaner Peter Pienaar. There was an affinity between the ideas of the South African leaders and those of the idiosyncratic Scots Tory.

And for both, race was essential to the story. For Buchan, as for Botha and Smuts, the story of modern South Africa was the story of the creation of a white nation, in which black people had no part. The South African Native Labour Contingent in France, for example, was pretty well overlooked in Buchan's official history. And Buchan certainly delivered on his ideological brief. In the *History*, participation in the Great War is the heroic act in which white South Africans fuse into a single nation. Significantly, Buchan links this achievement to their ancestors' triumphs over colonised peoples. Describing the South African role in the holding off of the German Spring offensive of 1918, he writes:

> In that last stand every man of the Brigade 'took counsel from the valour of his heart', and the glory became less that of the individual than of the race. Two strong stocks, coming together from the ends of the earth, had each of them in their blood the spirit that defends lost hopes and is undismayed by any odds. The kinsfolk of the men who shattered Dingaan's hordes and under Andries Potgieter beat off the indunas of Mosilikatse at Vechtkop, and those who had in their tradition the Ridge at Delhi and the laager at Rorke's Drift, joined hands in the wood of Marrierres in an achievement more fateful and not less heroic than any in their splendid past.[40]

This was Buchan's contribution to Smuts's ultimately doomed attempt to use a call for racial unity to overcome the intractable divisions among whites. Buchan had, as an administrator in the time of British direct rule of the former Boer republics, been part of a regime that had attempted to stimulate British immigration to create a permanent British majority in white politics, and had been notably unsympathetic to Afrikaner cultural and political aspirations. The desired result was not achieved, as United Kingdom emigration to South Africa collapsed after 1906. But subsequently, Buchan had become sympathetic to Smuts and Botha's imperial loyalist ideas. Thus in the passage quoted above, Buchan turned his considerable literary skills to ransacking history to establish the unique martial qualities of South Africa's two main white ethnic groups. He thus refers to the two major victories of the *Voortrekkers*, when they moved into the South African interior in the 1830s. One ('Vechtkop', now Vegkop) was the Boer defeat in 1836 of the Matabele. The other was the 1838 Boer victory over the Zulu army at Blood River. The latter event is then connected to a famous 1879 victory of a small contingent of British soldiers, again over the Zulu, at Rorke's Drift and to the siege at Delhi during the Indian Mutiny. The paragraph, however, does not quite work – the British heroes invoked are imperial troops, not colonials, and thus perhaps not the best vehicle for mobilising white South African identity.

In the aftermath of the war, the South African role in the conflict was extensively memorialised. As elsewhere in the empire, Armistice Day parades became a ritual for the army. An elaborate monument, designed by the imperial architect Sir Herbert Baker, was erected at Delville Wood and opened in 1926. Its centrepiece is a statue by Alfred Turner of two standing males reining in a horse – symbolising Afrikaner–British unity. And Scotland itself recognised the South African role. In the Scottish National War Memorial on Edinburgh's Castle Rock, a plaque commemorates the South African Scottish Regiment, within an overall design which gives a central place to 'The Outposts of Empire' and ' . . . Scotsmen of All Ranks Who Fell while Serving With Units of the British Dominions and Colonies, 1914–1918'.

Most Afrikaners were, in the long run, unable to join Smuts in forgiving the British for past injustices. And the material inequalities between them and British-origin South Africans, who largely controlled business and the professions, provided fertile ground for nationalist mobilisation. Smuts was to be driven from office by an Afrikaner nationalist regime in 1924. Later was to come the forty-year dominance of Afrikaner nationalist government which would commence in 1948 and, notoriously, the implementation the policy of *apartheid*. In the 1950s the defence ministry made active attempts to undermine the Scottish military traditions of South African regiments and to break connections with Britain. Over time though, the Afrikaner government would reconcile itself to the symbolism of both the Scots regiments and, in particular, of Delville Wood. By the early 1970s, with their dominance of white South African politics well established, and facing threats from African popular protests and guerrilla movements, the Afrikaner leadership was anxious to incorporate Anglophone whites in the common defence of white supremacy. In the interests of conciliation, the military hierarchy began to emphasise the value of regimental traditions, including those of the 'Scottish' units, in creating unit cohesion. And they sought to create a shared, heroic white military past, in which Delville Wood was given a central place. The regime also played on the theme of South Africa's past contributions to the defence of the West, insouciantly ignoring the fact that Afrikaner nationalists had opposed participation in both world wars. When President P. W. Botha was making hopeless attempts to sell his 'reforms' of apartheid to European leaders during a 1984 tour, the trip included a visit to Delville Wood.

With the fall of apartheid in 1994, it might have been expected that the all-white 'Scottish regiments' and their military heritage would be abolished. But in the context of Nelson Mandela's attempts at transcending past divisions they were maintained and incorporated into the new South African National Defence force. The Transvaal Scottish, for example, has continued to operate and has made a significant drive to recruit people of all races. So in Cape Town and Johannesburg to this date, the now multi-racial CTH and the TS take central parts in ceremonies that allude to Delville Wood.

Conclusion

For both Scotland and South Africa, the attempts to reconcile imperial and national identities were already starting to be problematic in the 1920s. The war had begun to set new social and political processes in motion. In Scotland, a young generation of nationalist intellectuals emerged to challenge the politics of British identification. The decline of Scotland's formerly prosperous heavy industries and the horrors of the Great War led to disaffection with the British state. Although these currents would take a long time to play out, the process of the unravelling of the secure pre-1914 Scottish loyalty to the empire was beginning. The Great War Memorial in Edinburgh could be both Scottish and imperial for the moment, but the two terms would begin to move apart. Similarly,

Smuts faced a rocky future for his vision of a strong, united white nation. The war stimulated inward industrialisation. Afrikaners moved into the cities in mass numbers, and there their grievances were, in the long run, mobilised by republican Afrikaner nationalists. To them, the loyalty of the SA Scottish at Delville Wood meant nothing. Also urbanising were the African people, who were themselves moving away from the legacy of imperial loyalty, which had been strong in the Cape black elite of the nineteenth century, towards anti-imperial radicalism. If African nationalist leaders remembered the war at all, it was through the story of the *Mendi*, a troopship on which hundreds of African soldiers has been drowned when it sank in the English Channel. The narrative as it came to be told was one of heroism, but also of the pointless sacrifice of black lives in a white man's war.

Military Scottishness retained an enormous, long-lasting appeal for, primarily, a section of white Anglophone men. But they were, after South Africa left the Commonwealth in 1960, forcefully separated from the British connection which so many of them cherished. They were in the end to serve an Afrikaner state, and then, remarkably, after 1994 an African nationalist one. But for most Afrikaners, the First World War was one in which South Africa had no interests at stake, and into which it had been dragged by traitorous leaders. For African nationalists, the conflict was one in which black soldiers had been placed in an inferior role and had suffered for a cause that was nothing to do with them. Delville Wood, and the kilted South African soldiers who died there, did not become part of either of the most powerful political narratives of modern South Africa.

Notes

1. Edward Paice, *Tip and Run: The Untold Tragedy of the Great War in Africa* (London: Phoenix, 2007) and Hew Strachan, *The First World War in Africa* (New York: Oxford University Press, 2007) pp. 131–84 give excellent accounts of the campaign. Although these authors tend towards the sceptical consensus on Smuts as a military leader in Tanganyika, these narratives show that by the time Smuts departed he had secured most of the north, the towns and communications routes. But on the other hand, he had failed to pin down Lettow in the field, leaving the German forces free to roam southern Tanzania and later even to enter Mozambique.
2. Bill Nasson, 'Delville Wood and South African Great War Commemoration', *English Historical Review*, vol. 119, no. 480 (2000), pp. 57–68.
3. Jonathan Hyslop, 'Cape Town Highlanders, Transvaal Scottish: Military "Scottishness" and Social Power in Nineteenth and Twentieth century South Africa', *South African Historical Journal*, vol. 47, no. 1 (2002), pp. 96–114.
4. *Mail and Guardian*, 13 June 1997.
5. John M. Mackenzie, 'Essay and Reflection: On Scotland and the Empire', *The International History Review*, vol. 15, no. 4 (1993), pp. 714–39.
6. John M. Mackenzie with Nigel R. Dalziel, *The Scots in South Africa: Ethnicity, Identity, Gender and Race, 1772–1914* (Manchester: Manchester University Press, 2007).
7. Heather Streets, *Martial Races: The Military, Masculinity and Race in Imperial Culture, 1857–1914* (Manchester: Manchester University Press, 2011).
8. Christopher Harvie, *Scotland and Nationalism: Scottish Society and Politics 1707–1994*

(London: Routledge, 1995), p. 59; Gordon Donaldson, *The Scots Overseas* (London: Hale, 1966), pp. 187–8.
9. Neil Orpen, *The Cape Town Highlanders 1885–1970* (Cape Town: Cape Town Highlanders History Committee), p. 4.
10. Hubert Calla Juta, *The History of the Transvaal Scottish* (Johannesburg: Hortors, 1933); James H. Mitchell, *Tartan on the Veld: The Transvaal Scottish 1950–1993* (Johannesburg: Transvaal Scottish Regimental Council, 1994). For more on these initiatives, see also chapters within this volume by Spiers and Bueltmann.
11. *Minutes of Evidence (With Appendices) of the Transvaal Volunteers Commission* (Pretoria: Transvaal Governmnent, 1906), p. 263.
12. For a discussion of the political role of Scots workers in South Africa in this period, see the debate between Dr Billy Kenefick and myself: William Kenefick, 'Confronting White Labourism: Socialism, Syndicalism and the Role of the South African Radical Left before 1914', *International Review of Social History*, no. 55 (2010), pp. 29–62; Jonathan Hyslop, 'Scottish Labour, Race and Southern African Empire c. 1880–1922: A Reply to Kenefick', *International Review of Social History* (2010), pp. 63–81.
13. W. J. De Kock and D. W. Kruger (eds), *Dictionary of South African Biography*, vol. II (Pretoria: Human Sciences Research Council, 1972), p. 157.
14. John Buchan, *The History of the South African Forces in France* (London: Thomas Nelson, 1920), pp. 16–17. There were certainly Scots in the other battalions of the SA Brigade, but it is unlikely that they would have been sufficient to make up a complete battalion.
15. Jonathan Hyslop, 'Making Scotland in South Africa: Charles Murray, the Transvaal's Aberdeenshire Poet', in David Lambert and Alan Lester (eds), *Imperial Careers Across the British Empire* (Cambridge: Cambridge University Press, 2006), pp. 309–34.
16. Charles Murray, *Hamewith: The Complete Poems of Charles Murray* (Aberdeen: Aberdeen University Press, 1979), p. 71.
17. Barbara Kinghorn, *Miss McKirdy's Daughters will now Dance the Highland Fling* (London: Black Swan, 1995), p. 14.
18. Buchan, *History*, pp. 11–22.
19. Ibid. pp. 23–42.
20. Ibid. pp. 43–82.
21. A good sense of the politics of this period is conveyed by P. S. Thompson, *Natalians First: Separatism in South Africa 1909–1961* (Johannesburg: Southern, 1990), pp. 29–49.
22. Buchan, *History*, pp. 83–256.
23. Deneys Reitz, *Adrift on the Open Veld* (Cape Town: Stormberg, 1999).
24. Ibid. p. 12.
25. Ibid. p. 12.
26. Mordechai Tamarkin, *Cecil Rhodes and the Cape Afrikaners: The Imperial Colossus and the Colonial Parish Pump* (Johannesburg: Jonathan Ball, 1996).
27. Reitz, *Adrift*, p. 275.
28. Ibid. p. 282.
29. Ibid. p. 285.
30. Ibid. p. 305.
31. Ibid. p. 299.
32. Ibid. p. 280.
33. Ibid. p. 302.
34. Ibid. p. 301.
35. Ibid. p. 315.

36. Buchan, *History*, p. 5.
37. Andrew Lownie, *John Buchan: The Presbyterian Cavalier* (London: Constable, 1995).
38. W. K. Hancock, *Smuts*, 2 vols (Cambridge: Cambridge University Press, 1962–8).
39. Lownie, *John Buchan*.
40. Buchan, *History*, p. 192.

8

Ngāti Tūmatauenga and the Kilties: New Zealand's Ethnic Military Traditions

Seán Brosnahan

New Zealand, to borrow from Rudyard Kipling's famous description of Auckland, is the 'last, loneliest, loveliest' domain of the Scottish diaspora. Furthest away of all Britain's white settler-dominated colonies from the homeland, it is arguably the one where the Scots were most numerous in proportion to population, and most influential culturally. It is perhaps surprising then, that unlike Canada, South Africa and Australia, New Zealand's First World War expeditionary force contained no units bearing Scottish names or drawing from Territorial units with Scottish identities, and apparently eschewed any links with Scottish military traditions. Instead, this national force marched under the New Zealand name, wearing plain khaki uniforms badged with New Zealand motifs and symbols. The sole exception to this assertion of a homogenous identity was an ethnically branded contingent of Maori, the native inhabitants of New Zealand, who served with distinction at Gallipoli and on the western front.[1]

This chapter will trace the evolution of both Scottish and Maori military traditions in New Zealand and their contrasting fates into modern times. In the twentieth century, distinctive Maori contingents went overseas to fight for 'King and Country' in both world wars, to wide acclaim.[2] Following the Second World War, as the imperial connection attenuated and a stronger national identity emerged, the significance of this indigenous warrior tradition steadily increased within the New Zealand military, eclipsing earlier manifestations of military Scottishness in the process. No other native culture has projected its military traditions onto the armed forces of a former British Dominion to a similar degree. This provides an intriguing point of comparison between New Zealand's two ethnically focused military traditions. As one has waxed – the New Zealand army becoming *Ngāti Tūmatauenga* (the tribe of the warrior God)[3] – the other has waned, with Scottish affiliations, dress distinctions and unit identities in danger of disappearing altogether at the start of the twenty-first century.

Scottishness in New Zealand

James Belich has made the point that it is the over-representation of Scots that most distinguishes settler New Zealand from nineteenth-century Britain. Whereas Scots made up about 10 per cent of the population of the British Isles, they made up 24 per cent of New Zealand's settler population. New Zealand was thus, according to this estimate, twice as Scottish as Britain.[4] The Scots, moreover, were both widespread across the country – in significant proportions in almost every province – and also concentrated, being clustered in the south in Otago and Southland. Continuing emigration into the twentieth century also meant that this ethnic over-representation stabilised into a long-term pattern. Up to the 1950s, ethnic Scots made up about 20 per cent of the New Zealand population. The Maori proportion by contrast was less than half that.

These figures set up an intriguing point of reference for the relative influence of Scottish and Maori traditions on the evolution of New Zealand's military forces, before, during and after the First World War. The country's two major cultural strands, Maori and Pakeha,[5] each had their own strong martial heritage. Maori society had impressed the earliest European observers with the primacy accorded the place of the warrior and the centrality of warfare in the Maori way of life. Captain Cook, for example, in 1771 described Maori as 'a brave war-like people'.[6] Cannibalism, *haka*,[7] *moko*[8] and the visceral ebullience of traditional Maori tribal warfare were reported in explorers' accounts to a fascinated European audience.[9] A wary respect for the Maori as a virile foe, willing and capable of defending their tribal territory, may explain the seventy-year gap between Cook's discovery of New Zealand in 1769 and the first waves of organised migration there in the 1840s.[10] European settlers, when they did finally come, nonetheless brought with them to New Zealand an overweening pride in British military superiority.

The nineteenth century had begun with British military triumphs on land and at sea over Napoleon's French forces, foreshadowing Britain's dominant position in world affairs through the century. The grim struggle against Russia in the Crimea was 'current news' as New Zealand's major settlements were establishing themselves in the 1850s. Almost a dozen British army regiments served in New Zealand in the same decade, with many soldiers remaining to settle in the colony permanently. Veterans of other British military campaigns also emigrated, particularly survivors of the Crimean War. By 1858 at least 6 per cent of New Zealand's total European male population consisted of British army veterans, ensuring that British military traditions would be a core component of emerging New Zealand colonial identities.[11]

Scottish settlers, in particular, had their own dual tradition of military valour. Broadsword-wielding clansmen of the Scottish Highlands had long been bogeymen figures to Lowlanders and those further south. Until perhaps the early nineteenth century it was these 'barbarians of the north' who provided the stock figure of the savage to most Britons. Indeed, failed risings in support of Stuart claimants to the throne in 1715 and 1745 had brought armies of Highland warriors through Lowland Scotland and deep into the heart of England, threatening the nation's peace and stability from within.[12] Brutal repression followed in the Highland region of Scotland, intended to destroy the military threat of the rebellious Highland clans forever. More positively, and ultimately more successful, was the development of Highland regiments in the British army, drawn particularly from areas of the Highlands where there was a closer interface with the infrastructure of the British state and where pro-government elites were more influential. Within fifty years their exploits overseas had transformed the image of the Highlander from barbaric 'outsider' to staunch defender of the empire.[13] Even the Jacobites were re-interpreted as tragic heroes, becoming a staple of Romanticism in British art and literature.[14] When Scots migrated to British colonies, whether in Canada, Australia, South Africa or New Zealand, they took an enthusiasm for Scottish-branded military units with them. Such units became a distinctive component of colonial armed forces and wider Scottish associational culture in all of these territories.

Scots and the New Zealand Wars

The first official representative of the British Crown to take up residence in New Zealand was a Scotsman: James Busby from Edinburgh. He arrived in the Bay of Islands in 1833 and built a two-room home at Waitangi which remains one of New Zealand's premier historic houses. As what was termed the 'British Resident', effectively a consular representative, Busby had wide-ranging responsibilities for relations between the indigenous Maori and European settlers in what was an often violent frontier territory. He was, however, provided with no means of enforcement and was 'expected to control contact through sheer force of character and moral superiority'.[15] He received little support from his Australian-based superiors, had no military background to draw on, and was mocked by Maori as the 'Man-of-War without Guns'. His extensive reports on the deteriorating situation in New Zealand did eventually lead to a decisive change in British policy towards the country, however. In 1840 a British naval officer, Captain William Hobson, was despatched to New Zealand with a small military force to negotiate a treaty of cession with Maori chiefs, a discussion which concluded in a monster *hui* (meeting) on Busby's front lawn at Waitangi.

The resulting treaty, known as the Treaty of Waitangi, is the founding document of the New Zealand nation. It set the context for the mass influx in subsequent decades of European settlers, who were overwhelmingly British or Irish in origin. It provided a right of settlement to these immigrants, while also guaranteeing the rights of the native inhabitants. The Treaty accorded the latter the same rights as British subjects, and recognised as well, in an ill-defined way, the authority of Maori chiefs. However, these ideals of partnership and racial equity were quickly dishonoured. Armed conflict between Maori and Pakeha broke out within five years of the Treaty signing and continued in various forms for more than thirty years. At issue was control of the land. As Europeans flooded into New Zealand through the mid-nineteenth century, pressure built up to wrest the land they desired from its native proprietors. These struggles, generally known as the New Zealand Wars (1845–72), offer our first case study for examining the relationship between New Zealand's Scottish and Maori military traditions.

The New Zealand army dates its origins to the Militia Act of 1845, passed in response to Maori aggression in the Far North region of the country. This Act established the first official New Zealand military units of the Crown. British troops were soon involved as well: various British regiments, including naval detachments, were sent to the colony to suppress the Maori rebellion. The regiments were mostly English units – though no doubt many included Scottish personnel, and certainly a large proportion of Irishmen. None of the Highland regiments was sent for service to New Zealand. The only Scottish unit to be involved was the 99th Lanarkshire Regiment, which spent two years in New Zealand from 1845 to 1847. The Lanarkshires lost twenty-four members during fighting in New Zealand who were subsequently commemorated on their return to their base in Hobart, Tasmania with the erection of a memorial monument.[16]

Thus, it would be hard to claim a major Scottish military influence on the basis of the dozen or so British regiments that served in the New Zealand Wars. One caveat to that might be the leadership of Lieutenant General Duncan Cameron, commander of the British forces in New Zealand from 1861 to 1866. He came from a long line of men from Clan Cameron who had made their mark in the British army since the defeat of the clans at Culloden in 1746. Duncan Cameron was commissioned to the Black Watch in 1825 and rose rapidly through the ranks. He made his name at the Crimea and succeeded his patron General Colin Campbell as commander of the Highland Brigade there. In 1860 he received the highly prized post of commander in chief in Scotland and was considered 'one of the most accomplished officers in the British Army'.[17] In 1861 he arrived in New Zealand to lead the invasion of the Waikato.

Cameron arrived to take charge of a campaign that was failing. There had been serious reverses and victory against the rebellious Maori forces was proving elusive. The Maori were well led by warrior chiefs like Rewi Maniopoto, renowned for his analysis of British military strategy and a master of the defensive withdrawal.[18] Rewi was repeatedly able to frustrate the superior British forces at Cameron's disposal, leaving the Scottish general to claim victories that were largely pyrrhic.[19] Eventually Cameron became disenchanted with government policy towards Maori and fell out seriously with the New Zealand governor, George Grey. Despite his ongoing professionalism, this political failure sapped his enthusiasm for the struggle; in his final years in New Zealand, Maori called him 'the lame seagull'. Duncan Cameron returned to Britain in 1865, the New Zealand chapter possibly the lowest point in his otherwise distinguished biography.[20]

Kūpapa: Maori fighting Maori on behalf of the Crown

Using imperial troops in New Zealand was hugely expensive for the colony, absorbing a significant proportion of limited colonial revenue.[21] In the latter half of the

1860s this cost prompted a change of strategy towards colonial self-reliance. The British regiments, which had peaked at 17,000 personnel in the mid-1860s, were gradually pulled out, the last leaving New Zealand in 1870. Home-grown forces – colonial militia and volunteers – now took over the struggle against Maori. Many of the professional British troops chose to take their discharge in New Zealand, however, and such veterans provided a core of experienced military men for the subsequent development of the New Zealand Armed Constabulary. This was a paramilitary force on the Irish model, combining policing and permanent militia functions. Military veterans, particularly those who had served in the Crimea or India, also constituted a significant proportion of the migrants coming to New Zealand in this period. There is evidence to suggest, however, that overall, former members of Scottish regiments made up only a small proportion of this veteran inflow.[22]

Scottish involvement in the New Zealand Wars was thus rather modest, especially compared to the English and Irish contribution. More important to this chapter is the pivotal role played by Maori fighting for the Crown against Maori. It was increasingly these 'Queen's Maori', known as *kūpapa*, who provided the cutting edge in campaigns against Maori rebels.[23] This was analogous to the way that 'loyalist' clans had been so important in fighting Jacobitism in Scotland. Like the clansmen, Maori were organised tribally and the tribes, or *iwi*, used the Crown's cause to carry on ancient rivalries under a new banner. Just like the pro-government clans of eighteenth-century Scotland, Ngāti Porou and Te Arawa proved eager to harry their traditional enemies with the full force of the new colonial state. They had both the bushcraft and the warrior élan to take the fight to rebel Maori on their own terms. So too, increasingly, did units of the New Zealand Armed Constabulary, who adapted to the guerrilla-style warfare of the bush more readily than British regulars had been able to.

The New Zealand Wars were over by the end of 1881.[24] Early in that year the Maori king had unexpectedly come out of his fastness in the King Country – a *de facto* Maori zone of control in the central North Island – to symbolically lay down arms, thus signalling an end to armed conflict. But there was to be one final act of armed aggression from the colonial forces. In November 1881 a massive force of police and militia gathered in Taranaki, supported by Volunteer units from across the North Island. They had come to crush the non-violent resistance campaign of the Taranaki prophet Te Whiti O Rongomai. His followers had developed effective strategies of passive opposition to Pakeha encroachment on Maori land. Parihaka, his model village, had become a symbolic thorn in the side of the New Zealand government. On 5 November 1881 the village was invaded with overwhelming force and hundreds of unresisting Maori were arrested and imprisoned without trial. A recent New Zealand army history calls this event 'a shameful episode', an assessment that few modern historians would dispute.[25] Among the 'invasion force' were the Thames Scottish Rifle Volunteers. This is the only time that a New Zealand Scottish corps has ever gone into 'action' as a discrete unit.

The Volunteers

The northern wars are only part of New Zealand's nineteenth-century military history. Defence arrangements in the colony were configured around two potential threats. The internal one posed by Maori resistance to Pakeha settlement preoccupied the settler governments of the first few decades of New Zealand's history as a national state. Yet the wars that followed were restricted in time and place. Even at their height in 1869, when the government faced separate insurrections on both the east and west coasts of the North Island, there was never any danger of the wars becoming general. Settlers on the southern island, for example, were unaffected. Though subject to the same regulations requiring militia service as their northern neighbours, South Island militia were never called into action.[26]

It was the external threat – attacks by foreign enemies – that dominated the second great skein of New Zealand military activity in the colonial period. This was the Volunteer movement, a patchwork of voluntary units of amateur soldiers and sailors that covered the country from north to south. Modelled on British precedents, the movement was a response to prospective invasion from the sea. The Volunteers were initially established in 1860 when fears were aroused by tension between Britain and the United States. It seemed possible that New Zealand could become a target of any American aggression. Russia was the next bogey figure, a potential imperial rival in the Pacific. Neither threat was very pressing; distance alone provided New Zealand with an excellent defence, such that military spending was never high on colonial government agendas. Volunteer corps largely organised themselves, coming together at their own initiative and thereafter bearing much of the cost of uniforms, arms and training. Essentially, the Volunteers were citizen soldiers whose enthusiasm underwrote a reasonable level of military preparedness at a very modest price.[27]

Ethnic identity among the Volunteers

Ethnic identity was one of the bases upon which New Zealand's Volunteer units constructed their *esprit de corps*, but only a minor one. It was mostly a Scottish phenomenon.[28] Not surprisingly, the first Scottish Volunteer unit was established in Dunedin, capital of Scottish-founded Otago. The Scots were the dominant ethnic group in Otago, a position occupied in all the northern regions of New Zealand by the English. It is important to note, however, that over 80 per cent of Otago's Scottish pioneers were Lowlanders. This cultural background was reflected in the creation of the No. 2 Company Scottish Rifle Volunteers in Dunedin in 1863. The company was the second Dunedin Volunteer unit to be established but, purloining the motto of the Scots Greys, held themselves to be 'Second to None'. Significantly, they were *not* a kilted unit. The foundation members initially intended to adopt the uniform of the recently established London Scottish Rifle Volunteers discussed in Stuart Allan's chapter in this volume. This did involve a kilt, but in hodden grey instead of tartan.[29]

Unfortunately the business of sourcing uniforms was a perennial problem in New Zealand. The Dunedin Scots quickly settled instead on the much more readily available option of a scarlet jacket with white facings, blue trousers and a half shako with horsehair plume. This uniform made them look little different from other colonial units.

However, No. 2 Company is the exception. Distinctively Scottish uniforms were otherwise both the defining feature of New Zealand Scottish Volunteer units and their biggest problem. Sourcing the right gear from overseas suppliers continued to be difficult. It also made specifically Scottish costumes and accessories very expensive. A second Dunedin Scottish unit, for example, was organised in 1864 explicitly to be a kilted corps. This 'Highland Company' of the Dunedin Rifle Volunteers planned to wear the Black Watch tartan, sourcing uniforms from Melbourne. It is difficult to tell from surviving references if they ever managed to kit themselves out properly as they were a short-lived unit. When Volunteer regulations changed in 1866, Dunedin's Highland Company decided to disband rather than meet a new, higher unit corps membership requirement.[30] In this they were typical both of the ephemeral existence of Volunteer corps and the shifting sands of New Zealand defence policy. Dunedin's No. 2 Scottish Rifle Volunteers likewise voted themselves out of existence rather than submit to new regulations a decade later, in 1874.

In all, at least fifteen Scottish units were established in New Zealand during the Volunteer era (1860–1910). The 1870s, for example, saw Scottish corps established in Auckland, Thames, Wellington and Invercargill, stretching from one end of the country to the other. Wellington and Invercargill's corps were Highland companies – the Wellington company also choosing to wear the Black Watch kilt, which seems to have enjoyed a particular esteem in the colony – while the other two were Rifle Volunteers, uniform option unclear. All had disbanded by 1882. Volunteering received a major boost in 1885, however, when deteriorating British–Russian relations led to a major invasion scare in New Zealand. New Volunteer companies sprang up in consequence all over the country, particularly around the main port cities. A Canterbury Scottish Volunteers corps was one of them. More significant, however, was a second incarnation of the Dunedin Highland Rifles (DHR).

It was later claimed that the DHR was established by former members of the Black Watch Regiment. At a fiftieth jubilee celebration in 1925, speakers made the claim that, 'Among the founders were many men who had seen service in the mother regiment, the Royal Highlanders (Black Watch) . . .', although this seems to be something of an exaggeration.[31] The martial reputation of this famous Highland regiment lent it a particular allure in colonial military circles. Linking a local Scottish corps to the Black Watch gave it a sense of distinction, not only among members but among a discerning public who could be expected to recognise the Black Watch tartan. The DHR wore the tartan of 'the mother regiment' in any case, apparently with approval from the Black Watch, and spent large sums of money on their kit. Such costs, and the free time required for participation in corps events, meant that Volunteers were disproportionately drawn from higher-status occupations.[32] This was even more the case with the kilted units. Notwithstanding the financial challenge, the DHR proved more enduring than its predecessors, remaining active and viable until the disestablishment of the Volunteer system in 1910. Former members then developed an ex-members' organisation that was still holding reunions into the 1960s (lasting longer in fact than the unit's official period of service). The Ex-DHR Association became a key agency for promoting the Scottish military tradition in New Zealand in the twentieth century, as discussed below.

None of New Zealand's Volunteers corps were very large; they averaged forty to sixty members in total. There were many of them, however, and they played a significant role in colonial society. Their military drills, parades, camps and shooting competitions were one part of this. Their bands, balls and general participation in social events, such as sports carnivals and civic occasions, were another. The Volunteers were a popular component of Victorian society, adding dash and colour to colonial life. Seen in this light, it is easy to understand why the 'kilties' were so popular.[33] The Highland companies, accompanied by their pipes and drums, *looked* good. And since the New Zealand Volunteers never had to fire a shot in anger, looking good was quite a major part of their role. The Highlanders simply bore a heavier cost in doing so. No systematic analysis of Highland company membership has so far been attempted but it seems likely that it held a particular appeal for those with Scottish ancestry.

At war and on show

New Zealand's first military engagement overseas was the South African War in 1899, which was supported with great popular enthusiasm. Ten New Zealand contingents (6,500 men in total) were sent to the war. They were organised separately from the Volunteer system, however, and no Volunteer corps was involved as a unit. Lots of Volunteers went to South Africa, including members of the DHR and other Scottish companies, but they did so as individuals, not members of their corps.[34] War fever stimulated a surge in new Volunteer corps being created at the turn of the century. The new units included Highland companies in Christchurch, Wellington (Seaforth Highlanders uniform) and Wanganui (a Gordon Highlanders uniform made in Dunedin). The Scottish units were vastly outnumbered by the profusion of new mounted rifles corps. In Waipu, New Zealand's other special Scottish settlement, they combined the two, forming the Scottish Horse Mounted Rifle Volunteers in 1906.[35]

The popularity of the mounted corps had direct linkage to their achievements on the field of battle.[36] This had, moreover, a distinctly colonial character. The rugged independence of the mounted troopers of the New Zealand contingents was commonly perceived as a reflection of their rural New Zealand backgrounds, as was their skill with horses and as marksmen.[37] The Highland companies' missing out on the public relations opportunity offered by active combat on the veldt probably undermined their traditional appeal and suggests, perhaps, the beginning of a marginalisation of the Highland military tradition in a New Zealand context. The mounted corpsmen looked at least as dashing as the 'kilties' on parade (and faced a comparable set of additional expenses in providing their own mounts). They had the added advantage, however, of serious military credibility after the success of the New Zealand mounted troopers in South Africa.

After the South African War there was a serious reappraisal of New Zealand's defence arrangements which saw a strategic refocusing on forward defence. New Zealand forces would be designed to combine with imperial forces abroad, on the South African model. The deficiencies of the Volunteer system – the sturdy independence of the corps, the election of officers, the system's inherent inefficiencies – also came under close scrutiny. Reform, such as enforcing the adoption of a standard khaki uniform, for example, soon gave way to complete abolition. In 1910 the whole fifty-year-old corps structure was disestablished and a new Territorial Force army was created in its place, along with compulsory military training. The NCOs of Dunedin's Volunteer units gathered together for a final group portrait at this end-point. The assembled group, arrayed in distinctive unit uniforms, underscores the relatively modest numbers of the Scottish component; the kilted NCOs were visibly a small minority, no more than a minor key even in the Scottish heartland.[38]

After the end of the New Zealand Wars, race relations in New Zealand had stabilised. Maori resistance to European colonisation, which involved the often forced expropriation of tribal lands and resources, had garnered considerable respect. The race seemed to be doomed to extinction, however, as disease, poverty and high mortality rates saw Maori population numbers decline rapidly. A low-point was reached in 1896 when the Maori population was just 42,211.[39] Official policies were configured around a notion of 'smoothing the pillow for a dying race'.[40] Systematic expropriation of remaining areas of Maori land continued apace. Maori struggled on in their rural enclaves, largely apart from the European mainstream though with no formal barriers to Maori participation in colonial society and quite a lot of intermarriage. Maori could join Volunteer corps, and there were apparently some specific Maori Volunteers corps, based among the *iwi* who had been *kūpapa*. Maori leaders also offered to raise a 500-man contingent for service in South Africa in 1899 but this was turned down: imperial policy held that this was a 'white man's war' and no native troops were to be deployed. Nonetheless many Maori were keen to be part of the adventure and joined the New Zealand contingents, especially those of mixed heritage who had European names that they could use to enlist.

Maori were welcome, however, as display troops in ceremonial contingents sent overseas from New Zealand at this time. The first group went to London for Queen Victoria's diamond jubilee in 1897. A twenty-strong Maori unit was assembled for inclusion in the New Zealand party that joined hundreds of others from all over the empire for the ceremonials in England. Members were selected for their physical stature, and their tribal pedigrees. Another unit was assembled for the Australian Federation celebrations in 1901 – this one serving alongside a

Highland contingent drawn from the DHR and the Wanganui Highland Rifles. The same pattern was followed for King Edward's coronation in 1902 and King George's in 1911. Each contingent wore a standard khaki uniform (except for the 'kiltie' components) similar to that worn by New Zealand troops in South Africa. But the Maori units were expected to perform *haka* and *waiata*[41] alongside their soldierly drills and parades, and proved enormously popular with British and Australian crowds. Like the kilted Highlanders, their value, it seems, was performative rather than military in essence.

These ceremonial contingents were of huge importance to *iwi*, especially those with *kūpapa* histories. Their members were often the grandsons of men who had fought in the New Zealand wars, a record of service that they were designed to commemorate. Two of the men selected for the diamond jubilee contingent, for example, were nephews of the *kūpapa* chief Henare Tomoana, who had been presented with a sword of honour by Queen Victoria in 1869. The old chief entrusted this sword to the young men to take with them to England and to carry in the jubilee procession.[42] But while British defence planners were happy to have 'tame' Maori for show on such ceremonial occasions, they seem to have forgotten the formidable military record that went with the Maori warrior ethos. Thus, when war was declared in 1914, there was again an initial government refusal of a Maori contingent offered by the *kūpapa* tribes. This was quickly overturned, however, when news came through of Indian troops heading to France, and *Te Hokowhitu a Tū*, the First Maori Contingent, was established for service overseas in September 1914.

The First World War

The Maori first went into action at Gallipoli in 1915. They had originally been held back to serve as garrison troops and sent to Malta. The fearsome casualties experienced by New Zealand units in the first months at Gallipoli, however, saw the Maori called in as reinforcements, arriving on the peninsula on 3 July. After the famous attack on Chunuk Bair a month later, in which the Maori soldiers played a critical role, New Zealand troops recalled their excitement at tracking the progress of New Zealand advances by the sound of *haka* coming from cleared Turkish trenches.[43] A decision was quickly made, however, to turn the Maori contingent into a Pioneer Battalion. This support role, digging trenches, forming roads and performing other labouring tasks, was apparently based on fears that the small Maori population, which had reached an historic low-point of 42,000 in 1896, would not be able to maintain the flow of reinforcements required for a front-line battalion.[44] Maori leaders accepted this rationale, if reluctantly.

It is worth noting that many Maori served in the New Zealand Expeditionary Force (NZEF) outside the Maori Contingent. There were no restrictions on Maori service in any of the other New Zealand units and it was entirely a matter of personal choice for Maori recruits as to which option they might take. Thomas Grace, of Ngāti Tuwharetoa, provides one example. An old boy of Wellington College and a top Maori representative rugby player, Grace was working as a civil servant and serving in the Territorials when he enlisted with the Wellington Infantry Battalion on 13 August 1914. Appointed sergeant, he was subsequently commissioned at Gallipoli. More significantly, the battalion's commander selected Grace to head up a special unit to deal with Turkish snipers who exacted a terrible toll on the Anzac forces in the weeks after the landing. Grace's group quickly turned the tables, raiding and sniping the Turkish snipers until the New Zealanders had the ascendancy. Killed with his scouts in the August offensive, Grace was one of the outstanding New Zealand soldiers of the Gallipoli campaign.[45]

New Zealand's Scottish community fared less well than Maori in expressing its identity on the First World War battlefield. There were Burns Clubs, Caledonian and Highland societies and clan associations in many areas of New Zealand by the early twentieth century.[46] In September 1915 a combined conference was held in Palmerston North by representatives of these various Scottish organisations to consider a proposal to form a New Zealand Scottish Regiment for service overseas. A delegation led by Sir Walter Buchanan, a member of the Legislative Council, subsequently waited on the defence minister, James Allen. Their proposal was for a Highland regiment, similar to Canadian units and the London Scottish Regiment, and wearing a khaki kilt. It was to be composed of men of Scottish birth or parentage. This idea had been circularised previously among 135 Scottish organisations across New Zealand and the delegation considered itself as representative of 'united Scottish interests in the Dominion'.[47]

The deputation included one notable non-Scot in Sir James Carroll, a *kūpapa* veteran and the leading Maori politician of the day. Sir James had been intimately involved in the formation of the Maori Contingent the year before and no doubt the Maori precedent was part of the Scots' arsenal of arguments. So, too, was their claim that New Zealand Scots were heading for 'Home' to join kilted regiments there.[48] Their offer was rejected, however. The minister pointed out that any unit so created would also need to be sustained for at least two years with further batches of reinforcements.[49] More important though was the precedent that a Scottish regiment would create: 'If such offers were accepted the New Zealand Forces would not be a national army, which had been the desire at the back of its formation.'[50] The government's policy was hostile to the principle of units with alternative identifications, be they Scottish, or Irish, or English.[51] Maori identity was to be the unique exception to this rule.

Those of Scottish birth or descent thus took their place in the Expeditionary Force as New Zealanders, and nothing else, just as they had had to do in the earlier conflict in South Africa. There was no place for kilts, not even the khaki version that the Scottish societies had offered to fund for their planned regiment, nor any tartan or thistles in the NZEF's uniform or accoutrements. Bagpipes were another matter. A number of the New Zealand infantry battalions operated pipe bands, though these do not seem to have enjoyed official status.[52] Dunedin's Scottish societies – the Burns Club, Gaelic Society and Caledonian Society – presented the Otago Infantry Battalion of the Main Body of the NZEF with eight

Figure 8.1 The Dunedin Highland Rifles pose with rifles and kitbags in central Dunedin. Collection of Toitū Otago Settlers Museum.

Figure 8.2 Inscribed pipe band from the Dunedin Scottish Societies' bagpipes recovered from the battlefield at Gallipoli. Collection of Toitū Otago Settlers Museum.

Figure 8.3 Cap badge of the New Zealand Scottish Regiment. Collection of Toitū Otago Settlers Museum.

sets of bagpipes before it embarked for war service abroad in September 1914.[53] The troops piped their way through Dunedin prior to their departure, played the pipes at sea en route to Egypt, in camp while training there and at Gallipoli.[54]

We also know that the pipes came ashore with the first New Zealanders at Anzac on 25 April 1915. Toitū Otago Settlers Museum in Dunedin has in its collection a silver band from one of the eight sets of pipes given to the Otago Battalion, inscribed with details of the Dunedin Scottish Societies' gift. It was picked up on the beach at Anzac Cove soon after the landing by a Canadian member of the Royal Naval Division, a Lieutenant Langley.[55] He took the silver band off the bagpipes 'which he saw lying on the beach smashed to atoms, and covered with human blood'.[56] Two years later the Canadian joined the Royal Flying Corps and trained with Ronald Burns Bannerman, a New Zealander from Dunedin. He was given the silver band to take back to Dunedin and return to the Burns Club, from which it eventually passed into the museum collection.

Perhaps the most noteworthy aspect of the distinctive New Zealand identity that war-time service did so much to foment among the soldiers of the First World War was its ready recourse to Maori words and symbols.[57] Maori and Pakeha had still lived largely in parallel societies in early twentieth-century New Zealand. War service brought their young men together, often for the first time, at Gallipoli and on the western front. The intensity of their shared experience, and the high reputation earned by the Pioneers among their fellow countrymen, helped to forge new bonds across the cultural divide. Lieutenant Colonel Hughes, commanding officer of the Canterbury Battalion at Gallipoli, writing of the Maori group attached to his unit during the assault on Chunuk Bair, testified that they were 'an object lesson to us white Maoris'.[58] It was an apt phrase, foreshadowing a sense of 'indigenisation' among the descendants of the European settler groups that would gather pace generation by generation.[59] Precursor ethnic identities among Pakeha – Scottish, Irish, English – would, meanwhile, inevitably begin to fade.

The inter-war years

The inter-war years were a difficult period for New Zealand's military. There was little appetite for defence spending, especially as the economy deteriorated in the 1920s. The Regular Force army was reduced to skeletal cadres and Territorial numbers slumped.[60] There were regular calls from Scottish societies to institute a kilted Scottish unit to foster martial enthusiasm but the army proved no more amenable to the proposal than it had been in 1915. An interview in 1937 between representatives of the Council of Dunedin Scottish Societies and the Dunedin area army commanding officer, Colonel Jeffery, had drawn the unsympathetic response from the latter that 'next the Irish, Chinese and others would all want their own regiments'.[61] In times of severely reduced defence funding, there was little appetite for a new unit, and especially one with a more expensive uniform requirement. There were no Maori units either. As war clouds gathered in the late 1930s, however, New Zealand began a belated re-armament and a rapid expansion of its territorial army. When recruiters struggled to secure sufficient volunteers, there was a change of heart on the value of the 'Kilties'.

The Dunedin Highland Rifles Ex-Members Association had been working with the Council of Scottish Societies for some time for the introduction of a Scottish unit to the Territorial Force.[62] It saw such a unit as being a successor to the old DHR and indeed a 'resuscitation' of the old Volunteer unit. The Council of Scottish Societies had broadened the pitch somewhat, suggesting that such units be set up in 'all the centres of New Zealand'.[63] In the final months of 1937, Fred Jones, the minister of defence and a Labour member representing the Dunedin South electorate, instructed the army to investigate the feasibility of raising a Scottish unit. In response the army proposed that a Scottish company be added to all the infantry battalions, and that it should wear the Black Watch tartan, with that regiment's permission. It would be up to the various Scottish societies to provide recruits 'of unblemished Scots descent' and contribute towards the cost of uniforms.[64]

Support for this scheme was offered by Scottish organisations in South Canterbury, Wellington, Auckland, Marlborough and Taranaki, as well as by national bodies like the Piping and Dancing Association.[65] The army noted, however, that the Scottish groups were generally not prepared to contribute to uniform costs. The commanding officers of the infantry battalions were all opposed to the idea, except for the Dunedin-based commander of 3 Composite Battalion. Thus, no action was taken. A request in 1938 from the commander of the Southern Military District to form an independent Highland Company in Dunedin was also declined. Scottish groups from around the country continued their advocacy and by late 1938 were prepared to contribute to the additional costs of a Highland uniform. In October 1938 the Chief of the General Staff added his support to the cause, noting how much of a contribution a 500-strong Highland Company would make to the under-strength Territorial Force.[66]

In January 1939 the creation of the New Zealand Scottish Regiment (NZ Scots) was gazetted. It was to consist of four companies of 125 men each, based in Auckland, Wellington, Christchurch and Dunedin. The Scottish societies were to play a role in recruit selection, which required Scottish ancestry regardless of birthplace. Each recruit was also required to contribute £1 on attestation, while the societies were to match this sum for each man selected. Their arguments about the appeal of the kilt to New Zealanders of Scottish ethnicity were borne out by the quick response to recruitment. Against the broader Territorial trend, all four companies reached full strength within five weeks and had waiting lists. Local fundraising also raised the Scottish societies' uniform contribution in short order. Formal agreement on affiliation with the Black Watch was concluded by the New Zealand army by March 1939 and permission granted for the New Zealand Scots to wear its famous tartan. Finally, a Gaelic motto was adopted: '*Mo Righ, Mo Dhuthaich* (My King, My Country).'

The Second World War

When war was declared in September 1939, New Zealand put together a second Expeditionary Force for service abroad on the same basis as in 1914. The country's eight Territorial battalions (including the New Zealand Scottish) were embodied for training in 1940 but candidates for overseas service would move on from training to newly formed battalions created solely for the war's duration. The New Zealand Scottish Regimental Association, formed to co-ordinate the Scottish societies' support for the NZ Scots, met with the minister of defence in January 1940 to pitch the idea of a Scottish battalion for overseas service. This, they maintained, would enable the Territorial unit members to retain their Scottish identity and build up a tradition. They also argued that with the precedent of a Maori battalion, discussed below, the Scots also deserved their own battalion for overseas service since the Scots ethnic group represented about one-sixth of the New Zealand population. New Zealand, they claimed, was the only Dominion without such a unit in its overseas forces.[67]

The minister took counsel from the army's director of mobilization, who was characteristically hostile to the Scots' cause. The New Zealand Division – the military form of the 2nd New Zealand Expeditionary Force – was, he claimed, 'too small for fractions; next the Irish would want their own battalion.'[68] Minister Jones therefore denied the Scottish request, commenting that 'the main purpose of the New Zealand Expeditionary Force was to create an esprit de division not an esprit de corps within units'. This went to the nub of the issue. New Zealand's military authorities believed that their formations were simply too small to allow for such strands of identity to be embodied in separate units. The New Zealand Division was to be a vehicle for national identity formation. The sole exception, as in the First World War, was for the country's indigenous people who could logically be seen as expressing a sub-set of New Zealand identity in a way that ethnic Scots did not.

As in the First World War, Maori leaders were determined to have a distinctive Maori unit serving overseas. They were insistent, moreover, that this time Maori troops should see front-line service, both to fulfil Maoridom's warrior heritage and, as Sir Apirana Ngata, the foremost Maori politician of the day, argued, as 'the price of citizenship'.[69] As he asserted, 'We are of one house, and if our Pakeha brothers fall, we fall with them. How can we even hold up our heads, when the struggle is over, to the question, "Where were you when New Zealand was at war?"'[70] Grievances over land loss and discriminatory treatment in New Zealand were put aside for the war's duration. The Maori population had bounced back dramatically from its late nineteenth-century nadir, more than doubling between the wars to 87,000, or 5.4 per cent of the total population, in 1938. Sir Apirana pushed the recruitment cause remorselessly, confident that his people could supply reinforcements for an infantry battalion. Ironically the existence of the NZ Scots was cited as a precedent for forming an ethnically based Maori unit.[71] The 28th (Maori) Battalion was the result. It proved to be New Zealand's flagship unit of the war, unrivalled in the highly regarded New Zealand Division with a record of valour through Greece, Crete, and the Middle East and Italian campaigns, and the highest casualty rates of any of the New Zealand battalions in the New Zealand Division.[72]

The Maori Battalion had no dress distinctions and it outwardly conformed to the structure and military culture of the New Zealand army. It was, however, steeped in the Maori warrior ethos, organised around tribal identities and *tikanga Maori* (Maori cultural protocols). As in the First World War, the *haka* beloved of British crowds in the turn-of-the-century imperial celebrations, were performed, both as entertainment and as an actual prelude to battle in the traditional manner. *Haka* also erupted spontaneously in the heat of battle, allied to vicious bayonet charges and hand-to-hand combat that terrified the pride of the German army and recalled ancient inter-tribal warfare.[73] All of New Zealand thrilled to the exploits of the Maori Battalion, and other New Zealand troops took pride in serving alongside them.[74] Comparisons were made with the martial reputation of Highlanders.[75] On one famous occasion the two martial traditions came together. At El Alamein in a night attack on 23–4 October 1942, the Maori *haka*'d as they advanced while on their flank the Highland Division marched into battle to the sound of bagpipes: 'From their right flank the New Zealanders heard the wail of bagpipes calling the Highland Division to battle, while their own battle cries, and the *haka* of the Maori Battalion rose and fell against the roar of the guns.'[76]

The New Zealand Scottish Regiment meanwhile languished at home as a Territorial training unit. It was, however, expanded into two battalions in December 1940, one in the North Island, one in the South. Briefly, in 1942, it looked as though the North Island-based 1st Battalion might see active service overseas. As in the First World War, the army worked on the principle of a 'national army', with the Territorial battalions feeding into Regular Force battalions, organised geographically. But, exceptionally, a couple of the Territorial battalions were to go overseas as distinct units. In late 1942, the 1st Battalion New Zealand Scottish Regiment was despatched to New Caledonia to train for service in the Solomon Islands as part of the New Zealand 3rd Division. Six months later, however, and without any warning or reason being given, the battalion was disbanded, broken up to provide reinforcements to other active service units. The unit's Scottishness had nothing to do with the decision. It was simply a by-product of New Zealand's growing manpower shortages and the challenges of supporting two divisions of infantry overseas. The same fate befell the 2nd Battalion back in New Zealand which had trained over 1,800 men over its four-year existence. Officially the NZ Scots went into suspended animation.

Post-war to the present

New Zealand's Maori and Scottish military strands had experienced sharply different trajectories during the war. Their fates in post-war New Zealand were equally contrasting. Briefly, the New Zealand (NZ) Scottish Regiment was revived in 1948 in a Cold War expansion of the New Zealand Territorial Army that saw the re-introduction of peace-time conscription, or compulsory military training. Almost immediately, the infantry regiment was converted into an Armoured Corp unit, with a squadron in each of the four main centres. Hundreds of men went through the NZ Scottish Regiment in this era and a strong esprit de corps developed around its Scottish identity, which was based on recruits having at least a Scots-born grandparent. This identity was particularly strong in Dunedin and Auckland.[77] The uniforms funded by the Scottish societies in 1939 (the Black Watch kilt) were still being used for ceremonial purposes. The NZ Scottish Territorial Association also offered strong support and a link with other Scottish cultural organisations.

Compulsory military training ended in New Zealand in 1960. Volunteer recruits provided a much-reduced flow of personnel thereafter and many Territorial units were combined or disbanded. In 1963 the NZ Scottish Regiment was reduced to two squadrons, both based in the South Island. Its role and designations changed repeatedly[78] and in 1980 it was proposed to disestablish the regiment altogether. A rearguard action was mounted from Dunedin; there was a petition supported by all the city's Scottish societies. Perhaps more crucially, there was a public meeting with ex-members of the regiment, fronted for the army by a Maori brigadier, Brian Poananga. The brigadier was surprised to find himself being harangued in Maori by a former NZ Scottish member about the importance of the Scottish military tradition and comparing this with the Maori warrior heritage.[79]

The regiment survived but was soon reduced to a single, Dunedin-based squadron. Over time this remnant of the sole New Zealand Scottish army unit atrophied to the point where it existed in name only.[80] With the regionalisation of the New Zealand Territorial Force between 1998 and 2000, the 'NZ Scots' was subsumed into the Otago Southland Regiment. To begin with it remained a distinct element as a company and then a platoon but eventually the NZ Scots personnel simply filled roles within the regiment with no distinct Scottish element. The NZ Scottish had been 'suspended' as an entity since 2001 and in 2014 it was planned to formally de-activate the unit and lay up its colours. This did not happen. Instead, the title has been transferred to a squadron of the Queen Alexandra's Mounted Rifles, New Zealand Armoured Corps, based at Linton Army Camp near Palmerston North. Intended to 'maintain a historical link and keep some of those past units [sic] traditions alive', the identity is vestigial at best. Meanwhile, the unit's kilts can still be worn by officers on the retired list, former unit members now posted to the southern 2/4 Infantry Battalion, or by personnel parading the regimental colours.[81]

The 28th (Maori) Battalion, meanwhile, passed into history on its return to New Zealand in 1946. No specifically Maori units were created in either the Regular Force or the Territorials in its wake. What happened instead was a steady 'browning' of the army in general. Young Maori took inspiration from the 28th Battalion and developed career paths in the military at a much higher rate than in other sectors of the New Zealand job market. In a 1977 survey, for example, almost 34 per cent of the Regular Force and 16 per cent of the Territorials identified as Maori, a much higher proportion than in the general population (11.6% in 1976).[82] A cultural resurgence of Maori across New Zealand life also swept through the army. During the army's sesquicentennial in 1995 it formally adopted a Maori name – Ngāti Tūmatauenga (tribe of the warrior god) – and opened a national army marae at the main army base at Waiouru. Since then, Maori tikanga has infused army institutional life at every level.[83] Perhaps most dramatically, the *haka* has become a key expression of New Zealand military identity. This is true for all the members of the 'tribe', Maori and Pakeha.

Outside the dominant 'English' military culture, which informs so much of New Zealand's military customs and traditions, there has been little room for alternative expressions of ethnic military identity. In fact, however, the desire for ethnically branded military units has been unique to the Scottish and Maori communities in New Zealand. Despite the New Zealand authorities' oft-cited fear that acknowledging one ethnic tradition would open the floodgates to other claimant ethnicities, there were only ever these two. Military Scottishness was early in the ascendant, with over a dozen Scottish units striding out in their kilts in the heyday of the Volunteer movement. Yet in the wider scheme of things, this was a rather modest expression of cultural identity, limited in numbers and light on long-term military and cultural impact. Military Scottishness proved to be no more than a thin veneer and its failure to embed itself in the history-making New Zealand expeditionary forces of the two world wars arguably doomed it to long-term irrelevance.

The Maori warrior tradition, on the other hand, did implant itself in an emerging New Zealand military culture through action on the field of battle. Rooted in the very landscape of New Zealand as an integral part of Maori culture, the cult of *Tūmatauenga* (the God of War) forged for itself a primacy in expressing a distinctive New Zealand military identity that no imported ethnic tradition could compete with. As Scottish military traditions have faded, along with a general 'ethnic fade' that has sapped the vitality of New Zealand's Scottish associational culture, Maori elements have come increasingly to the fore.[84] Increasingly, New Zealanders wanting to express their distinctiveness in a globalised world reach for symbols and cultural practices unique to New Zealand to do so.[85] Tribal tattoos, pounamu charms and *haka* have thus spread well beyond the Maori community as expressions of New Zealand-ness. And so too, New Zealand soldiers, whatever their ethnic background, have become the tribe of the warrior god, *Ngāti Tūmatauenga*.

Notes

1. Christopher Pugsley, *Te Hokowhitu a Tu* (Auckland: Reed, 1995).
2. '... the Maori Pioneer Battalion ... [was] an outstanding unit, not easy to command but responsive to good leadership. Its reputation has been overshadowed by its successor in the Second World War, the 28th Maori Battalion, yet the second built on

the spirit and experience of the first.' Pugsley, *Te Hokowhitu a Tu* (1995), p. 78. See also Monty Soutar, *Nga Tama Toa: The Price of Citizenship: C Company 28 (Maori) Battalion 1939–1945* (Auckland: Bateman, 2008).
3. Ngāti Tūmatauenga became the official Maori name of the New Zealand army during its sesquicentenary in 1995. Richard Taylor, *Tribe of the War God: Ngati Tumatauenga* (Napier: Heritage New Zealand, 1996).
4. James Belich, *Making Peoples: A History of the New Zealanders from Polynesian Settlement to the End of the Nineteenth Century* (London: Penguin, 2007), p. 315.
5. *Pakeha* is a term used to denote New Zealanders of European descent, or more broadly for non-Maori New Zealanders.
6. Quoted in Anne Salmond, *Between Worlds: Early Exchanges between Maori and Europeans 1773–1815* (Auckland: Viking, 1997), p. 25. This work and its predecessor, *Two Worlds: First Meetings between Maori and Europeans 1642–1772* (Auckland: Viking, 1991), offer the best modern overview of early contact between Maori and the European world.
7. *Haka* is sometimes called a 'war dance'. It is actually something more than that, part of the ritual of engagement of traditional combat. *Haka* is probably most familiar to international audiences in the pre-game performance of the *haka* 'Ka Mate' by the New Zealand All Blacks rugby team.
8. *Moko* is the facial and body tattooing that was an important component of traditional Maori culture.
9. See Salmond, as above.
10. Distance of course was probably the major factor. Belich notes that New Zealand was considered alongside New South Wales as a site for Britain's penal colony in the 1780s, 'but the natives were thought to be too dangerous and bloodthirsty'. Belich, *Making Peoples*, p. 129.
11. Peter Cooke and John Crawford, *The Territorials: The History of the Territorial and Volunteer Forces of New Zealand* (Auckland: Random House, 2011) p. 31. The dominant ethnic group among nineteenth-century New Zealand immigrants was the English component, with Scots and Irish the other major strands. Proportions varied at different times, and between the various settlements, but Scots were the major group only in the southern part of the South Island. For a detailed overview, see Jock Phillips and Terry Hearn, *Settlers: New Zealand Immigrants from England, Ireland & Scotland 1800–1945* (Auckland: Auckland University Press, 2008).
12. At the same time, many clans remained loyal to the Hanoverian regime and anti-Stuart. Thomas M. Devine, *The Scottish Nation 1700–2007* (London: Penguin, 2006), p. 40.
13. Edward M. Spiers, *The Scottish Soldier and Empire, 1854–1902* (Edinburgh: Edinburgh University Press, 2006), p. 112.
14. Charles Withers, 'The Historical Creation of the Scottish Highlands', in Ian Donnachie and Christopher Whatley (eds), *The Manufacture of Scottish History* (Edinburgh: Polygon, 1992), pp. 143–56.
15. Belich, *Making Peoples*, p. 134.
16. The monument erected to their memory at the regiment's Hobart base is actually the first war memorial in Australian history.
17. James Belich, 'Cameron, Duncan Alexander – Biography', from the *Dictionary of New Zealand Biography, Te Ara – the Encyclopedia of New Zealand*, http://www.TeAra.govt.nz/en/biographies/1c2/1 (last accessed 10 September 2014).
18. Rewi is credited with the famous riposte to Cameron's call to surrender at Orakau in 1864: 'Ka whawhai tonu matou, Ake! Ake! Ake!' (We will fight on for ever and

ever). Manuka Henare, 'Maniapoto, Rewi Manga', from the *Dictionary of New Zealand Biography. Te Ara – the Encyclopedia of New Zealand*, http://www.TeAra.govt.nz/en/biographies/1m8/maniapoto-rewi-manga (last accessed 14 September 2014).

19. The best modern account of the wars is James Belich, *The New Zealand Wars and the Victorian Interpretation of Racial Conflict* (Auckland: Penguin, 1988).
20. Belich, 'Cameron, Duncan Alexander'.
21. The British government was also becoming reluctant to use imperial troops for garrison duties in the colonies and by the mid-1860s was considering levying colonial administrations a charge of £40 per annum for each imperial soldier on its soil. See Taylor, *Tribe of the War God*, p. 27.
22. An analysis of the birthplaces of soldiers from four regiments (18th, 58th, 65th, 68th) who took their discharges in New Zealand showed just 2.3 per cent were Scots compared to 39.7 per cent who were English or Welsh and 50.3 per cent who were Irish. In actual numbers, those analysed are 2281 out of the 3601 discharges to 1870. Figures supplied by Dr Brad Patterson from 'Green Redcoats? The Irish as a Component of the Imperial Military Forces in Early Colonial New Zealand', unpublished paper delivered to ISAANZ Conference, University of Otago, November 2012, pp. 11–12. His data is drawn from Hugh and Lyn Hughes, *Discharged in New Zealand: Soldiers of the Imperial Foot Regiments who took their Discharge in New Zealand 1840–1870* (Auckland: New Zealand Society of Genealogists, 1988). The proportion of Scottish veterans does not seem to have risen much through the subsequent migrant inflow. In 1902, while he was governor of the colony, the earl of Ranfurly gathered information on surviving veterans resident in New Zealand who had served in imperial forces anywhere in the world between 1840 and 1902. Scottish regimental affiliations are very poorly represented on his list. *Roll of honour, 1840–1902 [microform]: Defenders of the Empire Resident in New Zealand* (Auckland: New Zealand Society of Genealogists, 1988).
23. Although this is really a term of abuse, essentially meaning 'collaborators'.
24. The last actual combat engagements were in 1872 but the threat of further armed insurrection by Maori remained for another decade.
25. Cooke and Crawford, *The Territorials*, p. 79.
26. Service in the New Zealand militia units was restricted to a 30-mile zone around each militia district's central post office.
27. The capitation grant paid by the government to 'efficient Volunteers', for example, did not cover the costs incurred by the various corps, who made up the difference from their own funds. See Cooke and Crawford, *The Territorials*, p. 84.
28. There were also one or two Irish units but they proved relatively short-lived and made little long-term impact on New Zealand's military tradition.
29. This was a deliberate strategy by the London company's first commanding officer (CO), Lord Elcho, to avoid any clan rivalries in a unit developed (in 1859) to cater for a pan-Scottish identity. See Stuart Allan's chapter in this volume.
30. *Otago Daily Times*, 9 April 1866, p. 4.
31. Toitū Otago Settlers Museum Archives (TOSM), Dunedin, AG-143. Newspaper cutting, Dunedin Highland Rifles Ex-Members' Association. The uniform used as a model was that of former Black Watch member Sergeant James Kennedy, brought with him to New Zealand in 1883. *Otago Daily Times*, 24 September 1945, p. 8. In later years this uniform was displayed at gatherings of the Dunedin Highland Rifles Ex-Members' Association and Kennedy described as one of the corps' founding members. In 1945 Kennedy's uniform was offered to the Otago Early Settlers Museum (now Toitū Otago Settlers Museum) but turned down as having 'no connection with the Early Settlers'. OESA Archives, letter to Mr G. W. Hill, 9 November 1945. I was

unable to find any other founding member of the corps with a verifiable Black Watch pedigree.
32. Cooke and Crawford, *The Territorials*, p. 84.
33. 'Kilties' was commonly used in newspaper accounts as a short-hand term for the Highland units.
34. An illuminated address was published in 1902 giving the names of all the Dunedin Volunteer corps members who had served. The largest number, fifteen names, were credited to the DHR. TOSM 1979/104/7. *1st Battalion Otago Rifle Volunteers List Of Officers & Men Belonging To The Battalion Who Served In The War In South Africa, 1899–1902* (Dunedin: J. Wilkie & Co. Ltd, 1902).
35. Stephen Ladanyi, 'The New Zealand Scottish Regiment: a Brief History 1939–1982', extended essay for Master of Arts degree, University of Canterbury, Christchurch, New Zealand, 1982, p. 33.
36. The rapid growth in mounted Volunteer units after the war in South Africa, in Otago growing from 256 in 1899 to 981 in 1903, indicates how the war 'had enhanced the prestige of the mounted rifles'. Don Mackay (ed.), *The Troopers' Tale: The History of the Otago Mounted Rifles* (Dunedin: Turnbull Ross Publishing, 2012), p. 85.
37. 'Indeed the [New Zealand] "Rough Riders" with their dusty mounts, bandoliers of bullets, weaponry and swaggering gait evoked images every bit as romantic as those of the American frontier.' Michael King, *The Penguin History of New Zealand* (Melbourne: Penguin, 2003), p. 288.
38. Dunedin NCOs' Club last parade, 1910, photograph in TOSM collection, Album 38, p. 29. Even in Dunedin, the acknowledged stronghold of Scottish identity in New Zealand, there were only ever three Scottish Volunteer units among the dozens of military corps established there between 1860 and 1910. The Scottish units' membership may have numbered in their hundreds over this period but that was dwarfed by the thousands involved in the wider Dunedin Volunteer movement. Though a large proportion of Dunedin Volunteers would have been of Scottish ethnicity, most did not join the Scottish corps.
39. *Total and Māori populations, 1858–2013 Censuses of Population and Dwellings* (Statistics New Zealand, 2014).
40. This paraphrases colonial politician Dr Isaac Featherston's 1856 statement that the duty of Europeans was to 'smooth down . . . [the] dying pillow' of the Māori race. Quoted in Peter Buck (Te Rangi Hīroa), 'The passing of the Maori', *Transactions and Proceedings of the Royal Society of New Zealand*, 55 (1924), pp. 362–75, at p. 362.
41. Waiata are songs, often performed with actions.
42. *Feilding Star*, 28 July 1897.
43. The Maori companies were in fact distributed among the New Zealand battalions for this action and both Maori *and* Pakeha New Zealanders used the *haka* as they fought together up the hillsides. Second Lieutenant Tikao, leading a party of southern Maori alongside the Otago Battalion, recorded that, 'In the meantime my South boys under Captain Dansey, were charging on our right about half a mile away from us. As soon as we had cleared our first trench, when we heard them screaming "Ka mate, ka mate" we knew they were at it too. This started the ball rolling, and every charge the New Zealand pakehas made that night you would hear "Ka mate, ka mate, ka ora, ka ora!"' Monty Soutar, 'Kua Whewehe Matou! Breaking up the Maori Contingent and the Ordering Home of Four of its Officers', in Charles Ferrall and Harry Ricketts (eds), *How We Remember: New Zealanders and the First World War* (Wellington: Victoria University Press, 2014), pp. 46–79, at p. 53.
44. The casualties experienced at Gallipoli had highlighted the numbers that maintain-

ing a front-line fighting force would entail. By September 1915 there were only sixty fit members of the Maori Contingent left of the 477 who had arrived there in July. See Pugsley, *Te Hokowhitu a Tu*, p. 44.
45. Ibid. p. 40.
46. 'The overall number of Scottish clubs and societies in New Zealand is remarkable. Up to 1930, there were at least 155 Scottish associations, 102 of which were Caledonian societies.' See Tanja Bueltmann, *Scottish Ethnicity and the Making of New Zealand Society, 1850–1930* (Edinburgh: Edinburgh University Press, 2011), p. 66.
47. *Evening Post*, 13, 25 and 28 September 1915.
48. This claim was made by Hugh Morrison of Wairarapa. There were certainly a small number of New Zealanders who set off for Britain to join Scottish regiments on the outbreak of war. See http://freepages.genealogy.rootsweb.ancestry.com/~sooty/nzers-inscottishregiments1914.html (last accessed 10 March 2014).
49. This was also the argument which had seen the Maori Contingent withdrawn from front-line service after Gallipoli, see above.
50. *Evening Post*, 28 September 1915. Allen also revealed that he previously turned down a similar 'very generous offer' from the Legion of Frontiersmen.
51. The Legion repeated its offer immediately after the Scottish delegation had met with Allen. 'He had been offered a Scottish regiment that afternoon also. And he anticipated offers of Irish, English, and Welsh regiments, but he had to be absolutely fair. Individuals must register in the ordinary way, and allow the authorities to have our army as a national army.' *Evening Post*, 29 September 1915. Allen was being disingenuous; no English, Irish or Welsh military unit was in prospect or even suggested.
52. Bandsmen are not identified as such in their service records, for instance, and seem to have served in the bands on a voluntary, perhaps semi-official, basis. There are numerous photographs, however, of pipe band groups among successive drafts of reinforcements to the Otago Regiment and others in the Auckland Infantry Regiment.
53. *Otago Witness*, 23 September 1914, p. 27.
54. *Colonist*, 7 January 1915 and *Feilding Star*, 8 September 1915. The *Otago Witness*, 12 May 1915 reports on Private Gordon Fraser of the Otago Battalion being elected pipe-major of its pipe band and acting in that capacity in Egypt.
55. *Wanganui Chronicle*, 30 January 1918.
56. TOSM catalogue, 1998/56/400.
57. This is evident in much of the trench art, souvenirs and ephemera generated by New Zealand soldiers, as well as the badges adopted by New Zealand military units. Geoffrey Oldham, *Badges and Insignia of the New Zealand Army* (Auckland: Oldham Books, 1997). Distinctive New Zealand symbolism inevitably drew on native flora and fauna as well as Maori language and culture. The same phenomenon can be observed during the Second World War, for example, in the Maori mottoes and symbols adopted by almost all of the squadrons of the Royal New Zealand Air Force, even though few Maori served in that arm of the New Zealand forces. See Paul Harrison and Brian Lockstone, *Courage in the Skies: New Zealand Airmen at War* (Wellington: Grantham House, 2011), pp. 62–5.
58. James Cowan, *The Maoris in the Great War: A History of The New Zealand Native Contingent and Pioneer Battalion: Gallipoli, 1915, France and Flanders, 1916–1918* (Auckland: Maori Regimental Committee, 1926), p. 54.
59. But 'ethnicity is situational' as Angela McCarthy notes in her book, *Scottishness and Irishness in New Zealand since 1840* (Manchester: Manchester University Press, 2011), p. 6. Modern New Zealanders might express their Scottish heritage in some contexts, establishing their ethnic roots and their commonality with a diasporic identity world-

wide. To express the *distinctiveness* of a New Zealand identity, however, there is no substitute for the culture and language unique to New Zealand.
60. In 1931 the Territorial Force's establishment was reduced from 16,000 to 10,000 but its actual strength was a mere 3,655 all ranks. See Cooke and Crawford, *The Terriorials*, p. 220.
61. Ladanyi, 'New Zealand Scottish Regiment', p. 1. No specific date in 1937 is given. This echoed James Allen's response to the Scottish delegation seeking a Scottish unit for the NZEF in 1915 discussed above. In fact, however, the desire for ethnically branded military units has been unique to the Scottish and Maori communities in New Zealand.
62. There had also been an initiative from Christchurch in 1931–2 to establish a Scottish regiment affiliated to the Gordon Highlanders. Ibid. pp. 5–6.
63. TOSM, AG-143, undated newspaper cutting, Dunedin Highland Rifles Ex-Members' Association.
64. Ladanyi, 'New Zealand Scottish Regiment', p. 2.
65. For an overview of Scottish associational culture in New Zealand, see Bueltmann, *Scottish Ethnicity*.
66. Ladanyi, 'New Zealand Scottish Regiment', p. 5.
67. Ibid. p. 9.
68. Report of Lieutenant Colonel Conway to minister of defence, quoted by Ladanyi, p. 10.
69. This catchcry was used as the title of a pamphlet written by Sir Apirana Ngata in 1943 after a member of the Maori Battalion, Second Lieutenant Moananui-a-Kiwa Ngarimu, was posthumously awarded the Victoria Cross. It was also the sub-title of a recent history of C Company of Maori Battalion, Soutar's *Ngā Tama Toa*.
70. Soutar, *Ngā Tama Toa*, p. 35.
71. The irony is emphasised by the Scottish Regimental Association's citing in their turn the formation of 28 (Maori) Battalion as a precedent for the hoped-for Scottish battalion.
72. The battalion suffered 649 fatalities from the 3,600 men who served overseas from 1940 to 1945. This was more than 10 per cent of all 2NZEF deaths in the Middle East and Europe. Another 1,712 were wounded and 237 taken prisoner. According to 2NZEF commander Lieutenant General Bernard Ferguson, 'no infantry battalion had a more distinguished record, or saw more fighting, or, alas, had such heavy casualties as the Maori Battalion'. J. F. Cody, *28 (Maori) Battalion* (Wellington: War History Branch, Department of Internal Affairs, 1956), p. v.
73. Their Pakeha commanding officer Lieutenant Colonel Humphrey Dyer later recalled an action on Crete: 'The spontaneous charge by the Maoris in the last evening at Maleme was the finest action that I saw. I believe that for sheer courage it was unsurpassed in the Middle East . . . The pride of the German army turned and fled.' Soutar, *Ngā Tama Toa*, p. 144. A battalion commander wrote home to Sir Apirana Ngata of the Maori action at Tebaga Gap in North Africa, 'The Germans were slaughtered there. Wiwi Teneti was the one who disembowelled the Germans on the hill . . . He is the one who maintains the battle practices of old in this company. The only thing he did not do was eat their flesh . . . That is why I said I saw the spirit of our warrior ancestors over our boys that day . . .' Soutar, *Ngā Tama Toa*, p. 255.
74. Lieutenant Colonel Burrows, commanding officer of the 20th Battalion, wrote of 'the truly terrible clamour that went up every time an assault was made on an enemy post. My admiration and respect for the Maori as a fighting soldier is great and it has never wavered.' Ibid. p. 142.
75. 'Good infantry, wrote Dyer, are born and raised close to the soil . . . Gurkha,

Highlander, Pole, Maori . . .' Wira Gardiner, *Te Mura o Te Ahi: the story of the Maori Battalion* (Auckland: Reed, 1992), p. 73.
76. Taylor, *Tribe of the Warrior God*, p. 72.
77. Personal communication from Les Cantwell (ex-NZ Scots), February 2012. An indication of the strength of ethnic Scottish numbers in southern New Zealand was captured in 1953 when Major General Douglas Wimberley of the Queen's Own Cameron Highlanders wrote to the honorary colonel of the Otago-Southland Infantry Regiment (to which his unit was affiliated) seeking information on how many members of the New Zealand regiment had clan surnames. The answer was 417 out of a thousand or so members, a number which surprised the Scottish enquirer. 'I am duly impressed with your Clan names . . . Twenty-two Camerons and thirty-five MacDonalds is most impressive to a Cameron Highlander.' Hocken Collections, Dunedin, Falconer Papers, MS-0804, Wimberley to Falconer, 10 September 1953.
78. A formal sequence of these roles and designations is outlined in a statement emailed to the author by the Heritage section of the New Zealand army, 4 February 2015.
79. Personal communication from Les Cantwell (ex-NZ Scots), February 2012.
80. Personal communications: Les Cantwell, Colonel Roger McElwain, Major Terry Kinloch, February–March 2012.
81. Personal communication, New Zealand Army, 4 February 2015.
82. Cooke and Crawford, *The Territorials*, p. 371. In 1976 there were 270,035 Maori among a total population of 3,129,383. '1858–2013 Censuses of Population and Dwellings' (Statistics New Zealand, 2014).
83. Even the Otago-Southland Regiment has a Maori motto – *Kia Mate Toa* – and a Maori warrior on its corps badge (though this was inherited from the Southland Regiment and goes back to its formation).
84. The decline of the Scottish associational culture is evident in the shrinking numbers and faltering activity of traditional stalwart groups like the Caledonian Society of Otago and the Dunedin Burns Club, while the Gaelic Society of New Zealand folded altogether in 2006.
85. This may be particularly important for New Zealanders, coming as they do from a small and geographically isolated country that plays a very modest part in the tide of international affairs.

9

Scottish Ethnic Associationalism, Military Identity and Diaspora Connections in the Late Nineteenth and Early Twentieth Centuries

Tanja Bueltmann

In 1856 Sydney-based *Freeman's Journal*, a paper catering for the Catholic Irish immigrant community in the city,[1] reported on the patriotism of the Scots. The paper was asking why 'a Scotchman [is] a more genuine, more unmistakable patriot than an Englishman – a Frenchman – an Irishman', and the answer was clear for the writer:

> Because there is no cant about his [the Scot's] patriotism. He does not love Scotia so much as he loves Scotchmen; he does not allow his mind to rest satisfied with a mere pleasing sentimentalism; he thinks and acts for his countrymen. This is the sovereign test of true patriotism.

Consequently, the paper went on, 'true love of country . . . is best recognized by deeds',[2] and in the Scottish immigrant community such deeds were carried especially well by means of ethnic clubs and societies. Through these, the report concluded, the Scots were 'acting together for each other's benefit' – and 'no matter how long he may have been absent from his native land'.[3] In fact, so profound was the Scots' commitment to ethnic associations – at least according to a story published in the *Belfast News-Letter* – that two Scots shipwrecked on a remote island in the Atlantic, by the time the captain of a ship who came upon them by coincidence, had founded on that island a variety of associations, including a St Andrew's Society and a Burns Club. The two were also hosting Highland Games and had established both a curling and a golf club.[4] As the newspaper aptly concluded, the Scots 'may be defined as an Association-forming people'.[5]

This humorous take on the Scots' propensity to come together in ethnic clubs and societies should not detract from a critical fact: Scottish associationalism remains one of the defining characteristics of the Scottish diaspora near and far to this day. In New Zealand, the British Empire's farthest outpost, there were at least 130 Scottish ethnic associations by the early twentieth century; these were chiefly comprised of Caledonian societies, but also Burns clubs and Gaelic societies. A few decades later, the 1928–9 *Scots Year Book* lists 1,288 Scottish societies around the world, though not all of them were actually ethnic societies. Still, even if the non-ethnic associations are taken out, for instance Presbyterian church groups,[6] nearly 600 associations remain. First carried overseas in the 'cultural baggage' of Scottish migrants, the Scots soon developed a rich panoply of ethnic clubs and societies in the new worlds in which they settled. But the gathering together of migrants with shared ethnic origins is, of course, not a characteristic specific to the Scots: in fact, it remains a common migrant response post-migration and settlement in a new place.[7] This is the case first and foremost because ethnic associations, together with kinship networks, are key tools migrants can use to counteract a sense of dislocation: both associations and networks have the power to serve as safety nets, for the purpose of utilising patronage or to generate social capital.[8]

Yet while the Scots' case of ethnic associationalism was not exceptional, they deserve particular attention because they were its original facilitators in many, if not most, places of settlement, spearheading their establishment. This was a direct result of the way in which Scots utilised their ethnicity in an active way: acting, as the *Freeman's Journal* had aptly noted, for their countrymen. In so doing, those Scots who founded ethnic clubs and societies became agents in the making of their collective identity, utilising and actively employing their Scottishness: they became active agents within the structures offered by associations.[9] This is a critical point of difference to migrant groups whose identity is largely determined by the ascriptions of others: as I have explained elsewhere, 'active agency vests definatory power with the ethnic group itself rather than others'.[10]

But although Scottish migrants showed great zeal in establishing a plentiful array of clubs and societies around the world, the rich story of their associational culture has received only patchy coverage. The principal reason for this is that, for a long time, ethnic associations have been hidden behind a terminology of nostalgia and romantic sentiments echoing those of the literary Kailyard school,[11] with associational activities being perceived by many to simply replicate old world traditions for the purpose of keeping alive the memory of the native land. This view of ethnic associationalism has been further entrenched by the idea that immigrant associations were a preserve for an urban middle-class elite that was, according to Charlotte Erickson, 'not in touch' with the wider immigrant community.[12] This view has been challenged recently by scholars, including myself, who recognise that ethnic associations serve much more varied purposes, providing a unique means to capture the experiences of migrants, their activities and networks, while also helping to unravel how they shaped host societies and cultures more broadly.

The development and global spread of Scottish ethnic associations

The Scots' ethnic associations were modelled on early modern British county feast societies. Organised in the seventeenth century in the major urban centres of the British and Irish Isles, regional or 'county feast' societies were generally composed of merchants, traders and lesser gentry who originated from common counties. These societies were characterised by their annual meetings, processions, sermons and dinners, which were held for the purposes of charity but also to facilitate the integration of members into urban society.[13] Among the Scots these early associations were founded, first, in the population centres of England, Scotland's near diaspora. In the early development period this essentially meant a concentration in London, though other centres such as Norwich and Bristol were also important.[14] But the tradition of associationalism soon extended its reach, crossing the Atlantic in the seventeenth century. The first Scottish ethnic society in North America was founded in 1657, when the Scots' Charitable Society was set up in Boston, Massachusetts.[15] This association was not only the first Scottish ethnic organisation founded in the New World, but also the first such society of any ethnic group; moreover, it is the oldest charitable society still in existence in the United States today.[16] The Boston Society was established to provide 'temporary relief'.[17] With this a charitable tradition was established that was to become the *sin qua non* of Scottish ethnic associations in North America.

Scottish migrants who made their way to North America from the eighteenth century onwards followed this spirit of clubbing together, focusing on the provision of charity in combination with elements of sociability.[18] The union of 1707, through which Scotland gained access to the British Empire and began peopling it in great numbers, facilitated the proliferation of Scottish clubs and societies in the settler colonies and beyond. The principal carriers of the charitable tradition were St Andrew's societies, the first of which was founded in Charleston, South Carolina, in 1729, with Philadelphia (1749), Savannah, Georgia (1750) and New York (1756) following suit. The origins of the New York St Andrew's Society offer a more detailed view on how and why St Andrew's societies were founded. On 19 November 1756 'a number of gentlemen, natives of Scotland or of direct Scottish descent' had gathered in New York City for the purpose of forming a Scottish society. The express role of the new society was 'to be the charitable relief of those fellow-Scotsmen, resident in New York, who might be in want or distress'.[19] Activities came to a halt during the American War of Independence, but resumed quickly thereafter with a new constitution. This, finalised in 1794, sets out:

> When people fall into misfortune and distress in any part of the world, remote from the place of their nativity, they are ever ready to apply for relief to those originally from the same country, on the supposition that they may possibly have connections by blood with some of them, or at least know something of their relations. For these reasons, the natives of Scotland, and those descended of Scotch Parentage, in the State of New York, have formed themselves into a Charitable Society, the principal design of which is to raise and keep a sum of money in readiness for the above laudable purpose.[20]

The New York Society was led by a president, two vice-presidents, six managers, two chaplains, a physician, a treasurer, a secretary and an assistant secretary – an organisational framework that was common for most St Andrew's societies. Membership was restricted to 'Scotsmen and the children and grandchildren of a native of Scotland', with the payment of a $12 entrance fee, and an annual subscription of $2.50, securing membership. This type of exclusive, Scots-only approach was common in North America, but not automatic: some organisations used membership definitions that were less tight. Moreover, parameters certainly changed over time: when it became more difficult for associations to maintain a healthy membership, criteria for becoming a member were often relaxed.

Overall, Scottish ethnic associations were slower to emerge in Canada. This is not, however, a sign of a protracted development, but rather an immediate result of migration trends as Canada only emerged as a more prominent destination for Scottish emigrants after the American Revolution, with migration only significantly proliferating from the mid-nineteenth century. The earliest Scottish association in Canada was set up in Halifax, Nova Scotia 'by local, mostly Lowland, Scottish elites in 1768'.[21] Originally called the North British Society, or Scots Club, 'the objects which our founders had in view appear to have been the assistance of Scottish emigrants landing in the Colony, and the establishment of a medium of communication with kindred Societies in the neighbouring Provinces'.[22] Inland, in Montreal, the St Andrew's Society developed out of the St Andrew's Day Dinner Committee in 1835.[23] Political currents, especially the 'instability caused by the rebellions in both Canadas',[24] had also played their part in the city and elsewhere in Canada, contributing to a heightened sense of ethnic identity and expression among the British immigrant community in the 1830s.[25] In Canada, too, charity lay at the heart:

> To a person far removed from the land of his nativity, and at a distance from those friends, to whom he could apply for relief when in the hour of misfortune and distress, the friendly assistance of those who own a common home and boast a common origin is always cheering to the heart and acts as a balm to a wounded spirit ... With a view to regulate charity in a systematic manner, to prevent imposition on the one hand and to relieve the truly indigent and distressed on the other – to afford advice and information to fellow countrymen far from the scene of their nativity – to promote the welfare of the emigrant and to aid him in forming a settlement, from which he is hereafter to derive happiness and independence, it is proposed to form among the Sons of Scotia resident in Montreal, a charitable Society, based upon these principles and directed solely to advance the cause and welfare of Scotchmen and their descendants.[26]

The relief provided by St Andrew's societies in North America came in diverse forms, ranging from the handing out of cash to the provision of meal tickets and support with finding employment. This could include arrangements for rail tickets to other cities where job prospects were better. At times, when other measures had failed, societies also offered return passages to Britain. The Montreal St Andrew's Society's annual report for 1867 documents 'that 105 persons had been helped on their way, at a cost of $224.65; that 192 cords of wood had been distributed to the city poor, with 1,120 loaves of bread, 2,400 lbs. Meal, and $69.47 in small sums of money – the whole work of the committee costing $1,341.05.'[27] Generally the charity provided by most St Andrew's societies followed the ideal expressed in the motto of the Toronto St Andrew's Society – 'to help them to help themselves' – stressing that the best charity was one that enabled migrants to better their situation long term rather than just carry out short-term fire-fighting.[28] The type of aid provided also depended on the recipient, however: widows or old people, for instance, frequently received cash in support, while those who could work – and were thus considered able to actively improve their lives themselves – tended to be given other forms of support. From the late nineteenth century helping the elderly became a particular focus in a number of cities. The St Andrew's Society of Illinois, for instance, established a Scottish Old People's Home in 1901 to address the issue of poverty in old age.

Yet while charity was critical in the Scots' ethnic associational culture in North America, it was changing in light of the continuous arrival of new migrants from Scotland, and also the increasing pressure through alternative social pursuits on offer for people. It was partly as a response to these pressures that two new, and distinct, types of Scottish ethnic associations developed in North America: Caledonian societies, which brought with them the proliferation of Highland Games, and Scottish mutual benefit societies.

In the US it was only after the Civil War that Highland Games expanded their reach, establishing a permanent footing; by 1875 there were a minimum of eighty Scottish associations holding annual Games, and their spectator numbers grew.[29] While early events may have attracted a few hundred people, by the 1870s the Games held by the Brooklyn Caledonian Club could boast 5,000 spectators; but even this paled when compared to New York, which saw the arrival of 20,000.[30] Games were not restricted to the east coast, however, the Caledonian seed having spread to the Midwest and then through to California, also establishing roots in the Canadian west.[31] In California, Games took place, for instance, in San Francisco, where a Caledonian Club had been set up in 1866 for the express purpose of providing 'encouragement and practice of the Games'.[32]

The tradition of Caledonian societies, therefore, was a fundamentally different one when compared to that of St Andrew's societies. This is a point that becomes all the more clear with reference to the Antipodes. Here the tradition of providing benevolence, though often listed in association rules, was rather pale: in fact, in New Zealand the St Andrew's tradition was effectively non-existent. The Scots' associational roots there lay in the provision of leisure – a leisure associational activism – rather than philanthropic associational activism.[33] In both North America and the Antipodes the Games' growing popularity was a result of their ability to provide entertainment for a wide range of people and to promote field athletics.[34]

Alongside this expansion in leisure pursuits, ethnic mutualism developed as a distinct pillar in the Scots' ethnic associational world. The Sons of Scotland (SoS) association was established as a mutual aid society in Toronto in 1876 to provide insurance to its members for protection, also including in its remit elements of sociability and the celebration of Scottish culture; likewise, in the United States the Order of Scottish Clans (OoSC) began to serve that purpose, also developing in the 1870s. Organised in so-called 'camps' and 'clans' respectively – hence essentially through a lodge system akin to that of freemasons and other friendly societies – the SoS and OoSC had an estimated 200 and 250 branches respectively, boasting a combined membership of well over 20,000 by 1900.[35] In numeric terms these associations quickly eclipsed St Andrew's and Caledonian societies. But they were also characterised by a different membership: while Caledonian societies also tended to be more working class, the SoS and OoSC were distinctly so. St Andrew's societies, by contrast, attracted a membership from the higher echelons of society. Recognising these differences in membership is critical, also emphasising again the importance of giving voice to the migrants' active agency in setting up associations. Scottish migrants chose associational structures according to their needs; these varied over time, as well as by location.

By the time Scottish ethnic associations were first established in the Antipodes they could look back to a nearly two-century-long history. Still they developed their own distinct patterns of associationalism: both the Scots in Australia and New Zealand did not simply copy developments from elsewhere in the Scottish diaspora, they put in place a system of ethnic associations with its own discrete and distinct characteristics. First and foremost it was characterised by the relative absence of charity. While Australia saw a number of significant benevolent projects channelled through Scottish ethnic societies in the 1840s and 1850s,[36] all of them were short-lived. Across the Tasman, in New Zealand, such initiatives rested on even feebler foundations. There is no clear evidence that explains the exact reasons for this difference between the Antipodes and North America, but it seems plausible that the later timing of the Scots' migration to Australia and New Zealand, together with their generally better socio-economic profile, were critical in the different foci. Ultimately, the Scots in the Antipodes were as committed to fellow Scots as those elsewhere, but they did not channel that commitment through charity, focusing instead on the provision of leisure.

The need for such appreciation of the distinct local developments of Scottish ethnic associations becomes clearer when broadening the geographic remit further. While there undoubtedly were synergies in the evolution of associations in Africa too, the role of the frontier zone as a stimulus for the development of Scottish clubs and societies is notable. In southern Africa in particular this was important, first, because the idea of the frontier zone as a buffer zone directly resulted in the arrival of new migrants, but, secondly, also because it brought them in contact not only with African tribes – a group that could clearly be marked out as a racial 'other' – but also the Dutch, a distinct European 'other'.[37] Elsewhere, in British East Africa, we find the strongest evidence of Scottish ethnic associations serving as platforms for political engagement, so much so, in fact, that we can speak of quasi-parliamentary functions in some locations, most notably in Nairobi.[38]

Further east, in Asia, another characteristic was paramount in shaping Scottish ethnic associationalism: the high level of transience. Scottish arrivals there were, to a significant degree, sojourners rather than settlers. If not already reasonably well off, they were intent on using their time in Asia as a springboard for social advancement after their return home – the eventual return usually being the goal from the outset. These Scots came from a limited range of occupational backgrounds: a focused mix of elite, bureaucratic, commercial and military migrants. The latter group of migrants was especially important in the early days of Scottish connections with Asia: Scots served, for example, as soldiers in the East India Company (EIC).[39] Overall, McGilvary suggests that around 3,500 Scots were present in the Indies between c. 1720 and 1833.[40] While this number also included civil servants, military personnel – both ordinary soldiers and officers – made up the bulk. This was the case not least because service in India was viewed by many as an attractive route for acquiring wealth, especially for members of the lower gentry and the sons of gentry families, the result of the often large number of offspring and resultant concerns about their future inheritance.[41] For many of these young men, ethnic networks and patronage systems played a crucial role in facilitating employment with the EIC. As such, these military migrants and other Scottish elites that came were part of a fairly small group of whites that was surrounded by non-white ethnic majorities. This had an immediate impact on the development of Scottish ethnic associations in Asia: more so than anywhere else in the diaspora, they served as a preserve for the colonial elite. This was a characteristic that found expression annually in the large-scale Caledonian balls held throughout the Far East and on an unprecedented scale.

Within this general developmental context and global spread of Scottish ethnic associations, war provided a particularly potent hook for associational activities. This was the case because of the connection between Scottish ethnic associations and Scottish military identity, a connection tied up in particular with the promotion of Scottish regiments by associations, as well as war and post-war relief schemes and initiatives in support of the war effort. In combination, these themes permit analysis of how Scottish ethnic associations actively fostered Scottish military culture to promote a broader spirit of patriotism not only within their respective sites of settlement, but also throughout the diaspora and in Scotland itself. It is to these themes that the remainder of this chapter will turn.

The South African War and the British Empire

While Scottish ethnic associations had been engaged with supporting soldiers and smaller-scale war relief efforts for a long time, it was at the end of the nineteenth century – and with the outbreak of the South African War – that efforts became more significant. Intrinsic to these efforts, as Edward Spiers' chapter in this collection makes clear, was a profound sense not simply of Scottishness, but of Scottishness in the British Empire, combining a spirit of empire with militarism. This generally worked well as a profound sense of Scottish heritage, and the role the Scots had played in fighting for empire, provided an immediate hook. As the Johannesburg Caledonian Society stated in the greetings sent in 1901 to its Bulawayo counterpart: '"The Empire never shall recede while Scottish chiels wi' Scottish wit, wi' Scottish pluck and Scottish grit, stand steady in our Empire's need."'[42] Or, as noted at a later dinner in 1910, 'where the dead have laid thickest, where the world has stretched widest, there you [Scottish soldiers] have been; the skirl of the pipes sounds through the story of Empire.'[43]

The sense of duty many Scots felt towards the empire is most immediately seen in one particular activity several Scottish ethnic associations in Africa pursued: the formation of Scottish units in support of the South African War. In Johannesburg the Caledonian Society supported the formation of the Scottish Horse, a cavalry regiment raised under the leadership of Lord Tullibardine which is addressed elsewhere in this volume.[44] What marks out the Scottish Horse – apart from its promotion by Scottish ethnic associations – is that it recruited a large number of volunteers from Australia for its second battalion, chiefly from Victoria.[45] In terms of measuring the strength of a diaspora – but also the ties that bind it together – war provides key evidence: the Scottish Horse recruited volunteers not only from Australia and Africa itself, but also from Scotland and England. For the latter, Tullibardine relied on the support of the Highland Society of London, asking for its 'co-operation . . . in raising two hundred and fifty men (Scotsmen preferred)'.[46] The fact that the Highland Society was approached does not surprise given its involvement in the organisation of the London Scottish Volunteer Corps in 1859, as discussed in Allan's chapter.[47] It certainly took the call for help seriously, raising, through the Volunteer Corps, '400 men'.[48] Through these links the story of the Scottish Horse powerfully documents the sense of diasporan duty Scots felt within the context of the British Empire.

In southern Africa the South African War had an even more direct effect on Scottish ethnic associational culture: it served to boost the idea of federation. First proposed in the early twentieth century, federation was framed as a unifying movement in what was – post-war – a fractured society. Perhaps as one might expect, however, association members were initially more concerned with restoring to normality their own lives, and hence no action was taken immediately. The outbreak of the First World War provided another impetus, however, and the Federated Caledonian Society of South Africa was eventually established in 1918. Initially it operated only in the Transvaal, but it soon extended its reach to other parts of South Africa. Federation gave stability to associational endeavours, and helped consolidate Scottish activities in a large area.

Military identity and Scottish ethnic associations

The examples documenting the connection between Scottish ethnic societies and regiments during the South African War reflect more broadly on the role Scottish military identity played for many Scottish ethnic associations. In part this was a result of membership composition: many a military man can be found among the members of Scottish ethnic clubs and societies. But the connection to the military was also a critical building block in the Scots' identity as empire-builders. It is this link that brings us to early twentieth-century Australia: it was there that the proposed abolition of national, and therefore also the kilted, regiments emerged as an issue that greatly antagonised Scottish ethnic societies in the country.

The debate concerning national regiments had been smouldering for some time,[49] but it was in 1912 that the situation reached boiling-point. Early in the year Senator James McColl from Victoria had sent a letter to the minister of defence at the request of the Bunyip Caledonian Society 'regarding the wearing of kilts by the Australian Scottish regiments'.[50] The answer he received did not go down well with the Scots and their supporters, it being noted that Highland uniforms may only be worn 'on certain occasions', and that 'the uniform to be issued in future to all members of the Australian defence force will be of a uniform type'.[51] The end of national regiments had come.[52] This was, however, not the view of Scottish ethnic associations throughout the country, who mounted a sustained attack on the proposed changes.

For many Scots the proposed changes were very serious indeed, as was noted in the *Scottish Australasian*, a Scottish community paper:

> It is stated that the retention of the Highland Dress is a matter of 'mere sentiment.' It may be admitted at once that the retention of the kilt is just sentiment, – true national sentiment, the God-given endowment of patriotism. By its aid work of majestic import may be accomplished, and without its inspiring impetus the Commonwealth will never attain to a leading position among the nations of the world. The value of such patriotism to the community cannot be too highly regarded . . . Now the loyal enthusiastic and patriotic Australian Scot, with the blood of a heroic ancestry flowing through his veins, and the history of his race in his mind, tenders his services for the defence of Australia. He wishes to do in defence of his country what his forefathers did for the Old Land, and, when the time arrives, write his name on Australian history, which will commence on the day in which he falls in the hour of victory, full clad in the kilt . . .[53]

For the *Scottish Australasian* it fell to the Highland Society of New South Wales to lead the protest. The Society was established as a merger of the Caledonian and Gaelic societies of Sydney in 1877,[54] and, by the time of the debate about national regiments, the Society was regarded as one of the lead organisations in Australia's Scottish community. Hence, the Highland Society was happy to answer the call issued by the *Scottish Australasian*, writing in protest to the minister of defence on 14 June 1912, including with that letter a resolution passed by its Council, which:

1. Records an emphatic protest against the abolition of the Kilt in the Scottish Regiments of the Commonwealth Forces.

2. Resolves that the Minister of Defence be approached with the earnest request that provisions be made which, while meeting all the necessities of modern warfare, will permit, as in the Forces of the United Kingdom, and in those of other British Dominions, of its retention.
3. Considers that the desire to live up to the high traditions of those who have worn it on the battlefields of history is the strongest incentive to the production of the best and bravest soldierly qualities in the wearer of to-day.

The kilt, the Highland Society's letter noted at the end, is 'symbolic of the loyalty and patriotism towards the Empire of Scotsmen and their descendants throughout the world'.[55] So although the kilt was recognised as Scottish, its purpose was much wider: it served to show loyalty to the empire. Framed in this way, the Scottishness the kilt represented was neither insular nor exclusionary, but, in the words of Hugh Sinclair MP, a manifestation of the Scots' willingness 'to spill their blood in the service of the Empire'. Consequently, Sinclair continued, the proposed abolition of national regiments would only 'damp the enthusiasm'[56] of the soldiers concerned.

The Highland Society did not only send its resolution to the minister of defence, however, but copies were also widely disseminated among other Scottish clubs and societies in Australia. A letter directly addressing these other associations accompanied the resolution, stressing the need for 'simultaneous and united action'. If taken, and if members 'will individually undertake to influence their friends, and if the local papers will take the matter up wholeheartedly', so the argument went, 'we cannot fail to shake the confidence of those officials who . . . have dared to assume that they can ride roughshod over the wishes of such a large and influential body of Australian Citizens as our Scottish community'.[57] Those groups who had received the Highland Society's resolution adopted it, and also proceeded to send it to the minister of defence,[58] also asking their respective local senators to take action.[59] As a result, the Australian press was filled with headlines including 'Passing of the Kilts'; '"Scots Wha Hae": United Action in Defence of Kilts'; '"Scottish Blood Rebelled"'; 'Killing the Kilt' and 'The Last of the Kilties'.[60] So vocal was the campaign that it was also picked up in the Scottish press. Under the headline 'In Defence of the Kilt', the *Dundee Courier* noted that Scots in Australia were 'much exercised in mind over the attitude of the Minister of Defence towards the kilt', lobbying against the kilt's abolition 'as a symbol of loyalty and patriotism towards the Empire of Scotsmen and their descendants throughout the world'.[61]

Yet little positive came of the flurry of activity. The Victorian Scottish Union, the federation of Scottish societies in Victoria, made a final effort in August 1912, sending a deputation from various states to meet the minister of defence. Yet while the minister showed some sympathy, in the end, as was reported in the press, he believed that 'Australian soldiers could cultivate a national sentiment, and be proud of the uniform typical of the present Defence scheme'.[62] He also deemed kilts to be too costly. Still members of the Scottish community were not willing to concede defeat. As the *Scottish Australian* observed, this was the result of the 'racial sentiment . . . one of the hardest things . . . to extinguish. It is as subtle, as mysterious, as intangible, and as puissant as electricity.'[63] It was partly as a result of such statements, and ongoing lobbying activities, that a lengthy debate on the question of national regiments took place in the Senate in November 1912. Previously encountered Senator McColl moved that national regiments be kept. Referring to the many Scots in Australia, and their role in building the country, he was keen to point out that nothing 'has disturbed Scottish feeling and blood so much as has the proposed abolition of these regiments'. This was the case, McColl went on, because the Scots' deeds are 'so closely associated with [the] characteristic dress'.[64] One suggestion, also by McColl, was to adopt an Australian tartan – though another senator, Hugh De Largie, immediately called it 'nonsense'.[65] Debates continued for some time,[66] but eventually the fight was lost as national regiments were abolished. Notwithstanding defeat, this episode of co-ordinated and collective action from a subscriber democracy, channelled through ethnic associations, powerfully underpinned the standing of Australia's Scottish community, as well as the connection between its sense of Scottishness and military identity.

The First World War and war relief

Federation in South Africa was, as we have seen, important in the development of the Scots' associational culture there, particularly after the First World War. In London too there was a link as the Federated Council of Scottish Associations was a federation set up during the First World War 'for the co-ordination of Scottish effort' in the city,[67] particularly in relation to war relief efforts and to help Scottish soldiers. Hence, in the summer of 1915, it was announced that the London Federation distributed '35,000 articles of warm clothing during the past months to Scottish regiments', and a new appeal was made 'for socks, shirts, and other articles of warm clothing'.[68] Items were also sent to Scottish prisoners of war in Germany. These efforts continued after the war, for instance when the Federation was involved in garnering support for the establishment of the Scottish National War Memorial at Edinburgh Castle, securing significant subscriptions and donations.[69]

It was through such activities connected to war relief that Scottish ethnic associations had the most profound impact during and after the First World War. Importantly, it was a genuinely diasporic and transnational effort, as associations thus engaged were located all over the world.

With the commencement of the First World War a range of charitable initiatives developed, for instance, that linked the Scots in Asia directly back to Scotland; these links proved enduring long past the end of the war. Hence, in 1914 the Colombo St Andrew's Day dinner organised by the Society did not take place as a result of the outbreak of the war. The suggestion was made that, instead, those who had planned to attend the ball should donate the money they would have spent on a dinner ticket to the Ceylon branch of the Prince of Wales'

Fund.[70] This was a practice followed in other centres in Asia. In Singapore, ball preparations were abandoned in 1914 after the outbreak of the war,[71] and members were asked 'to contribute to a war relief fund the amount they would individually have spent on the St Andrew's Day Ball'.[72] This type of activity in support of the British war effort, the president of the St Andrew's Society stressed, was crucial: they had to 'cease for the time being to think of [themselves] as English, Irish or Scottish, and remember only that [they] are Britons'.[73] This was further emphasised by the sums collected through the selling of war bonds or fundraising concerts. The Singapore St Andrew's Society had thus raised over $16,000 since 1914 for war relief purposes. Designated collections were also made 'to the purchase of Comforts for Scottish troops and to the relief of Scottish War Prisoners', an initiative that was supported by the help of the Edinburgh St Andrew Society.[74] In Hong Kong, in 1915, $2,650 was raised at a St Andrew's Day concert in the City Hall for the Scottish War Charities,[75] and in 1917 the Society organised a Heather Day and a St Andrew's Fair expressly for the purpose of raising funds 'to help the ever growing needs of the Home hospitals in which our brave wounded soldiers are being treated'.[76] At the fair there were shows and merry-go-rounds, and golf competitions were held; in the evening a dancing floor was put down, 'and there the lightfooted tripped it merrily to the tune of the pipe until a late hour'.[77] It was anticipated that $40,000 had been collected through raffles, auctions and fair takings. Further east, in Shanghai, in 1916, a mere eight people came together at the Astor House as guests of the St Andrew's Society's president, Gavin Wallace, to celebrate the saint's day. The meeting was not public, however, and designed primarily to announce that $10,000 had been collected from Society members for the Scottish Red Cross Fund.[78] Moreover, the Shanghai St Andrew's Society also responded to appeals from Scotland, for instance by the Soldiers' and Sailors' Help Society, for which a total of £500 was collected and 'sent home'.[79] Another way in which Scottish ethnic associations sought to support the war effort was through sponsoring hospital beds at the front, with the St Andrew's Society of Shanghai sending £250 to establish 'beds in the hospital at Rouen'.[80] Even more directly, the First World War provided another impetus for the mobilisation of the Shanghai Volunteer Corps, which had a Scottish unit.[81]

It was partly as a result of the First World War that links with Scotland were strengthened through charity and donations: a sustained form of transnational charity developed that was maintained long after the war. The most impressive example comes from Calcutta, where Scots raised a significant £13,000 in 1917 in support of Scottish Women's Hospitals. While this initiative was launched by a Mrs Abbott rather than a Scottish ethnic association, the Calcutta Caledonian Society opened the first subscription list.[82] Moreover, the transmission of donations to Scottish hospitals became an established annual practice of the Selangor St Andrew's Society (Kuala Lumpur) in the 1920s. While the sums were nowhere near as high as those raised in Calcutta, the Selangor Society continued its donations for many years. Among the hospitals that received support were the Royal Aberdeen Hospital for Sick Children, the Aberdeen Royal Infirmary and the Dundee Royal Infirmary.[83] As was reported in 1927, '[e]ach year the Selangor St Andrew's Society, Kuala Lumpur, sends a cheque to be distributed amongst the deserving Scottish hospitals, and yearly £5 is allocated to Dundee Royal Infirmary'.[84] *The Scotsman* newspaper at times served as the distributor of funds received from Scots in Asia. In 1928, for instance, the Negri Sembilan St Andrew's Society, Federated Malaya States, had sent £50 that *The Scotsman* distributed to various hospitals throughout Scotland. This was a practice it had already been doing for the Selangor St Andrew's Society 'for a number of years' and, as was observed, 'we welcome the further evidence provided by the Negri Sembilan St Andrew Society of the practical interest taken by Scotsmen abroad in the work of Scottish charitable institutions'.[85]

Conclusion

From the earliest days of Scottish expansion abroad, ethnic clubs and societies developed as a prominent characteristic of the Scots' life in the diaspora near and far. The organisations that were founded were not uniform, being characterised instead as direct responses to the New World contexts in which they were set up, as well as the background of the migrants who established them. Consequently, any study concerned with Scottish ethnic associations must give recognition to the distinct nature of organisations. While commonalities undoubtedly existed, and shared cultural traditions played their part in sustaining Scottishness, the Scots' ethnic associations are much more multifaceted than is often acknowledged. Consequently, in North America the provision of charity was their *raison d'être*, while it played a comparatively smaller role elsewhere. In the Antipodes, for example, it was the provision of leisure that carried Scottish ethnic associational life.

Within this wider context of development, military identity was a constant point of reference for many Scottish ethnic associations. It provided impetus for the Scots engaged in ethnic clubs and societies to promote the establishment of Scottish regiments – or prevent their de facto abolition – as well as run and support war and post-war relief schemes. In so doing, the Scottish ethnic associations themselves actively fostered Scottish military culture to promote a broader spirit of patriotism. This was a patriotism framed firmly as Scottish, but, importantly, as Scottish *within* the British Empire. This the associations did not only in their respective sites of settlement, but also transnationally and globally, connecting them with Scots elsewhere in the diaspora as well as in Scotland itself. Moreover, throughout the First World War in particular, a very practical and directed form of diasporic consciousness and connection was channelled through Scottish ethnic associations and their relief projects. Military identity was critical to it, providing the initial motivation for action.

Notes

1. The paper is still published, though it now runs under the name of *Catholic Weekly*. Some of the paper's editors were ardent nationalists; see, for instance, Patrick O'Farrell, *The Irish in Australia: 1788 to the Present* (Notre Dame: University of Notre Dame Press, 2000), p. 209.
2. *Freeman's Journal* (Sydney), 31 May 1856.
3. All quotations from ibid. In terms of the role of ethnic associations the writer specifically refers to the St Andrew's Society of Launceston as an example of such a Scottish organisation.
4. *Belfast News-Letter*, 24 November 1888. Story cited and explained in more detail in Kyle Hughes, 'The Scottish Migrant Community in Victorian and Edwardian Belfast', unpublished PhD thesis, Northumbria University, 2010, pp. 1, 4.
5. Ibid.
6. While Hughes, for example, has aptly referred to Presbyterianism as 'the largest Scottish association of them all' (Hughes, 'Scottish Migrant Community', p. 4), among the Scots overseas its primary function was neither the maintenance of ethnic identity, nor continued orientation to the old homeland. Moreover, while there clearly were ties between ethnic societies and Presbyterian churches in many of the sites studied for this chapter, Scottish ethnic associational culture is intrinsically secular: they deserve a separate study with a more broadly framed definition of associationalism. See also S. Karly Kehoe, *Creating a Scottish Church: Catholicism, Gender and Ethnicity in Nineteenth-century Scotland* (Manchester: Manchester University Press, 2010) and S. Karly Kehoe, 'Catholic Identity in the Diaspora: Nineteenth-century Ontario', in Tanja Bueltmann, Andrew Hinson and Graeme Morton (eds), *Ties of Bluid, Kin and Countrie: Scottish Associational Culture in the Diaspora* (Guelph: Guelph Series in Scottish Studies, 2009), pp. 83–100.
7. A substantial body of work is available that has explored migrant groups from the British and Irish Isles in diverse locations, including Charlotte Erickson, *Invisible Immigrants: The Adaptation of English and Scottish Immigrants in Nineteenth-Century America* (Coral Gables: University of Miami Press, 1972); Ronald L. Lewis, *Welsh Americans: A History of Assimilation on the Coalfields* (Chapel Hill: University of North Carolina Press, 2008); Angela McCarthy, *Irish Migrants in New Zealand, 1840–1937: 'The Desired Haven'* (Woodbridge: Boydell Press, 2005); Brad Patterson (ed.), *The Irish in New Zealand* (Wellington: Stout Research Centre, 2002); Malcolm Prentis, *The Scots in Australia* (Sydney: University of New South Wales Press, 2008); Peter E. Rider and Heather McNabb (eds), *A Kingdom of the Mind: How the Scots Helped Make Canada* (Montreal and Kingston: McGill-Queen's University Press, 2006); and William E. Van Vugt, *British Buckeyes: The English, Scots, and Welsh in Ohio, 1700–1900* (Kent, OH: Kent State University Press, 2006). In the context of the principal nineteenth- and early twentieth-century settler destinations other migrant groups have also found their historians: John Bodnar, *The Transplanted: A History of Immigrants in Urban America* (Bloomington: University of Indiana Press, 1985); Stanley Nadel, *Little Germany: Ethnicity, Religion and Class in New York City, 1845–80* (Urbana: University of Illinois Press, 1990); or Jürgen Tampke, *The Germans in Australia* (Cambridge: Cambridge University Press, 2006).
8. See, for example, John Belchem, 'Priests, Publicans and the Irish Poor: Ethnic Enterprise and Migrant Networks in Mid-Nineteenth-Century Liverpool', in Enda Delaney and Donald M. MacRaild (eds), *Irish Migration, Networks and Ethnic Identities Since 1750* (Abingdon: Routledge, 2007), pp. 62–86; or Angela McCarthy

(ed.), *A Global Clan: Scottish Migrant Networks and Identities Since the Eighteenth Century* (London: Tauris Academic Studies, 2006).
9. For more on the idea of diaspora agents and structures, see Figure I.2 in Tanja Bueltmann, *Clubbing Together: Ethnicity, Civility and Formal Sociability in the Scottish Diaspora to 1930* (Liverpool: Liverpool University Press, 2014), p. 13.
10. Ibid. p. 4.
11. See, for instance, David McCrone, *Understanding Scotland: The Sociology of a Nation* (second edition, London: Routledge, 2001), p. 136ff.
12. Charlotte Erickson, 'English', in Stephan Thernstrom, Ann Orlov and Oscar Handlin (eds), *Harvard Encyclopaedia of American Ethnic Groups* (second edition, Cambridge, MA: Harvard University Press, 1980), pp. 320–39, quote at p. 333.
13. See Peter Clark, *British Clubs and Societies 1580–1800: The Origins of an Associational World* (Oxford: Oxford University Press, 2000), pp. 274–95. For later development patterns and a useful wider discussion of urban associations, see Robert. J. Morris, 'Urban Associations in England and Scotland, 1750–1914: The Formation of the Middle Class or the Formation of a Civil society?', in Graeme Morton, Boudien de Vries and Robert. J. Morris (eds), *Civil Society, Associations, and Urban Places: Class, Nation, and Culture in Nineteenth-Century Europe* (Aldershot: Ashgate, 2006), pp. 139–58.
14. Clark, *British Clubs and Societies*, pp. 274–5, 295.
15. As Dobson suggests, the formation at that point in time probably related to the fact that veterans were 'ending their years of servitude', requiring support. David Dobson, *Scottish Emigration to Colonial America, 1607–1785* (Athens: University of Georgia Press, 2004), pp. 36, 41–2.
16. See the website of the Scots' Charitable Society, http://scots-charitable.org (last accessed 6 August 2014).
17. See E. M. Bacon (ed.), *King's Dictionary of Boston* (Cambridge, MA: Moses King Publisher, 1883), p. 420.
18. See Georg Simmel, 'The Sociology of Sociability', *American Journal of Sociology*, vol. 55, no. 3 (1949), pp. 254–61.
19. This and the previous quote from George Austin Morrison, *History of the Saint Andrew's Society of the State of New York, 1756–1906* (New York: St Andrew's Society, 1906), p. 7.
20. Ibid. pp. 10–11.
21. See Michael Vance, 'Powerful Pathos: The Triumph of Scottishness in Nova Scotia', in Celeste Ray (ed.), *Transatlantic Scots* (Tuscaloosa: University of Alabama Press, 2005), pp. 156–79.
22. James S. MacDonald (ed.), *Annals of the North British Society of Halifax, Nova Scotia, For One Hundred and Twenty-five Years from its Foundation, 26th March, 1768, to the Festival of St Andrew, 1893* (Halifax: John Bowes, 1894), p. 6.
23. Montreal St Andrew's Society Archive, Minutes, 17 January 1835, First Minute Book.
24. Catherine Bourbeau, 'The St Andrew's Society of Montreal: Philanthropy and Power', in Bueltmann, Hinson and Morton, *Ties of Bluid*, p. 70ff. See also *Narrative of the Proceedings of the St Andrew's Society of Montreal* (Montreal: St Andrew's Society, 1844), p. 3.
25. See also Gillian I. Leitch, 'Scottish Identity and British Loyalty in Early-Nineteenth-Century Montreal', in Peter E. Rider and Heather McNabb, *A Kingdom of the Mind: How the Scots Helped Make Canada* (Kingston and Montreal: McGill-Queen's University Press, 2006), pp. 211–26.

26. Montreal St Andrew's Society Archive, Minutes, 17 January 1835, First Minute Book.
27. Montreal St Andrew's Society Archive, Annual Report of the St Andrew's Society of Montreal for 1867.
28. This, in turn, followed the tradition of self-help envisaged by Samuel Smiles. See also Robert. J. Morris, 'Samuel Smiles and the Genesis of Self-Help: The Retreat to a Petit Bourgeois Utopia', *Historical Journal*, vol. 24, no. 1 (1981), pp. 89–109.
29. Frank Zarnowski, *All Around Men: Heroes of a Forgotten Sport* (Lanham, MD: Scarecrow Press, 2005), p. 14. For useful wider context and some specific references to the role of Caledonian Games in the growth of organised sports, see also Nancy B. Bouchier, *For the Love of the Game: Amateur Sport in Small-town Ontario, 1838–1895* (Kingston and Montreal: McGill-Queen's University Press, 2003).
30. Zarnowski, *All Around Men*, p. 14.
31. See also Eric Heath, '"You Don't Have to Be a Scotchman": Sport and the Evolution of the Vancouver Caledonian Games, 1893–1926', unpublished MA thesis, Simon Fraser University, 2005.
32. From the Society's Bylaws, cited in Emily Ann Donaldson, *The Scottish Highland Games in America* (Gretna: Pelican Publishing Company, 1986), p. 32.
33. For details on the idea of different types of ethnic associational activism, see Bueltmann, *Clubbing Together*, Figure C.3, p. 232.
34. Graham Scambler, *Sport and Society: History, Power and Culture* (New York: Open University Press, 2005), pp. 44–5.
35. The *Scottish Canadian*, October 1897 and December 1900. See also Celeste Ray, 'Scottish Immigration and Ethnic Organization in the United States', in Celeste Ray (ed.), *Transatlantic Scots* (Tuscaloosa: University of Alabama Press, 2005), pp. 48–95, at p. 67.
36. For instance, the St Andrew's Immigration Society set up in Launceston, Tasmania, in 1853. See St Andrew's Immigration Society Records, TL PE 325.2411 SAI, LINC Tasmania, Hobart, Australia.
37. See also Alan Lester, *Imperial Networks: Creating Identities in Nineteenth-Century South Africa and Britain* (London: Routledge, 2001), pp. 48–54.
38. For details, see Bueltmann, *Clubbing Together*, Ch. 4.
39. H. V. Bowen, *The Business of Empire: The East India Company and Imperial Britain, 1756–1833* (Cambridge: Cambridge University Press, 2006), p. 272.
40. George McGilvary, 'Return of the Scottish nabob, 1725–1833', in Mario Varricchio (ed.), *Back to Caledonia: Scottish Homecomings from the Seventeenth Century to the Present* (Edinburgh: John Donald, 2012), pp. 90–108, at p. 91.
41. G. J. Bryant, 'Scots in India in the Eighteenth Century', *Scottish Historical Review*, vol. LXIV, 1, no. 177 (1985), pp. 22–41, at p. 26.
42. *Izwi Labantu* (East London), 10 December 1901.
43. *East African Standard* (Mombasa), 3 December 1910.
44. For further discussions of the significance of the Scottish Horse, see the chapters by Edward Spiers, Hew Strachan and Craig Tibbitts within this collection.
45. Prentis, *Scots in Australia*, p. 145.
46. *Morning Post* (London), 31 December 1900.
47. This was supported jointly together with the Caledonian Society; see John Douglas, *The Chronicles of the Caledonian Society of London* (London: Caledonian Society, 1930), p. 131.
48. *The Caledonian*, May 1920, p. 57.
49. The Highland Society of New South Wales, for instance, referred to the question of

'kilted regiments' in its annual report in 1910, State Library of New South Wales, Sydney, MLMSS.4738 2(7).
50. *Daily Herald* (Adelaide), 15 February 1912.
51. Ibid.
52. For further discussion on this debate, see Tibbitts' chapter in this collection.
53. *Scottish Australasian*, June 1912, p. 253.
54. See Constitution and Rules of the Highland Society of New South Wales, State Library of New South Wales, Sydney, MLMSS.4738 2(7).
55. Secretary of the Highland Society of New South Wales to the minister of defence, 14 June 1912, copy of letter contained in the records of the Caledonian Society of Adelaide, State Library of South Australia, Adelaide, SRG 279, box 8.
56. *Shoalhaven News and South Coast Districts Advertiser*, 20 July 1912.
57. Ibid.
58. See, for instance, *Western Campion* (Parkes), 28 June 1912; the article includes a reprint of the Resolution sent by the Highland Society of New South Wales, as well as a piece from the *Scottish Australasian*. This article was printed in a number of papers; see also *Forbes Advocate*, 28 June 1912, *Argus* (Melbourne), 17 July 1912 and *Malvern Standard*, 10 August 1912.
59. Letter from Senator McGregor's secretary to the secretary of the South Australian Caledonian Society, Melbourne, 25 June 1912; copy of letter contained in the records of the Caledonian Society of Adelaide, State Library of South Australia, Adelaide, SRG 279, box 8.
60. *Barrier Miner* (Broken Hill), 17 July 1912; *Advertiser* (Adelaide), 10 July 1910 and 16 August 1912; *Register* (Adelaide), 17 August 1912; *Argus* (Melbourne), 10 July 1912. For letters sent to the Ministry of Defence, see National Archives Australia, files MP84/1 2011/1/193, 2011/1/197, 2011/1/215, 2011/1/356, 2011/1/358, 2011/1/359, 2011/1/361 or 2011/1/364.
61. *Dundee Courier*, 25 July 1912.
62. *Kalgoorlie Miner*, 16 August 1912; see also *Advertiser* (Adelaide), 16 August 1912.
63. *Scottish Australasian*, September 1912, p. 520.
64. 'The Debate in the Senate of the National Regiments', Parliamentary Debates, 21 November 1912, p. 2; copy contained in the records of the Caledonian Society of Adelaide, State Library of South Australia, Adelaide, SRG 279, box 8.
65. Ibid. p. 5.
66. *Advertiser* (Adelaide), 22 November 1912.
67. *Aberdeen Journal*, 10 February 1915.
68. Ibid.
69. *The Caledonian*, September 1920, p. 203.
70. *Ceylon Observer* (Colombo), 3 December 1914.
71. *Straits Times* (Singapore), 28 August 1914.
72. Ibid. 12 September 1914.
73. Ibid.
74. Ibid. 17 September 1918.
75. *South China Morning Post* (Hong Kong), 1 December 1915.
76. From the editorial, ibid., 3 December 1917.
77. Ibid.
78. *Shanghai Times*, 1 December 1916.
79. *North China Herald* (Shanghai), 19 October 1917.
80. *The Scotsman*, 17 July 1915; other societies also contributed and it appears that some sponsored beds together.

81. See Robert Bickers, *Britain in China* (Manchester: Manchester University Press, 1999), p. 84.
82. *Western Daily Press* (Bristol), 6 January 1917.
83. *Aberdeen Journal*, 27 August 1923; *Aberdeen Journal*, 12 October 1929; *Dundee Courier*, 20 May 1927; *Evening Telegraph* (Dundee), 7 July 1938.
84. *Evening Telegraph*, 19 May 1927.
85. *The Scotsman*, 20 April 1928; donations from the Selangor Society continued for some time; see, for instance, ibid. 21 May 1936 and 2 November 1949 (though donations had stopped during the Second World War).

Notes on the Contributors

Editors

David Forsyth is a Principal Curator in the Scottish History & Archaeology Department at National Museums Scotland. His particular area of interest has been in the material culture of the Scottish diaspora. Along with Wendy Ugolini he has acted as Principal Investigator on the Royal Society of Edinburgh/Scottish Government Research Workshop of which this jointly edited volume is the final output. In 2014 he and Stuart Allan curated the exhibition *Common Cause: Commonwealth Scots and the Great War* at the National Museum of Scotland, also co-authoring the book of the same name. He has curated numerous diaspora-themed projects at National Museums Scotland, including the major special exhibition *Trailblazers: Scots in Canada*.

Wendy Ugolini is a Lecturer in British History at the University of Edinburgh and an Associate Director of the Scottish Centre for Diaspora Studies. She has published extensively on the relationship between war and identities in twentieth-century Britain. Her monograph, *Experiencing War as the 'Enemy Other'. Italian Scottish Experience in World War II*, was awarded the 2011 Gladstone History Book Prize by the Royal Historical Society. Her current research addresses Welshness in England during the two world wars.

Contributors

Stuart Allan is Principal Curator of Scottish Late Modern Collections at National Museums Scotland. He specialises in the material culture of the Scottish military tradition, and the relationship between military service and Scottish identities. In 2014 he and colleague David Forsyth curated the exhibition *Common Cause: Commonwealth Scots and the Great War* at the National Museum of Scotland, also co-authoring the book of the same name. He is the author of *Commando Country* (2007) and, with Allan Carswell, of *The Thin Red Line: War, Empire and Visions* *of Scotland* (2004). He is currently working with colleague Henrietta Lidchi on the culture and practice of British military collecting of the non-European world, 1754–1904.

Seán Brosnahan is a Curator at the Toitū Otago Settlers Museum in Dunedin and an adjunct member of the Centre for Irish and Scottish Studies at the University of Otago. He recently fronted a documentary series, *Journey of the Otagos*, tracing Otago's military units across the battlefields of the First World War, which won the Best Museum Project award for New Zealand in 2015. He has published widely on Irish and Scottish settlement in southern New Zealand and curated numerous exhibitions on Scottish and military themes.

Tanja Bueltmann is Senior Lecturer in History at Northumbria University and an expert in diaspora history, especially ethnic associational culture. She is the author of *Clubbing Together: Ethnicity, Civility and Formal Sociability in the Scottish Diaspora to 1930* (2014), *Scottish Ethnicity and the Making of New Zealand Society, 1850 to 1930* (2011) and, with Andrew Hinson and Graeme Morton, *The Scottish Diaspora* (2013). Her current research focuses on a comparative longitudinal study of British and German expats in Asia.

Thomas (Tom) M. Devine is the Founding Director of the Scottish Centre for Diaspora Studies at the University of Edinburgh, where he previously held the Sir William Fraser Chair of Scottish History and Palaeography. He has held professorships at the University of Strathclyde and the University of Aberdeen. He has published widely in his field; in 2012 Penguin Books published his three-volume study on Scotland at home and abroad: *The Scotland Trilogy*. In 2014 he received a knighthood for services to the study of Scottish History. He is an Honorary Member of the Royal Irish Academy, a Fellow of the Royal Society of Edinburgh and a Fellow of the British Academy.

Jonathan Hyslop is Professor in the Department of Sociology and Anthropology, and in the programme in African and Latin American Studies, at Colgate University, Hamilton, New York. He has published widely on the social history and historiography of nineteenth- and twentieth-century South Africa, in journals including *Public Culture*, *Journal of Global History*, *Journal of Historical Sociology*, *International Review of Social History* and *Twentieth-Century British History*. He is currently researching the histories of the labour force of the British merchant marine in the steamship era, and of the port of Durban.

Andrew Mackillop is a Senior Lecturer in History at the University of Aberdeen. His research interests encompass the comparative study of Scotland, Ireland and Wales's contribution to British imperialism in Asia throughout the long eighteenth century and the nature of Scottish immigration into London during the same era. Recent and forthcoming publications include 'A North Europe World of Tea: Scotland and the Tea Trade, c. 1690–c. 1790', in Maxine Berg with Felicia Gottman, Hanna Hodacs and Chris Nierstrasz (eds), *Goods from* *the East, 1600–1800: Trading Eurasia* (2015) and '"Subsidy State" or Drawback Province? Eighteenth-century Scotland and the British fiscal-military complex', in Aaron Graham and Patrick Walsh (eds), *The British Fiscal-Military States, 1660–c. 1783* (forthcoming, 2015).

Jeff Noakes has been the Second World War historian at the Canadian War Museum since mid-2006. He is responsible for historical content in the museum's Second World War gallery, and is one of two historians jointly responsible for historical content in its LeBreton Gallery, which displays the CWM's collection of large military artefacts. He has presented numerous conference papers, and has also worked as a researcher on subjects related to Canada's military and diplomatic history during the twentieth century. Along with Janice Cavell, he is co-author of *Acts of Occupation: Canada and Arctic Sovereignty, 1918–25*, published by UBC Press.

Edward M. Spiers is a graduate of Edinburgh University and has spent forty years at the University of Leeds, where he has been the Professor of Strategic Studies since 1993, Pro-Dean for Research Evaluation (2012–14) and is currently the Dean for Postgraduate Research Studies. A Fellow of the Royal Historical Society, he has written sixteen books on military history and chemical warfare, including *The Army and Society 1815–1914* (1980), *The Late Victorian Army 1868–1902* (1992) and *The Scottish Soldier and Empire, 1854–1902* (2006). He co-edited *A Military History of Scotland* (2012), which won the Saltire Society prize (2012) and the Templer Medal (2012).

Hew Strachan has been Professor of International Relations at the University of St Andrews since 2015. He is a Life Fellow of Corpus Christi College, Cambridge, where he taught from 1975 to 1992, and was Chichele Professor of the History of War at the University of Oxford and a Fellow of All Souls College (2002–15). He serves on the Strategic Advisory Panel of the Chief of the Defence Staff and on the UK Defence Academy Advisory Board, as well as being a Trustee of the Imperial War Museum, a Commonwealth War Graves Commissioner, and member of the national committees for the centenary of the First World War of the United Kingdom, Scotland and France. His recent publications include *The Politics of the British Army* (1997), *The First World War: To Arms* (2001), *The First World War: a New Illustrated History* (2003) and *The Direction of War* (2013).

Craig Tibbitts is Senior Curator of Official and Private Records at the Australian War Memorial where he has worked since 2000. He is a professional member of the Australian Society of Archivists and is convenor of their Australian Capital Territory Branch. He maintains a lifelong passion for military history and Australian history, and is currently writing a book about the 56th Australian Infantry Battalion in the First World War. Although not of Scottish descent, his parents met playing in Scottish pipe bands in Sydney, New South Wales in the 1950s.

Index

Aboriginal Peoples, 6, 97
affiliations, regimental, 111, 131, 144, 168, 188n22
Africa, xi, 34, 35, 129, 150, 198, 200
African Canadians, 108
Allen, James, 178, 191n61
American Revolution, 20, 93, 94, 196
anti-modernism, 98, 101
Antipodes, 197, 198, 205
Anzac, 53, 65, 139, 144, 146, 178, 181
Armistice Day, 65, 93, 113, 115–16, 124n102, 158, 163
Asia, xi, 13, 15, 18–19, 20, 24, 26, 199, 203, 204, 205
associational culture, 6, 7, 74, 77, 78, 86, 170, 186, 192n84, 195–205
  Burns clubs, 178, 193; Dunedin Burns Club, 181, 192n84
  Caledonian societies, 32, 36, 43, 132, 152, 154, 155, 156, 190n46, 193, 197, 198; Brooklyn Caledonian Club, 197; Bunyip Caledonian Society, 201; Calcutta Caledonian Society, 204; Caledonian Society of London, 73, 78, 81, 86, 87; Caledonian Society of Otago, 192n84; Johannesburg Caledonian Society, 152, 200; San Francisco Caledonian Club, 197
  Club of the True Highlanders, 81
  Council of Dunedin Scottish Societies, 181

Federated Caledonian Society of South Africa, 200
Federated Council of Scottish Associations, 203
Gaelic Society of New Zealand, 192n84
Highland societies, 34, 41, 178; Highland Society of London, 73, 74–7, 78, 81, 86, 90n14, 200; Highland Society of New South Wales, 201, 208n49, 209n58
North British Society, 196
Order of Scottish Clans, 198
St Andrew's societies, 45, 193, 196–8, 204, 205; Edinburgh St Andrew Society, 204; Montreal St Andrew's Society, 196; Negri Sembilan St Andrew's Society, 205; St Andrew's Society of Illinois, 197; Selangor St Andrew's Society, 204, 205; Shanghai St Andrew's Society, 204; Singapore St Andrew's Society, 204; Toronto St Andrew's Society, 197
Scots' Charitable Society, 195
Sons of Scotland, 45, 197
Victorian Scottish Union, 202
Australia, xii, 1–5, 7, 34, 38, 39, 41, 42, 43, 46, 47, 53, 58, 63, 65, 88, 128–49, 158, 168, 170, 176–7, 187n16, 198, 200, 201–3
Australian Imperial Force (AIF), 5, 128–49

Australian units and formations
  4th Australian Infantry Battalion, 134, 135, 136–7, 140, 143, 144
  5th Australian Infantry Battalion, 133, 134, 135, 143, 144, 146
  25th Australian (Militia) Battalion, 133, 134, 136
  26th Australian (Militia) Battalion, 133, 136
  30th Battalion (New South Wales Scottish Militia), 5, 144
  52nd Australian (Militia) Battalion, 133, 135
  56th Australian Infantry Battalion, 5, 128, 136–40, 143
  Adelaide Regiment of Volunteers (Scottish Company), 130
  Byron Regiment (New South Wales), 131
  Cameron Highlanders of Western Australia, 131
  Duke of Edinburgh's Highlanders (New South Wales), 131
  New South Wales Scottish Rifles, 2, 131
  Queensland Cameron Highlanders, 131, 144
  Queensland Scottish Volunteer Corps, 131
  Royal Victorian Regiment, 144
  South Australian Scottish Regiment, 131
  Victorian Scottish Regiment, 43, 131–5, 144–5, 147
  Victorian Scottish Rifles 132, 135

bagpipes, 21, 61, 85, 114, 136, 144, 154, 178, 180, 181, 184
Bannerman, Ronald Burns, 181
Battles (First World War)
  Delville Wood (1916), 5, 150–1, 156–8, 160, 163, 164, 165
  Gallipoli (1915), 53, 55, 58, 65, 66, 135, 136, 137, 138, 139, 158, 168, 177, 178, 180, 181, 190n44
  Loos (1915), 55, 56, 57, 60, 67
  Messines (1914), 7, 55, 88, 89, 91n49
  Somme (1916), 55, 60, 136, 137, 138, 150, 156, 158
  Vimy Ridge (1917), 65, 115, 126n120
Belfast News Letter, 193
Belich, James, 169
Boston, 109, 195
Botha, Louis, 150, 153, 159, 162, 163
Bristol, 195
British Army, units and formations
  1st Royal Scots Fusiliers, 27, 35, 49, 66, 159–60
  6th/7th Battalion Royal Scots Fusiliers, 160
  9th Scottish Division, 156
  42nd Black Watch, 23, 25, 35–7, 40–1, 44, 54, 58, 60, 66, 76, 131–4, 141, 144, 171, 174, 182, 188–9
  55th Regiment, 22, 30
  71st Fraser's Highland Regiment, 13
  77th Montgomery's Highlanders, 23
  78th Fraser's Highland Regiment, 23
  78th (72nd) Highland Regiment, 23, 32–3, 35, 45, 48–9
  84th Royal Highland Emigrants, 93
  89th Highland Regiment, 23
  99th Lanarkshire Regiment, 171
  Highland Armed Association, 74, 75, 76, 77, 84, 89
  Highland Rifle Volunteers, 81
  Liverpool Scottish, 73–4, 82, 84, 91–2
  London Regiment, 74, 82
  London Scottish, 74, 78–92
  Loyal North Britons, 76–8, 84, 89
  Royal Scots, 22, 35, 40, 50, 55, 60, 68, 74, 139, 160
  Scottish Artisans, 81
  Scottish Horse, 43–4, 65, 132, 147, 200
  Tyneside Scottish, 74, 88, 91
British Canadian Recruiting Mission, 109
British East Africa, 198
  British empire, 5, 16, 53, 61, 65, 75, 88, 93, 94, 95, 96, 97, 99, 113, 150, 152, 159, 162, 193, 195, 199–200, 205
Britishness, 13, 14, 96, 152

Brockie, Robert, 26
Buchan, John, 56–7, 59, 60, 65, 151, 161–3
Buchanan, Sir Walter, 178
Busby, James, 170

Calcutta, 204
Caledonian Asylum, 75
California, 197
Cameron, Lt-Gen. Duncan, 171
camouflage, 80
Campbell, Archibald, of Inverneil, 19
Campbell, John, duke of Argyll, 17
Campbell, John, earl of Loudon, 20, 21
camps, 85, 175, 198
Canada, 1–7, 34, 36, 38, 42, 44, 45, 46, 47, 51n51, 53, 58, 63, 65, 88, 93–127, 152, 161, 168, 170, 196
Canada, units and formations
    3rd Battalion CEF, 100
    15th Battalion CEF, 99, 100, 111
    16th Battalion CEF, 99, 108, 111, 120n53
    25th Battalion CEF, 121n54
    48th Highlanders, 2, 44, 95, 96, 99, 100, 108, 109, 111
    72nd Highlanders, 23, 45, 95
    79th Highlanders, 34, 95
    91st Highlanders, 44, 45, 49n21, 95, 120n53
    113th Battalion CEF, 108
    173rd Battalion CEF, 108, 123n81
    185th Battalion CEF, 123n81
    236th Battalion CEF, 104, 108, 109, 123n89
    Black Watch (Royal Highland Regiment of Canada), 44, 95, 101, 102–3, 104
    Calgary Highlanders, 113
    Cameron Highlanders of Ottawa, 93, 113
    Lake Superior Scottish Regiment, 115, 126n116
    Lorne Scots, 113
    Stormont, Dundas and Glengarry Highlanders, 113
    Toronto Scottish, 82, 88–9

Canadian Forces, 41, 44, 46, 94, 99, 115
    Royal Canadian Air Force, 93, 114, 115
    Royal Canadian Navy, 115
Canadian Women's Army Corps (CWAC), 114
Canadian Women's Army Corps pipe band, 114–15
Carroll, Sir James, 178
Ceylon, 36, 42, 203
Charleston, 195
Chunuk Bair, 177, 181
clans, 35, 82, 98, 114, 143, 170, 171, 172, 187n12, 198
Colombo, 203
Commando, 159
correspondents, 35, 36, 38

Dalrymple, Sir William, 154
De Largie, Hugh, 203
deer-stalking, 79, 82, 84
Diamond Jubilee (1897), 176, 177
Dominions, xi, xii, 2–4, 6, 32–52, 53, 59, 65, 93, 128, 150, 163, 202
Douglas, James, Lord Drumlanrig, 17
Dunedin, 61, 173–4, 175, 176, 178, 179, 180, 181–2, 185, 189n34,n38
Dunlop, John, 104

East India Company, 13, 19, 199
Elcho, Lord (Francis Wemyss-Cahrteris-Douglas, later earl of Wemyss and March), 73, 78–82, 84, 85, 88, 90n28, 92n51, 188n29
England, xi, 3, 4, 6, 15, 17, 23, 33, 53, 54–5, 60, 61, 63, 66, 67, 73–92, 100, 118n22, 133, 151, 156, 159, 170, 176, 177, 187n11, 195, 200
ethnicities, 5, 6, 108, 186

Far East *see* Asia
fiscal-military state, 14, 15
Freeman's Journal, 193, 194
freemasons, 73, 74, 78, 79, 80, 198
friendly societies, 198

Glasgow, 14, 25, 26, 55, 58, 59, 62, 63, 66, 85, 140

Gordon, Lieutenant Thomas Fowler, 138, 145
Grace, Thomas, 177
Grant, Lillian, Pipe Major, 114

haka, 169, 177, 184, 186, 187n7, 189n43
Halley, Dr Alexander, 78–82, 86, 90n18
Hamilton, George, earl of Orkney, 17
Hepburn, Robert, 78, 86, 87, 91n33
Highland games, 108, 111, 193, 197
'Highlandism', xii, 3, 14, 32, 34–5, 47, 54, 62, 77, 90n14, 96
Hobson, Captain William, 170
Hong Kong, 204
Hudson's Bay Company, 15
Hughes, Sam, 99

imperialism, 3, 5, 16, 20, 24, 26, 93, 95–8, 101, 113, 114, 116, 118n22
Industrial Revolution, 15
Ireland, xi, 1, 6, 13, 17, 23, 33, 66, 67, 94, 99

Jamaica, 19

kilts, 23, 61, 77, 82, 84, 108, 111, 115, 133, 144, 151, 178, 185, 186, 201, 202
kinship, 47, 67, 132, 194
Kuala Lumpur, 204, 205
kūpapa (Queen's Maori), 172

Lighthall, William, 98
London, 16, 17, 36, 41, 63, 73–92, 143, 161, 176, 195, 200, 203

McColl, James, 201
McCord, David, 98
Macdonald of Greshornish, 18
Macdonald of Kingsborough family, 19
McGhee, Sergeant John, 139
MacKenzie, John, 2, 152
Macleod of Ullinish family, 13, 14, 16, 20
Maniopoto, Rewi, 171
Maori, 6, 168, 169–73, 176–8, 181, 183–6, 188n24, 189n43, 190n57, 191n61, 192n82,n83

Marlborough, duke of, 17
martial races, 97, 98, 109, 111
masculinities, 77, 84, 98–9, 104, 108, 111, 115–16, 156
militarism, 3, 14, 25, 26, 46, 53, 98, 151, 200
'military Scottishness', 1–7, 38, 93, 95, 97, 98, 99, 100, 101, 108, 109, 111, 113–15, 141, 143, 151, 154, 165, 168, 186
Montreal, 36, 44, 95, 98, 99, 101, 111, 196
Munro, Hector, 26
Murray, Charles, 154, 155
mutual benefit societies, 197
music, 2, 22, 46, 75, 84, 109, 131, 144
Mysore, 26

Nairobi, 199
New Caledonia, 184
New South Wales, 39, 41–3, 51, 128–33, 135, 140, 187n10, 206n7, 213
New York, 109, 123n87, 195, 197, 206–7
New Zealand, 1, 3, 4, 6, 8n4, 34, 38, 42–3, 46–7, 51n51,n56, 53, 58, 63, 65, 69n21, 88, 132, 147n23, 154, 168–92, 193, 197–8, 206n7
New Zealand, military units and formations
  1st Expeditionary Force, 168, 177–8, 183, 186
  2nd Expeditionary Force, 183–4
  No. 2 Scottish Rifle Volunteers (Dunedin), 173–4
  2/4 Battalion (Royal New Zealand Infantry Regiment), 185
  28th (Maori) Battalion, 183, 185–7, 191
  Canterbury Scottish Volunteers, 174
  Dunedin Highland Company, 174, 179
  Dunedin Highland Rifles Ex-Members Association, 182, 188, 191
  New Zealand Army, 168, 171–2, 176, 178, 181–6, 190, 192
  Otago Infantry Battalion, 178, 181, 189–90
  Otago Southland Regiment, 185, 192
  Pioneer Battalion, 177, 181, 186, 190

New Zealand, military units and formations (*cont.*)
  Queen Alexandra's Mounted Rifles, 185
  New Zealand Scottish Regiment, 178, 180, 182, 184, 189, 191; Regimental Association, 183; Territorial Association, 185
  Scottish Horse Mounted Rifle Volunteers (Waipu), 175
  Thames Scottish Rifle Volunteers, 172
Ngata, Sir Apirana, 183, 191n69
Ngāti Tūmatauenga (New Zealand Army), 168, 186, 187
North America, 1, 3, 13, 18, 19, 20–1, 23–4, 25, 30n44, 32–3, 37, 48n2,n13, 93–4, 97, 115, 126n113, 128, 195–8, 205
Nova Scotia, 22, 26, 41, 51n61, 61, 100, 114, 116n3, 117n8, 121n54,n56, 123n81, 125n105,n106

Otago, 169, 173, 189

Pakeha, 169, 170, 172–3, 181, 183, 186, 187n5, 189n43, 191n73
Parihaka, 172
patriotism, 73, 96, 104, 123n87, 124n91, 193, 199, 201–2, 205
patronage, 17, 20, 22, 28, 30, 75–6, 86, 130, 194, 199
Pearce, George Foster, 133–4, 144, 147n26
Philadelphia, 195
pipe bands, 35, 109, 111–13, 115, 126n111, 132, 135, 144, 178
pipes, 21, 37, 85, 93, 98, 113–14, 123n87,n88, 124n91, 135, 147n10, 175, 181, 184
Pitt, William, the Elder, 23
plaid, *breacan an fheilidh*, 76–7, 90n13, 91n33
Poananga, Brigadier Brian, 185
poetry, 34, 40, 57, 69n17, 162
Prince of Wales' Fund, 204
proto-globalisation, 14–17, 19–20, 26, 28

Quebec, 26, 51n63,n65, 93, 122n64

racism, 108
recruiting posters, 101, 104, 108, 121n61, 122n62,n63
redshanks, 14
religion, 48n5, 68n4, 95, 140, 148n32, 159, 206n7
Remembrance Day *see* Armistice Day
Richardson, Piper James, 111, 124n93

St Andrew's Day, 196, 203, 204
San Francisco, 197
Scots Year Book, 194
Scottish Australasian, 201, 209n53
Scottish National War Memorial, 64–7, 70n33,n34, 143, 149n53, 163, 203
Shanghai, 204
Sinclair-Maclagan, Maj-Gen., Ewen, 132–3, 136, 147n24
Singapore, 204
Smollett, Tobias, 23, 29n27, 31n48
Smuts, Jan Christiaan, 150, 153–4, 158–9, 161–4, 165n1, 167n38
social capital, 194
South Africa, 1–6, 8n1,n4,n13, 9n30, 39, 44, 46, 47, 48n12, 49n28, 50n41, 51n51, 59, 61, 65
South African units and formations
  2nd South African Infantry, 158
  4th South African Infantry (South African Scottish Regiment), 4–5, 150, 155, 157
  Cape Town Highlanders, 8n1, 43–4, 51n54,n55,n59,n60, 52n75,n77, 118n21, 124n97, 151–3, 156, 165n3, 166n9
  South African Brigade, 5, 59, 124n97, 150, 153, 156, 158–60
  Transvaal Scottish Regiment, 151–3, 155, 164, 166n10
Stuart, Andrew, MP, 20
Stuart, James, of Torrance and Castlemilk, 19–20, 22, 26
Sussex, Duke of, Prince Augustus Frederick, earl of Inverness, 77

tartanism, 5, 113–14, 116n3, 119n34, 122n68, 125n104,n106

Te Hokowhitu a Tū (Maori Contingent), 177, 186–7n2, 190n44
The Expedition of Humphry Clinker, 23, 29n27, 31n48
Tomoana, Henare, 95, 177
Toronto, 44, 95, 100, 117n8, 119n25, 120n46, 121n, 122n71, 197
Treaty of Waitangi, 170
Trekking On, 69n27, 161
Tullibardine, Marquess of (later 8th duke of Atholl), 4, 43–4, 65, 152–3, 200

United States of America, 36, 56, 65, 94, 108–9, 117n11, 123n81, 173, 195, 198, 208n35

Victoria, 7, 43, 130, 132–5, 144, 200–1

Waiata, 177, 189
wars
  American War of Independence (1775–83), 21, 24, 195
  First World War (1914–18), 1, 3–7, 9n26, 24, 53, 54, 57, 59–60, 62–3, 65, 68n4,n7, 68n12,n25, 70n34,n42, 74, 88, 92n51, 94–9, 111, 113–16n4, 120n45, 121n58, 124n89n98, 126n115,n120, 128, 130, 133, 136, 140–1, 143, 151, 153, 156, 162, 165n1, 168–9, 177–8, 181, 183–4, 189n43, 200, 203–5
  French Revolutionary War (1793–1802), 18, 30n41, 32, 74–5
  Napoleonic War (1803–15), 18, 30n41, 32, 49n15, 89n6, 169
  New Zealand Wars (1845–72), 170–2, 176–7, 188n19
  Nine Years War (1688–97), 17, 32
  Second World War (1939–45), 7, 114–15, 125n107n110, 126n112, 144, 168,183–4, 186n2, 190n57, 210n85
  Seven Years War (1756–63), 3, 20, 23, 53, 93
  South African War (1899–1902), 3, 38, 41–7, 50n41,n45, 51n56,n64 61, 65, 73, 84, 85, 88, 96, 119n25, 132, 134, 147n23, 152, 162, 175–6, 199–200
West Indies, 19
Williams, Lt Harold Roy, 139–40, 144n3, 148n36,n39, 149n43

EU Authorised Representative:
Easy Access System Europe Mustamäe tee 50, 10621 Tallinn, Estonia
gpsr.requests@easproject.com

Printed and bound by CPI Group (UK) Ltd, Croydon, CR0 4YY
17/06/2025
01902870-0005